Contents

Authors Introduction

I wish to especially thank Michael Thompson (Past Deputy Editor of the Herald Express) and Martin Harris (MD of Creative Media) for their patience in awaiting the completion of this publication.

The fifty two famous individuals included in this book were selected for no particular reason other than they are in some way remarkable people. Many are widely known or famous whereas others will be less known but in my view equally outstanding with a good story to impart. In choosing to include many of the lesser famous individuals I hope my book will become a useful reference tome for students, archivists and historians of the future as well as making a good read for you.

The researched material was often not easily found and therefore some of the more obscure personalities are being especially remembered and honoured by being included in the book.

The majority of the photographs included were supplied by the Herald Express and the Western Morning News although I also wish to thank here the many families that provided pictures. There are far too many individuals to name but it is right I confirm many of the pictures have never been published before including some of those appearing on the pages of; Agatha Christie, Arthur Hyde Dendy, Henry Brunel, Oliver Heaviside, Sean O'Casey, Eden Phillpotts, John Snelgrove, and Edward Vivian. Finally, individual photographs were taken or provided by; Mr J Bagwell, Mr K Day, Mr N Drew, Mr A Heather, Mrs R Hicks, Mr P Levie, Mr J Pentney, Mrs R Selous, Mr J Rowland and Mr M Thompson who are also formally thanked here.

I hope you find this publication and my style of writing makes for an easy read.

Ian L Handford – September 2007

TORBAY CIVIC SOCIETY

Famous
DEVON
FIGURES

52 short biographies of famous figures,
past and present, associated
with Devon

Compiled by
Ian L. Handford

cmp

First Published in Great Britain in 2007 by
Creative Media Publishing

Copyright © 2007 Ian L. Handford

ISBN 0-9546071-0-4

Design and production
Creative Media Ltd, 35 Woodland Park, Paignton, TQ3 2ST
www.mhcreativemedia.co.uk

Foreword

The idea of producing a series of biographies of famous local people of Torbay came about following the election of Ian Handford as the newly elected Chairman of Torbay Civic Society in 2001. It seems that one of his first acts was to ask the editor of the local daily newspaper the Herald Express whether or not the Society might allow him to provide a weekly cartoon so that society name might enjoy a higher public profile in Torbay.

Having had the editor reject that idea by coincidence Michael Thompson (Deputy editor at the paper) was wishing to reduce his workload which at that time involved four pages of the long standing and highly successful "Bygones" feature produced every Tuesday in the centre pages of the Herald Express. With the editor offering the Society the option to provide a biography of a famous person of Torbay each week this was too great an opportunity to miss. That series under the title of "Great Victorians" ran for fifteen months involving 60 separate features before the concept was seen as having run its course.

The editor now suggested that Ian widen his research to include famous individuals drawn from the whole of the circulation area of the paper. So it was that the new series "Famous Devon Figures" commenced and this second "Bygones" series ran for another two hundred and seven weeks before finally ending in February 2007. With a new editor appointed at the Herald Express the Society are now providing a weekly panel rather than a full biography, which can still be seen every Tuesday entitled – Famous People of Devon Remembered.

The fifty two biographies included in this book have largely been drawn from across the 267 featured in the Herald Express articles although most have now been amended or updated and there are many new pictures. The list of individuals have been drawn from across a variety of careers yet all of the people chosen have had some association with Devon.

WILLIAM FROUDE - Pioneer of safer shipping

A BRONZE plaque in Torquay Town Hall records that William Froude was a "genius whose pioneer research and experiments with ship models at Torquay greatly contributed to the science of naval architecture and to improvement in ship design".

WHEN HE DIED THE LORD Commissioners of the Admiralty told his family they considered his death a "national loss" and paid tribute to his "great service to the Navy and the country".

In 1871-1872 Froude started a chain of events in Torquay which led to the development of the world's leading ship model research establishment in Portsmouth, and put Britain at the forefront of technological innovation.

The pioneer of tank testing with scale models was born at Dartington Vicarage in 1810 to a literary and academic family. A graduate from Oriel College, Oxford, in 1837 he worked for Isambard Kingdom Brunel, and was soon in charge of the Exeter section of the Bristol & Exeter Railway.

Forced to give up full-time work to look after his ill father, he continued his pioneering work and also kept in touch with Brunel.

An example of this came in 1850, when he carried out tests on propellers using clockwork models made of tin-plate, and also investigated friction problems on Brunel's Great Eastern launch-ways. His delicate recording apparatus made out of tin and solder are now preserved in the Science Museum at Kensington.

With his many experiments on the River Dart, his knowledge of the river was such that he was appointed one of the first Dart Harbour Commissioners in 1862. The next year he took a lease on land at Cockington and in 1867 built his new home Chelston Cross (until 2003 the Manor House Hotel) in Seaway Lane. In the entrance hall is still the "flying staircase" designed by Henry Marc Brunel

(Isambard Kingdom's son, see No. 22) and built especially for Froude and his family.

His new house soon included a small covered water tank and workshops for making model ships. This became the first ever ship-tank used with model ships anywhere in the world, a significant historic event and, bearing in mind the problems, a great achievement.

The official history of the Admiralty Experiment Establishment at Haslar, Portsmouth, begins: "The first ship model tank in the world originated from a proposal by William Froude, a Civil Engineer of considerable ingenuity and skill who had for many years been ship model testing. William and R Edmund Froude (his third son) were to establish the foundations for almost all the experimental techniques used on models of surface ships. The frictional resistance coefficients obtained from those early experiments are still in use today".

In 1868, Froude had approached the Navy, pointing out there were serious discrepancies in the then current ideas about ship design as, particularly in those days, it was not an exact science. For example, a large steamship turned turtle in the Bay of Biscay losing hundreds of passengers and crew.

The disaster much upset Froude and spurred his determination to resolve the recurring problems in ship design.

He told the Admiralty Board his work with models in the Dart had shown him that accurate estimates of ship resistance could be made from tests using specially designed models. But it took the Lords Commissioners two years to sanction the plan and give a grant of £2,000 for the work.

In 1870 a large partly-covered tank was built on the other side of Old Mill Road from Chelston Cross. An official biographer wrote: "The enterprise soon attracted the attention of other governments. Admiral Popoff, on behalf of the Czar, having come all the way from Russia... and the rumour that Mr Froude was conducting a series of mysterious experiments which bade fair to revolutionise the naval architecture of the

TORBAY CIVIC SOCIETY

IN 1867
WILLIAM FROUDE
BUILT CHELSTON CROSS
(MANOR HOUSE HOTEL)
AND SET UP
ADMIRALTY EXPERIMENT WORK
RESULTING IN THE
CONSTRUCTION HERE OF
THE WORLD'S FIRST
SHIP TEST TANK
IN 1872.

Above: Chelston Cross tank at Torquay circa 1871

world, stirred interest in many men of mark - statesmen and others who were far from being naval experts".

Chelston Cross was to become a site of pilgrimage by English, continental and American admirers of his work.

The first vessel tested was a miniature version of HMS Greyhound on March 3, 1872.

Evidence tells us: "By the time the lease ran out in 1886, as well as testing models in the Dart Froude had constructed a tank in the roof of his home with an external gravity weight enabling the models to be pulled along at a constant speed.

"As a result of all of this work he had formulated his 'Law of Comparisons' - in effect, that real ships behave at sea in an identical way to especially constructed models tested in a tank."

Over the next century and a half this pioneering work revolutionised ship design throughout the world, and Froude's Law is still used in boat design today.

Today there are more than 300 ship-testing tanks world-wide, in itself a major testament of Froude's foresight and innovation.

The results of his mathematical analysis on the rolling of ships stood until the advent of computers in the late 1970s.

Froude died in May, 1879 in Cape Town, South Africa, but his work was continued by his son Robert Edmund.

Even before Robert's official appointment as superintendent of works in 1890, the Admiralty had realised the Torquay tank was far too short and that the building needed replacing.

A new site was sought, and eventually the Gun Boat Yard at Haslar, Portsmouth, was chosen, and the Torquay operation closed down on February 3, 1886.

Before then, some 46,000 experiments had been carried out at the "Admiralty Experiment Works", as it had become known, in Torquay.

Japan for many years held Froude in high esteem for his contribution to naval architectural principles and many Japanese visitors still seek out his Torquay home. The house looked over an unspoilt shoreline across Torbay, and in spite of the vast changes at Cockington the building still enjoys the same open views.

Torbay Civic Society unveiled a plaque to honour Froude on October 5, 2001, at the Manor House Hotel.

Below: Chelston Cross as it was in the 1950's

PHILIP HENRY GOSSE - Religion takes on evolution

PHILIP HENRY GOSSE, zoologist and renowned writer on natural history, was born at Worcester in 1810, the son of Thomas Gosse.

THOMAS, AN UNSUCCESSFUL WRITER but talented miniature-painter, moved the family to Coventry but eventually settled them in Poole, Dorset.

It would be an aunt that spotted Philip's special talent; the mother of Professor Thomas Bell. She was a woman with many scientific attainments.

Darwin's theories on evolution would one day completely divide the scientific community, bringing tremendous controversy even to the general public. An intellectual battle raged between distinguished men like Lyell, Darwin, Romanes, Rendle-Short and son, each determined to get his theory accepted.

Philip Gosse, however, would live completely in the atmosphere of God, praying every day and seeing little significance in ritual. He, an earnest student of holy scripture and an ardent believer in doctrine, would today be an extremist, with human pleasure being found only in the word of God.

He and his wife would have endless discussions on the scriptures at the end of each hurried day, a religious fervour that would see him eventually totally isolated from the world.

Philip's debut as a writer came in 1826, though he later went to Newfoundland to work in a whaler's office until 1835 and there became a naturalist, his speciality being insects, studied under his first microscope.

In 1836 his first work, *The Entomology of Newfoundland*, with drawings of the flora and fauna, was produced but not published.

Leaving Newfoundland for Philadelphia in 1838, he was warmly received at the Academy of Natural Sciences, before moving to Dallas where he spent five months as a teacher; he returned to Liverpool in 1838.

Completing *The Canadian Naturalist* on the voyage home, there were difficult negotiations before this manuscript was sold. Arriving in London Philip opened a school, and completed and sold his second manuscript, *Introduction to Zoology*.

At 33 and now noticed by the scientific community, he was commissioned by the British Museum in 1844 to collect undescribed birds and insects of Jamaica. Back in England by 1846, he never left its shores

again. *Birds of Jamaica* was published in 1847 and a year later Philip, a Wesyelan, married Emily Bowes, who was from an Anglican tradition but shared his attitude towards the divisions affecting the Protestant church.

Emily spoke three languages and was much the stronger personality, unknowingly having a magnetic power over the will and nature of Philip.

Their son Edmund would later write: "Here was a perfect purity, perfect intrepidity, perfect abnegation, yet also narrowness, isolation and an absence of perspective, an absence of humanity, entire resignation to the will of God and not less entire disdain of the judgement and opinion of man."

Into this most strange household was born the unwelcome Edmund in 1849. On hearing of the birth Philip recorded in his diary "E. delivered a son. Received green swallow from Jamaica". Edmund was to be an only child.

By 1851, *A Naturalist's Sojourn in Jamaica* (considered by some to be Philip's best work), was published, to be followed by *The Antiquities of Assyria* and other written work for the Society for the Promotion of Christian Knowledge (SPCK).

A now overworked Gosse, having been advised to retire, turned his attention to marine invertebrates, and in January 1852 came to St Marychurch, but soon moved on to the North Devon coast and at Ilfracombe.

These shoreline exploits resulted in *A Naturalist's Rambles on the Devonshire Coast*, published in 1853, together with an announcement that he could keep marine animals alive in captivity for 11 months, a feat previously thought impossible.

The family returned to London in December, 1852 and with the cooperation of the Zoological Gardens in Regents Park, Philip set up a large glass tank stocked with plants and marine animals. The first "Fish House" aquarium was financially successful and highly popular.

Now Philip moved the family to Weymouth, where work continued unabated and correspondence started with the Rev Charles Kingsley, a distinguished novelist, poet and innovator. But with Emily and himself in ill health, a return to London away from the cold winter of Weymouth was the order of the day.

When Kingsley came to Torquay in 1853, he became a regular supplier of "beasts" to Philip in London. Specially prepared wicker covered jars were sent to him for the purpose. Whilst in Torquay he completed his book *Wonders of the Shore*.

The Gosses journeyed to Tenby in 1854, to stay for eight

weeks, leaving in August. On return and in spite of undertaking much scientific work, both were in better health.

The Aquarium, with its five coloured plates, was published, much to the dismay of irritated amateurs who had no handbook to check the findings. The publication sold like wildfire, and was Philip's most successful book commercially.

Criticism levelled against *The Aquarium* resulted in two volumes of a *Manual on Marine Zoology*, embellished with 700 illustrations drawn during 1855-56. This saw Philip elected a Fellow of the Royal Society and a regular contributor to their publication, *Philosophical Transactions*.

But academic storm clouds were gathering, with evolution and geology at odds with the six days of Creation as described in the book of Genesis.

Tenby was published in 1856 and dealt with the scientific study of Welsh fauna, but also touched upon the controversial subject of evolution. With Darwin's theory of evolution now in vogue, and with Lyell's geological research having "rubbished the idea that Noah's flood covered the whole earth", there was now open hostility from the Christian Church.

Science, it seemed, had proved not that God was dead but that there had never been such an individual. Even today, however, insurance companies still quote the phrase "Act of God" to deny claims, so it appears the academic argument is far from resolved!

With the issue of evolution agitating public and scientific minds, 1857 was a turning point for Philip Gosse. Leaving London in despair he came to Torquay to live at Sandhurst in St Marychurch Road, where he wrote two volumes, *Life*, and *Omphalos*, to combat natural selection, and animal development versus deity.

These books, rejected by academics, showed his "fanciful theories" and approach to religion to be outdated.

In 1857 Emily died and was greatly missed, as her intellectual sympathy had become a necessity to Philip.

He, refusing to accommodate the "new order", reacted by isolating himself physically, mentally and spiritually from society and expecting the same from his son.

Philip's publication in 1858-60 of *Actinologia Britannica* included coloured illustrations of every known species of British sea-anemones and remains an accepted authority on the subject.

In 1860 he married his second wife, Eliza Brightwen, and as a member of the Plymouth Brethren during this period he made provision for building a Gospel Hall in St Marychurch.

Philip now devoted his time to the cultivation of orchids and microscopic studies of rotifera, a section of zoology until then wholly neglected.

He was a virtual recluse, and Kingsley would be the only person able to occasionally entice him out. Crushed between the seemingly irresistible force of science versus the immovable inerrancy of scripture, he continued to live a hermit's existence at Sandhurst.

Edmund refused his father's total rejection of the world, and instead rejected his father, confessing to having become "a militant evolutionary atheist".

In his seventies Philip was still drawing microscopic plates, collected with others drawn over a 20-year period, and his final volumes were published in 1886.

He died on August 23, 1888 aged 79; a latent cardiac disease developed after he contracted bronchitis while at his microscope in the winter of 1887.

No plaque has yet been unveiled to the memory of Philip Henry Gosse.

Philip Goss's son, Edmund, was eight years old in 1857 and later remembered his father at Torquay and his intense dislike of what he called Christ's Mass: "... on the subject of all feasts of the Church he held the view of an almost grotesque peculiarity. He looked upon each of them as nugatory and worthless, but the keeping of Christmas appeared to him by far the most hateful, and nothing less than an act of idolatry.

"On Christmas Day of this year 1857 our villa saw a very unusual sight. My father had given strictest charge whatsoever was to be made in our meals on that day; the dinner was to be neither more copious than usual nor less so. He was obeyed, but the servants, secretly rebellious, made a small plum pudding for themselves. Early in the afternoon, the maids - of whom we were now advanced to keeping two - kindly remarked that 'the poor dear

child ought to have a bit, anyhow', and wheedled me into the kitchen, where I ate a slice of plum-pudding.

'Shortly I began to feel that pain inside which in my frail state was inevitable, and my conscience smote me violently. At length I could bear my spiritual anguish no longer and bursting into my study I called out 'Oh Papa, Papa, I have eaten of the flesh offered to idols!' It took some time between my sobs, to explain what had happened. Then my Father sternly said: 'Where is the accursed thing?' I explained that as much as was left of it was still on the kitchen table.

"He took me by the hand, and ran with me into the midst of the startled servants, seized what remained of the pudding, and with the plate in one hand and me still tight in the other, ran till we reached the dust-heap, when he flung the idolatrous confectionery on to the middle of the ashes, and then raked it deep down into the mass. The suddenness, the violence, the velocity of this extraordinary act made an impression on my memory which nothing will ever efface."

Top picture: *Gospel Hall in St Marychurch*
Bottom picture: *Cartoon of Philip Gosse taking the pudding to the Fire*
Text - *Christmas in Devon by Todd Gray - seasonal tit-bits from the 13th century onwards. Published in 2000 by the Mint Press, Exeter.*

ANGELA BURDETT COUTTS -
The 'queen of the poor'

ORPHANED at the age of eight, Angela Burdett had to learn independence and self-reliance at an early age.

BORN IN 1814, SHE WAS THE DAUGHTER of the reformist MP Sir Francis Burdett and Lady Sophia Burdett.

Lady Sophia died when Angela was still a young child, and her father died when she was only eight.

At 23 she inherited her fortune from her grandfather, Thomas Coutts, banker to George III, through her step-grandmother, the Duchess of St Albans.

Perhaps to keep alive the memory of her mother's famous grandfather she also took his name and became known as Angela Burdett Coutts.

By then the richest heiress in Britain, she became a lavish society hostess, received at all the European courts, and a patron of the arts and theatre, friendly with Charles Dickens, the Duke of Wellington, William McCready and Henry Irving.

The question must have arisen, what should she do with this enormous wealth?

With her strong will and strong sense of purpose, and in an understanding and imaginative way, she decided to give it away — and she gave away £3 million, eventually earning the title of "the queen of the poor" for her philanthropic work.

Miss Burdett Coutts first came to Torquay in 1856, to live at Meadfoot House, No 1 Hesketh Crescent. Her immediate neighbour at No 2 was Charles Darwin, who at the time was "taking the waters" in Torquay, and believed to be working on the third edition of his historic book *Origin of the Species*.

She finally settled for a large property named Ehrenburg Hall in Chelston Avenue (now known as Chestnut Avenue), which was situated immediately behind what we now call Abbey Gardens, just off the seafront of Torquay.

Angela Burdett Coutts was apparently a woman with great intellectual interests, and having attended a William Pengelly (see No. 16) lecture at the Torquay Natural History Museum in Babbacombe Road she was to become a friend, student and collaborator with him on many projects in years to follow.

She gave money or help to finance churches and schools at home and abroad, in places as far distant as the East End of London and South Africa.

Her benefactions were as varied as they were numerous. She was particularly interested in science and gave money to that area of life, but also helped in the establishment of schools to prepare orphaned children for emigration, and even helped "fallen women".

Many of her gifts to the district of Torbay reflected her pioneering interests in education, which emanated from the friendship and joint interests she shared with William Pengelly.

Angela, like Pengelly, was a teacher, having been employed on a peripatetic basis to assist and train teachers at the Dame schools of neighbouring villages of the area, including Barton, Cockington, and Shiphay.

The enlargement of the Brixham British Seamen's Boys' Home became possible because of her monetary assistance, once again showing her specific interest and commitment to orphans, mirroring perhaps her own situation in early life.

She lived at Ehrenburg Hall from 1862 until 1877, and this home welcomed and entertained many local notables of the time, including Bishop Phillpotts of Exeter, Lady Brownlow, Lord Churston, the Vivian family, March Phillipps and the Pengellys.

Other distinguished visitors included royalty such as Sophia, Queen of Holland, and

A late 19th century view of Hesketh Crescent, where Angela lived at Meadfoot House

Rajah Brooke from Sarawak, together with Sir John Lubbock and the geologist Sir Charles Lyell, a friend and backer of William Pengelly during his excavation work at Kents Cavern.

In 1871 Angela was the first woman to be honoured with the title Baroness in her own right, by Queen Victoria, and was the first woman to be given the Freedom of the City of London.

Later, she met her future husband at a function at which she was guest of honour. Held at Apsley House, a building rather hidden away close to what is now known as the Lincombe Hall Hotel, in Lincombe Road, Torquay, the function was the annual prize-giving at a school. The head boy, an American called William Ashmead Bartlett, so impressed her with his speech of thanks in Latin that she arranged to pay for him to go Oxford. At the age of 27 he returned to Torquay, and eventually was to become her husband.

Marrying for the first time at the age of 67 seemingly caused little consternation amongst her immediate friends, and the marriage seems to have been happy, though she had to give up her right to transfer the Coutts fortune to her husband on her death.

Baroness Burdett Coutts left Ehrenburg Hall in 1877;

it underwent many changes, eventually becoming Erin Hall and then part of a complex which included the Rosetor Hotel. This was one of the hotels which were closed and demolished to make way for Torbay's Riviera International Centre, which opened in 1987.

The Baroness died childless, aged 92, in 1906, five years after her Queen, and is buried in Westminster Abbey. Torbay Civic Society erected one of their commemorative plaques in the entrance of the Riviera International Centre, in 1987.

Below: A newspaper depiction of Angela's wedding

Below: The Rosetor Hotel in Chestnut Avenue

EDWARD VIVIAN –
Educator of the working class

TORQUAY historian Arthur Ellis wrote of Edward Vivian: "No man did more to mould Torquay's character, advance its interests or extend its fame." Another local historian, Frank Cawson, described him as "one of the eminent Victorians of Torquay, active in public affairs, prominent in its educational institutions and a luminary in its social life".

VIVIAN WAS A LOCAL BANKER, MAGISTRATE, insurance agent, hotelier, writer and public speaker; together with William Pengelly he played a leading role in the exploration of Kents Cavern.

He has, however, been most remembered as a benefactor to the poor of Torquay.

Though he spent much of his life concentrating on a variety of aspects of local good works, he was also a keen sportsman, horticulturist, photographer and a notable artist.

A nephew of Lord Vivian, Edward was born in April, 1808, one of three brothers.

He went to Oxford, eventually graduating as BA and MA, and in 1828 with two friends of the Yacht Club, bought a yacht and sailed around the coasts of Wales and Devon, which ultimately led to him selecting the now well known "watering place" of Torquay as his permanent home.

He is known to have first lived with his brother-in-law at Hampton House, St Marychurch, Torquay.

In 1833 William Kitson, together with Edward's brother, Captain W. Vivian of St Catherine's in Torre, founded a bank in Vaughan Parade known as the Vivian & Kitson Bank. It was taken over and renamed Lloyds (now Lloyds-TSB) in 1900.

Early in his life this extraordinary man quickly determined that he wished to "lend assistance to anything and everything that has a tendency to elevate the moral and intellectual condition of the working classes".

As one of the Newton Board of Guardians, he arranged for firms in Manchester to take whole families of unemployed workers from St Marychurch to this industrial centre of the North, where there was more demand for labour and at wages far in excess of what could be earned in Devon.

He was treasurer of many local societies, notably Torquay Parochial Charities Group and Torbay Hospital. He was elected a Town Commissioner in 1840, a role he would hold for three years. (Town Improvement Commissioners were responsible for the then expanding local government). He was also one of the eight officials elected to the Local Board of Health formed in 1850, becoming a vice-president. From 1841 he served as a magistrate, finally becoming a Senior Justice in 1880.

He was also chairman of the Baths Corporation — a principal source of attraction for tourists of elegance, before his new venture, that of revealing the riches that lay buried in the caves of Kents Hole.

The full exploration of Kents Hole dates from September 1845, when two members of the newly-formed Torquay Natural History Society asked Sir Lawrence Palk for permission to explore Kents Hole "for the purpose of obtaining fossil remains for a proposed new museum in Torquay".

Edward Vivian and William Pengelly led "a major investigation" between 1846 and 1847, but the results were said to be "meagre and misunderstood".

In 1847 Edward Vivian read a paper to the London Geological Society on the serious work they had done in the cavern and soon afterwards a Kents Cavern "dig" was agreed. Conducted by Vivian and Pengelly, this major excavation, overseen by a committee of the British Association, lasted over 10 years until 1858. The committee included Edward Vivian as an active member, and although emphasis has been placed on Pengelly's name in connection with Kents Cavern, Vivian made a major contribution towards changing "the course of our knowledge of English prehistory".

Vivian was also a keen botanist and horticulturist, and from his new home at Woodfield in Lower Woodfield Road, Torquay, with its six acres of grounds, he possessed some of the finest collection of sub-tropical plants in the area.

The gardens would from time to time be used for social gatherings, often involving the Torquay Voluntary Artillery Band, who would entertain his guests in the gardens.

He was also so fascinated by Torquay's changing climate that for 30 years from 1848 Vivian recorded temperatures and meteorological notes at his home, which would be regularly

Above: The old Vivian Institute in Braddons Hill Road West, is now the Plazza

reported in the Torquay Directory newspaper which he had edited since the mid-1840s.

With political unrest rife, he decided in 1848 to split up his beautiful gardens to rent to 16 members of the Chartist Association, in an effort to allay further public agitation between rich and poor.

Despite his privileged upbringing, Vivian was acutely aware that many of his fellow countrymen were for a number of reasons poor, hungry and needy, and he identified three specific problems - drunkenness, low wages (particularly in the agricultural sector), and a lack of educational opportunity.

To address these problems he formed a Temperance Society, and although this had limited success, he maintained a continuing interest in its work. The second problem was attacked by encouraging everyone to grow more of their own food, hence his decision to divide his own acreage into quarter-acre plots and to lease land in the Lincombes to increase the number of plots he could offer.

But above all he came to realise that the underlying cause of poverty was the lack of educational opportunity for the "lower classes". Surprisingly, education for this group was still frowned on by the Church and secular authorities of the time. The Archbishop of Canterbury is quoted as believing "education would be prejudicial to their morals and happiness, and would teach them to despise their lot in life".

Vivian, on the other hand, devoted great enthusiasm to the educational needs of working people, and for many years lectured at the Mechanics' Institute, assisting in the Mutual Improvement Societies and Reading Room schemes, and had even backed many of the unsuccessful attempts to secure a local public library.

He realised that one of the first priorities required to help the poor was an ability to provide working people with practical training in or at work, and leisure skills, at a time and at a price they could afford.

Vivian was also involved in the Volunteer Movement which was very strong in Torquay in the late-1850s. By December 1859 the Fourth Devon Volunteer Artillery Battery was formed under Vivian's command, and he became Major Vivian.

An ardent supporter of Gladstone in 1865, Vivian had unsuccessfully contested the Parliamentary seat of St Ives, Cornwall.

In addition to all this activity he was made president of the Devonshire Association for the Promotion of Science and Art in the year that it met in Torquay, and became the second president of the Torquay Natural History Society.

Vivian, who was red/green colour-blind, was nevertheless a talented artist, and some sketches of Torquay and South Devon were lithographed, and shown at local art exhibitions.

It was largely though his efforts that a School of Art was to be founded in Braddons Hill Road West.

TORBAY CIVIC SOCIETY

"WOODFIELD"
HOME OF
EMINENT VICTORIAN
EDWARD VIVIAN M.A., J.P.
FROM 1842 TO 1893.
BANKER AND
RENOWNED BENEFACTOR
TO THE POOR

Originally built as the Salem Chapel in 1839, the building had been a church for 30 years before being purchased by public subscriptions and converted to the Institute for the Promotion of Science and Art in 1878 in his honour.

On reaching the age of 70, Vivian would see the Institute renamed the Vivian Institute (later to be called the School of Art). Through its early work in vocational and adult education, the Institute was recognised as one of the most important buildings of Torquay of the time.

As a keen photographer, Major Vivian was president of the Torquay Photographic Association, presiding at its opening exhibition in February 1893, the year of his death.

He died aged 84, and the wreath for his funeral carried no fewer than 62 different cuttings of shrubs from his garden. One, from the Indian Cedar, which he had grown from a seed from the Himalayas and planted when he was a boy, is still to be found at Woodfield.

Torquay Civic Society first unveiled a blue plaque to honour Edward Vivian at the former Vivian Institute in Braddons Hill Road West in 1987. Unusually, a second plaque was erected in November, 2001 at his home, Woodfield, in Lower Woodfield Road, Torquay.

Below: Edward Vivians Home, Woodfield

ELLA ROWCROFT –
The first lady of Torbay health

THIS AMAZING BENEFACTOR touches all Torbay residents and visitors who need medical treatment. In 1988 Torbay Civic Society honoured her by the installation of a plaque to her memory.

AT THE END OF THE 1914-18 WAR, Torbay Hospital was still lit by gas, had only 64 beds, and other than the provision of a children's ward in 1909 the building had not substantially changed since its construction in 1850.

With such outdated buildings and, perhaps more importantly, having being built on a quite unsuitably small site at the top of Union Street, (now known as Castle Chambers, across Trematon Road from the Magistrates' Court), it was time for a reappraisal.

With no National Health Service, (this would not come until 1948) hospitals were paid for by voluntary contributions and public subscriptions.

Residents were encouraged to pay 1d (one "old" penny) a week for those over 14, and 2d per week for children of the family. Where a regular subscription was not paid, any individual (non-member) who fell sick would be charged three shillings (15p) at admission, and also had to undertake to become a subscribing member on recovery. Failure to do so brought an automatic penalty of five shillings (25p) per person.

Born in 1860 Ella Wills was the daughter of Sir Edward Payson Wills, a director of the Imperial Tobacco Company. Married to Francis G. T. Rowcroft in Bristol Cathedral on November 25, 1905 she came to live in Torquay in 1912. Her husband was the son of Lieut Col T. T. Rowcroft of the Bengal Army, but little else is known other than that he had come from Tilehurst in Berkshire.

When Ella Rowcroft came to Torquay she initially lived with her sister, Violet Wills, in a house called Barcombe Hall at Paignton. In 1920 the sisters moved to Pilmuir, a large house above Torre Station that had just been built on the site of a demolished Georgian residence, previously the home of Lord Sinclair.

With the local population having doubled in the period to 1891 and then doubling again in the period to 1925, the needs of the hospital were obvious but as always with large institutions, particularly public ones, the problem was lack of money.

To address the problem, a town meeting was called and a hospital committee was set up, chaired by the Mayor. It was to be Ella Rowcroft who agreed to fund the subsequent project.

After some initial opposition from Paignton, which thought any new hospital should be built in the middle of Torbay, the committee eventually agreed that Hengrave House, a freehold property owned and offered by Major R. P. Kitson, should be purchased.

Ella Rowcroft then produced the £8,000 required to buy the property, but also went much further. In the words of a contemporary she then offered "a gift of such magnificence as has not been equalled in Torquay before".

She wrote to the committee and offered a sum of £100,000, a staggering amount of money in those days equating to millions of pounds today, and in addition she and her sister then also found a further £13,000 to set up an endowment fund to pay for the stipend of a hospital chaplain in perpetuity.

Her letter setting out the conditions of the gift is business-like and very illuminating, stating that the gift would not meet all costs, and was subject to the committee not relaxing its efforts in raising the additional money required. A further condition sought to ensure that no vivisection would be permitted at the new hospital.

The foundation stone was laid by Mrs Rowcroft, sadly by then confined to a wheelchair, on June 23, 1926, with the hospital being officially opened by Lord Mildmay of Flete, Lord Lieutenant of the County of Devon, on November 17, 1928.

Mrs Rowcroft also had very definite views on spiritual

Above: Rainbow House, on the heights above Torre.

matters. Her gift ensured that a chaplain would always be present at the hospital and there were several strict stipulations. Eventually the new chapel in the hospital was dedicated on August 12, 1930 by the Rt Rev Lord William Cecil, Bishop of Exeter. Unfortunately, Mrs Rowcroft was unable to attend the official opening of the hospital, or the chapel dedication ceremony.

By 1933 Mrs Rowcroft had commissioned a second home to be built in the grounds of Pilmuir and, as the story goes, because a rainbow appeared on the picture she was shown of the new house, it was named "Rainbow" there and then.

In 1937 "the modest, retiring Freeman of Torquay" announced that she would also give her former home, Pilmuir, and its five acres of grounds to Torbay Hospital in memory of her parents and to commemorate the Coronation of King George VI.

In 1938 a trust and an endowment fund were set up to manage Pilmuir as a convalescent home catering for up to 20 patients. The home opened in April 1939, exclusively catering for females from Torquay and Bristol. Mrs Rowcroft felt that women had a special need, since without some form of convalescence, they went straight from hospital to their home and the responsibilities of family and house, etc.

Although Rainbow House had been built for use by her long term companion and housekeeper, a Miss Mary Delve, she died shortly after its completion. After her death Mrs Rowcroft made the house her own home, and with the threat of an impending Second World War spent £24,000 on building an air raid shelter in the grounds, reached by lift. However, as she preferred to stay in her home with her 18 servants and her

Bible at her side, the shelter was never used.

During her life the financial contributions to charity were numerous and diverse, and included a rescue home for girls in Japan and a YMCA hut for soldiers in France.

Her first benefaction to the townspeople of Torbay had come through a public relations exercise. With the effect of the 1914-18 War still apparent, local activists of Torquay had started to look at ways of putting the area back on the tourist map.

It was agreed to publicise Torquay more widely, and newspaper representatives from throughout the United Kingdom and abroad were accommodated and entertained in Torquay. A massive promotions exercise for the time saw around 100 leading representatives of national newspapers coming to Torquay in May 1924, followed in June by 170 Canadian journalists with their wives.

An international advertising convention to show what this beautiful area had to offer was now held. Mrs Rowcroft provided £3,000 towards the project. Mrs Rowcroft died on January 26, 1941 leaving £1,623,000, most of which went to her sister Violet, who in 1937 had become Dame Violet.

By 1975 and as a result of inflation, her endowment fund was no longer adequate to sustain Pilmuir, and it closed. In 1981, following the creation of a Rowcroft Hospice Project Committee on the initiative of the Torquay Lions Club, came the announcement that up to 18 beds would shortly be made available at a newly established "Rowcroft Hospice" which would offer comfort and care to terminally ill people.

By May 1982 the first patients were being admitted to Rowcroft Hospice. Torbay Civic Society unveiled a Blue Plaque at the Rainbow in 1988.

OLIVER HEAVISIDE -
The spark of electrical genius

OLIVER HEAVISIDE was one of Britain's most eminent physicists in the new world of electricity in the Victorian era.

H E WAS A RENOWNED ELECTRICAL engineer, an outstanding mathematician and a forward thinking scientist.

He is possibly known best to the public for his brilliant prediction of a layer of ionised particles being present in the earth's upper atmosphere, off which would bounce all radio waves - a theory only proven in 1924, the year before his death in Torquay.

His early theory that radio waves would follow the earth's curvature would ensure his name being permanently linked to the phenomenon.

Today it is called "The Kennelly-Heaviside Layer" as a joint recognition, a similar prediction having been made by Arthur Kennelly of Harvard University, USA.

It was Marconi in 1901 who provoked Heaviside's theory, when he arranged for the first ever radio signals to be sent across the Atlantic.

Although at a loss to explain how they had followed the curvature of the earth, Heaviside's prediction that wireless waves might be "caught" by a layer in the atmosphere was included in the 10th edition of Encyclopaedia Britannica in 1902.

Andrew Lloyd Webber, in his musical Cats, based on the poems of T. S. Eliot, later wrote a song called *Journey to the Heaviside Layer*:

Up up up past the Russell Hotel

Up up up to the Heaviside layer...

Born in the same London slums as Dickens on May 13 1850, Heaviside left Camden House School, London in 1866, learned the Morse code, studied electricity and became a telegraph operator in Denmark, following another of his loves, languages.

He was publishing papers on electricity at age 22, having taken inspiration from James Maxwell, another expert in the field of electricity and magnetism, and his uncle, Charles Wheatstone.

Wheatstone, in 1837, in conjunction with a W. F. Cooke, had patented the electrical telegraph, and later devised an electrical network for measuring resistance, eventually to be known as the "Wheatstone bridge".

With this background Heaviside seemed destined to become a scientist and mathematical genius, obsessed by the electromagnetic and electromotive forces of the planet. Between 1870 and 1872 his first significant paper, entitled *Comparing Electromotive Forces*, was published.

In 1871 he returned to England to work for the Great Northern Telegraph Company, who were then dealing with overseas telephonic traffic. In 1873 he published a further paper which attracted the attention of Maxwell, who incorporated the results in the second edition of his own *Treatise on Electricity and Magnetism*.

This book so fascinated Heaviside he devoted years to studying and understanding the treatise and he wrote later: "I saw that it was great, greater, and greatest with prodigious possibilities in its power. I was determined to master the book.

"It took me several years before I could understand as much as I possibly could. Then I set Maxwell aside, and followed my own course. And I progressed much more quickly".

Heaviside eventually simplified Maxwell's equations by replacing them with variables.

Another notable of the time, the brilliant mathematical physicist George Fitzgerald, wrote: "Maxwell's treatise is cumbered with the debris of his brilliant lines of assault, of his entrenched camps, of his battles. Oliver Heaviside has cleared these away, has opened up a direct route, made a broad road, and has explored a considerable trace of country."

It was during this period that his increasing deafness meant he had to leave the telegraph company, and continue his own studying and research.

The alternating current (AC) system of electricity had been commercially established 15 years earlier, but in 1874 it was

Heaviside who established the ordinary symbolic method of analysing alternating current circuits still used today.

He was also emphasising the role of metallic circuits as guides, rather than conductors, of alternating current.

Between 1880 and 1887 he developed an operational form of calculus, still used in different branches of pure mathematics, and his visionary idea of inserting induction coils along long distance telephone and telegraphy circuits was a milestone in the development of telephony.

He also greatly enhanced knowledge of the relationship between the sun and earth, and his theories correlating electromagnetism with gravitation still fit in with modern high energy research today.

In the publication *Nature* Heaviside was described as "a man whose profound research into electro-magnetic waves has penetrated further than anyone yet understands".

Eminent mathematician Edmund Whittaker at the same time described Heaviside's operational calculus as one of the three most important discoveries of the late 19th century.

It was therefore not surprising that for this work, in particular, he was finally honoured in 1891 by being elected a Fellow of the Royal Society, and later would become the first recipient of the society's Faraday Medal.

By 1893 the first volume of his research on electromagnetic theory was published, followed in 1899 by the second.

Heaviside's third volume on electromagnetism was published in 1912, but his fourth and final book was not printed until after his death.

Having moved to Devon in June, 1889 Heaviside first lived at Paignton with his parents at Palace Avenue, and then for 11 years at Bradley View, Newton Abbot. With ill health having forced him to move nearer his relatives he finally moved to the Warberries area of Torquay in 1908.

Apparently now a bitter man with evident signs of a persecution complex, and a virtual recluse, he was locally viewed as a hermit. Although in these latter years he was desperately unhappy, and always the odd one out at family reunions, he nevertheless could often be seen during his years around Newton Abbot cycling alone around the lanes of Devon.

His brother Charles ran a music shop in Torwood Street, Torquay, and Oliver as a musician played the aeolian harp.

With his early theories and innovations proven, he was responsible for a number of new words being accepted into the English language, including impedance, inductance and attenuation, and as with many mathematicians he was to have craters on the Moon and Mars (Crater Heaviside) named in his honour.

Heaviside's brilliance as a scientist and mathematician had seen his early research and work accepted and adopted worldwide.

But his odd lifestyle, self-imposed solitude, unkempt way of life and his lifetime recurring illnesses through jaundice eventually proved fatal.

Found unconscious at his home, Highfield, in Lower Warberry Road, he died some weeks later in a nursing home on February 3, 1925 aged 74.

The family grave in Colley End Road cemetery, Paignton, has become a place of pilgrimage for modern day admirers.

Below: A page of mathematics in Heaviside's own hand

Below: Heaviside's induction coils in long distance telegraphy circuits

WILLIAM KITSON -
'The maker of Torquay'

A COMICAL example of William Kitson's penny pinching came when he was asked to sign on behalf of the local authority the contract to light the area's gas lamps.

IN ENSURING THE LAMPS WERE TO BE ILLUMINATED throughout the year, he put in a condition that they were NOT to be lit on any night of a full moon - this despite him also being a director of the Torquay Gas Company.

This clause later caused chaos, when one cold cloudy winter night, with the full moon having fallen on a Sunday, parishioners leaving their respective churches after evensong were unable to find their carriages in the darkness.

Torquay in 1800 was little more than a fishing hamlet but by the vision of William Kitson, so-called "The maker of Torquay", it would by 1864 be transformed into what the Western Morning News called "the most opulent, the handsomest, and the most fashionable watering place in the British Isles".

This achievement was possible mainly due to the unique positions of authority held by Kitson over many years.

By 1835 he was chairman of the Local Board of Health, a churchwarden (at that time an office of some significance), a land agent, a local solicitor and a banker. In addition to all this he held many directorships.

His power base was realised through the Palk family. At the time, the Roman Catholic side of the Cary family, having been dispossessed of their lands during the Civil War, still owned and lived at Torre Abbey, west of Fleet Street. The hilly land on the east of Fleet Street (the Braddons, Lincombes, Warberries, etc) had been purchased by Robert Palk, ex-Governor of India, on his return to England.

On his death the estate had passed to Laurence Palk, and it was he who had plans to develop it to create a port to rival Dartmouth. On his death in 1813 the harbour plan was shelved and the estate passed to his son, the second Laurence Palk. He quickly appointed Kitson as his land agent, and then became an absentee landlord who spent his life "wasting his substance" by gambling, womanising and drinking, mostly abroad.

It was in 1828 that Kitson, already established as a solicitor, was elected chairman of the newly formed local authority, a role he would retain continuously for the next 32 years. By 1835 he was also chairman of the new Local Board of Health and, with his friend Edward Vivian, joined the Torquay Savings Bank, later known as the Vivian & Kitson Bank (Messrs E. Vivian, W. H. Kitson and J. Kitson, Torquay Bank) and later renamed Lloyds.

Thus the scene was set for the eastern hills of Torquay to be developed into a genteel residential area, with wide roads, gentle gradients and literally hundreds of two-acre plots of land offered for sale to wealthy clients, provided they were willing to covenant to build a substantial, quality Victorian dwelling.

But Torquay also had its poor. In July, 1847 the town witnessed 150 individuals being taken to court for taking part in the Bread Riots, and with no Devon Constabulary yet in place, it was the parish constables, not the local authority, who ruled.

At the time, Kitson, as chairman of the Teign Valley Railway Company (later to be taken over by the Great Western Railway), was witness to the railway reaching Torquay in 1849, and this obviously ensured easier access from the North. Torquay was now very much open for business, visitors and residential growth.

By 1850 the new roads policy saw the linking of Meadfoot to the Ilsham Valley, and in 1852 Isambard Kingdom Brunel purchased land to build homes, a school and a chapel at Barn Place, Barton to house his ever growing workforce.

Kitson was also witness to the doubling of the local population every 20 years, and yet there was still a gulf between rich and poor.

As well as continuing with the sale of plots for the building of villas, Kitson was instrumental in the building of many splendid Anglican churches, including St Marks, St Mary Magdalene at Upton, and St Matthias at Wellswood.

He was also chairman of the local water company and one of his greatest achievements had been to create a proper drainage system, along with in 1856 a constant supply of piped water to Torquay from Hennock reservoir on Dartmoor.

He served on the Turnpike Trust, the Torquay Market Company and the town regatta committee, and even created a gentlemen's club. But for William Kitson, times were about to drastically change forever.

In spite of creating more than 500 villas in Torquay, he had been unable to bring together the Cary and Palk families, in an effort to eliminate the slums in the centre of the town. By 1864 more than 2,000 people were being housed in Swan Street, Pimlico, George Street and Madrepore Road, and the long standing neglect of this area of the town had resulted in slums with an appalling stench, such that few visited the area. The west side of beautiful Torquay was an eyesore and a place to avoid.

On the death of the second Laurence Palk in 1860, his son, Laurence Palk the third (later to be Lord Haldon) made it clear he wanted to run his own estates. As a consequence Kitson lost his land agency job and, through the machinations of Sir Laurence, he also lost his position as chairman of the local authority. Nevertheless, he remained a member of the authority for 23 more years, until his death in 1883.

Although recognised early as a man who closely watched every penny, his own and others', and was eventually be nicknamed "penny bun Kitson", his 30-year influence on Torquay's development, due to the free hand through the trusteeship given to him by the second Sir Laurence Palk, had been unique.

But it would be another 100 years before Torquay's dreadful dereliction on the west of the main street would be razed to the ground, by the development of what we now know as Fleet Walk and Swan Street car park.

Lord Haldon's wish to resurrect his grand-father's harbour scheme came too late. Torquay's residents, its tradesman and its visitors were too entrenched. The town's prosperity was by now intrinsically linked to that of a "resort". The great villas, the churches and the roads had made Torquay a shining example of Victorian town planning, and this mainly as a result of Kitson's autocracy, foresight, influence and perseverance.

Although the era of "the maker of Torquay" was at an end the people did not forget him. They celebrated his decades of work and commitment to Torquay with a great town dinner to which everyone was invited.

The speeches went on for hours and the event culminated in a salvo of guns being fired in his honour, off Corbyn Head. Later, in 1875, he was presented with a full length portrait, funded by public subscription recording his retirement from the Torwood Estate, which can still be seen at Torquay Town Hall.

He died in 1883 but the Kitson family continued to serve the local community for decades to follow. In 1966 the local council honoured Major R. F. Kitson and the family for the past extensive commitments to the community, by naming an adventure playground in Shiphay "Kitson Park". This ensured the name Kitson would live on and not be forgotten by later residents of Torquay.

Torbay Civic Society unveiled one of its blue plaques to "William Kitson - The Maker of Torquay" in 1988. It is fixed to the north facing wall of the former premises of Kitsons (Solicitors) at No 2 Vaughan Parade, facing Torquay's inner harbour. The firm has since become Kitson Hutchings and is now at No 4, and at The Terrace.

Below: William Kitson and his family with servants (circa 1880)

SEAN O'CASEY –
A theatre giant in South Devon

SEAN O'CASEY was born John Casey in 1880 in Dublin, and leaving school at 14 became variously employed in jobs of little skill.

LATER, THROUGH HIS BROTHER, he became attracted to the theatre, and would act in Dion Boucicault's play *The Shaughraun* at the Mechanics Theatre in Abbey Street.

From 1902 there were nine years of employment with the Northern Railway of Ireland, bringing a regular income to ensure his mother and family could eat properly.

The desperate financial status of his family would not be resolved until late in life, and many plays would describe the poverty and experience of his youth.

In 1906 John got involved with the Irish Gaelic Revival Movement, resulting in him learning the Irish language and changing his name to Sean O'Casey. His writing produced journalistic papers, and in 1918 his ballads *Songs of the Wren*, followed by *More Songs of the Wren*, were published. Other slender paperbacks came later that year together with his first play, *The Robe of Rosheene*. Next came the *The Frost in the Flower*, *The Harvest Festival*, *The Crimson and The Tri-Colour*, and *The Cooing of the Doves*.

Other plays and short stories came quickly, but in 1926 *The Plough and the Stars* would result in acrimonious debate due to the mention of prostitution in Ireland, resulting in rioting by those who felt this play insulted the heroes of 1916.

O'Casey met his wife Eileen in London in 1926, she aged 22, he 46. They married in 1927 and their honeymoon was spent in Ireland. After one further visit in 1935 he would never stay in Ireland again.

A variety of London homes followed, with the O'Caseys in contact with a virtual "Who's Who" of famous people, many remaining lifelong friends, including George Bernard Shaw, Ramsay MacDonald, H. G. Wells, Cyril Cusack, Sam Wannamaker, Peter Hall, Lord and Lady Asquith, Barry Fitzgerald, Eugene O'Neill, Tyrone Guthrie, Lady Astor and, from Number 10, Harold and Dorothy MacMillan.

September, 1938 saw the O'Caseys moving from London to Totnes, mainly to ensure that their sons Breon and Niall could go to the independent and progressive school at Dartington Hall, without having to board.

They settled down well in Devon, although on moving out of London O'Casey had apparently found living in the countryside very difficult. His biography states: "He feared the country, for it robbed him of much, his eyes were losing a lot of the power they had. In a city, the view was a short one, and his eyes hadn't to travel far to see things; all was at his elbow".

His wife later confirmed that he was always a townsman and yet "has taken to deep country Devon much better than I had guessed".

Constant debt and insufficient money eventually saw the local tax inspector threatening Sean with the bailiffs. After letters to London, an emissary from "Head Office" came to examine the affairs of this now world-renowned dramatist and soon discovered that although the Dubliner owed the Revenue £50, they owed him

Above: The O'Caseys lived at this house, Tingrith, on Station Road, Totnes.

£100 from forgotten post war tax credits he held. This resulted in a rare treat for the family and the London official - a celebration at a Totnes hostelry.

With the arrival of a daughter they stayed in Totnes until 1954, when they were given notice by the landlord. With their only daughter Shivaun at Dartington they moved to Torquay to rent a large first floor flat at 40 Trumlands Road, St Marychurch.

In spite of deteriorating eyesight, O'Casey continued to write plays, essays, a diary and further volumes of his autobiography, following the tragic death of his son Niall from leukaemia in 1957, aged 22.

Regarding his own health, London-based Dr Lyell told him: "Sean, I have done all I can. One eye is useless as you know, but I do not believe you will lose the sight of the other completely, it should last you". It did, but with very restricted sight, and major discomfort.

America and Russia were enthusiastic for Sean O'Casey's work and many trips were made to support plays on opening nights. But as in Ireland and London his work was always controversial, and the Wesleyans and Jesuits of the US united, to ban his play, *Within the Gates*, and a theatre company banned *The Silver Tassie*.

Nevertheless the American nation were generally kind to the Irish playwright. Income from Russia was difficult, but that nation remembered his 80th birthday, sending a gift of 80 red roses in 1960.

During the ten years at Torquay O'Casey published a comedy and such plays as *Behind the Green Curtains*, *Figaro in the Night* and *The Moon Shines on Kylenamoe*.

More amazing were the number of famous personalities that visited him in Torquay - Mai Zetterling, Adrienne Corri, Sybil Thorndike, Sam Wannamaker, Peter Hall, Alfred Hitchcock, Augustus John, Arthur Miller and his wife Marilyn Monroe, and O'Casey's long term friend, the comedian Barry Fitzgerald.

He welcomed two television companies, one being NCB from America to preview his plays and film in his small studio at home. The disruption saw his beloved "Eily" booking a room at the local Links Hotel, joining American friends staying over.

Although later years saw an easing of the struggle against debt, he was in poor health. His last published play was *Under a Coloured Cap* in 1963, although a series of articles and selected stories entitled *Blasts and Benedictions* were published posthumously.

O'Casey wrote over 20 published plays, numerous essays, verses, a history, journalistic articles and a four-volume autobiography. His most successful plays were *The Shadow of a Gunman* and *Juno and the Paycock*, (both 1925), but other plays remembered are *The Plough and the Stars* (1926), *The Silver Tassie* (1928), *Red Roses for Me* (1942), *Cock-a-Doodle Dandy* (1949), and *The Bishop's Bonfire* (1955) when "stink bombs" were thrown and riots occurred at a theatre performance in Ireland.

His son Breon became an artist and lived in St Ives, Cornwall, and daughter Shivaun became an actress. O'Casey in his final years continued to read his beloved Irish newspapers, write and watch TV, particularly sport and nature programmes, and listen to music by Mozart and Mendelssohn whilst always drinking copious amounts of tea, each with six or seven full spoons of sugar.

Sean O'Casey, an Irish protestant fanatical, fierce, determined and intolerant of compromise, yet also kind, gentle, witty, lovable and courteous, died on the way to Torbay Hospital from a thrombosis on September 18, 1964, aged 84.

After a service at St Martin's Church, Barton, this "international star" was cremated and his ashes taken to Golders Green, London to be scattered at the grave of his son, Niall.

A plaque to Sean O'Casey was erected by the residents of Totnes in 2002 on the gatepost of Tingrith, his former home in Station Road.

Below: The house in Trumlands Road where Sean O'Casey lived.

BENJAMIN DISRAELI - Friend of a Torquay widow

BENJAMIN D'ISRAELI was born on December 21, 1804, the second son of Isaac and Sarah, in a house that overlooked the gardens of Gray's Inn, London.

GAMES PLAYED AT AN early age included the forming of a Parliament with his brothers and friends. He, the permanent Prime Minister, saw no one else in power. Eventually, he did become Prime Minister - twice - and also a novelist, poet and orator.

By 1816, with his father inheriting a fortune from Benjamin's grandfather, the family moved to Bloomsbury Square, a stone's throw from the British Museum, where the young D'Israeli would bury himself in books for 12 of his formative years.

Although studying Greek and Latin at home, it would be politics that became the great delight of Benjamin's life. An agitated spirit, he followed his father's advice at 17, and become articled to a firm of solicitors in the City.

But it would be political achievements that created the amazing career for young D'Israeli who, during 1824, decided to drop the apostrophe from his name.

From the earliest years, Disraeli was an eccentric. With a florid delivery, a thirst for power, and a dress code which included rings, ruffles, coloured waistcoats and velvet jackets he was initially much mistrusted.

But he had a strong romantic streak and great patience. He said "everything comes if a man will only wait", and he waited 36 years to become Prime Minister. This was a man who was nicknamed "The Jew" and was not liked. He would often stand alone but never gave up.

In 1827, entering Lincoln's Inn with the intention of being called to the Bar, he took little interest in the calling. He had seen his satire *Popanilla* released and his novel *Vivian Grey* published, and by 1832 was well travelled and well read.

Determined not to be a lawyer, he stood instead for Parliament. It would take three more elections before his popularity reached a height where eight constituencies asked him to stand, including Ashburton, Barnstaple, Dartmouth and Taunton. Others in the chase were Chichester, Derby, Maidstone and Marylebone.

His choice ensured that in 1837 he was returned MP for Maidstone. The leader of his party in opposition, Sir Robert Peel, and Disraeli would both eventually achieve the office of Prime Minister.

Having always wanted to be "a great man", Disraeli, having looked at other professions, is quoted as saying: "To enter high society, a man must either have blood, a million or a genius".

He was certainly conscious of genius, but his blood was against him, so he speculated - and lost. His debts would take 30 years to clear and although bad management and the City crash colluded to bring about his downfall, it would be a lesson well learned. He would never again trust speculation or speculators.

Following a number of love affairs, marriage to Mrs Marie Anne Wyndham Lewis in 1839 was a controversial choice, she a widow and 12 years older than he. Nevertheless, their marriage was serenely happy until her death in 1872. He admitted "we have been married for 33 years and she has never given me a dull moment". He apparently delighted in domesticity.

Elections came and went, and with Parliament affectionately nicknaming him "Dizzy", he was to serve three times as Chancellor of the Exchequer. Once on the front bench of his party the colourful dress code was abandoned to the more customary suit of solemn black.

Between 1846 and 1851 he served as Leader of the Opposition and said of his great rival Lord Palmerston, who had served as War Secretary for 20 years under various Prime Ministers, that he had the only brain in the house that he really respected.

During 1851, a letter from an elderly widow in Torquay, Mrs Sarah Brydges Willyams, asked Disraeli to become an executor to her will, for which he would inherit part of her estate. She had apparently written to him on a number of occasions congratulating him on speeches, and was clearly an admirer.

An assignation in London was arranged but the appointment never kept by Dizzy. Later, a friendship developed and this saw the Disraelis holidaying in Torquay over the next 10 years. They always stayed at the Royal Hotel, although visits were made to Mrs Willyams's home at Mount Braddon, in the Warberries.

Regular and often intimate correspondence ensued, and gifts of Dizzy's books, photographs, flowers, newspapers, venison, grouse, partridge and trout were sent to Torquay.

Marie Anne also wrote in reply to some of Mrs Willyams's letters, and a great friendship ensued. On his becoming Chancellor of the Exchequer a telegram was sent, then a great novelty. Sarah's villa was eventually left to Dizzy together with £30,000, following her sudden death on November 11, 1863.

Sad that they had been unable to attend her interment, the Disraelis eventually built a special vault for her in Hughenden churchyard, where later both Marie Anne and Benjamin were also buried. All three, benefactress and beneficiaries, now lie together.

The Disraelis retained the villa for two years, finally disposing of it and seemingly their connection with Torquay. A private plaque in their memory was unveiled at Mount Braddon in September, 1929.

Having initially been despised by Queen Victoria, Dizzy's first audience in 1868 as her Prime Minister saw him achieving a lifetime ambition.

Below: Disraeli pictured with HM Queen Victoria

Above: This drawing shows Disraeli at Mount Braddon, receiving a bunch of primroses from Mrs Brydges Willyams. It is said that this incident was responsible for the name of the Primrose League.

The Queen would later dote on him, allowing him to address her in the first person and often visiting him at his home. For now, though, he would be PM for just nine months, as another general election saw the Whigs return to power.

With the death of his wife in 1872, condolence letters were received from a lifetime of connections, including the Queen and foreign monarchs, the Prince and Princess of Wales and a plethora of ambassadors from around the world. He grieved hard and long and apparently found much solace walking the parks and gardens of central London.

The general election of 1874 saw Disraeli getting a second term as Prime Minister, at the age of 70. He remarked: "Power, it has come to me too late," and, saddest of all, he had lost his partner in Marie Anne.

The 1874 Government was important, as it concentrated on social reform, clearing of slums, improving the conditions in factories and providing houses for working people.

Two years later, Dizzy made his final speech to the House on August 11, 1876 and later the same day was seen wearing a long white coat, with lavender kid gloves. The Times reported that his beloved Queen had created him Earl of Beaconsfield and Viscount Hughenden. The black parliamentary dress had gone forever.

Benjamin Disraeli died aged 76 in 1881. He declined a visit on his deathbed from the Queen, stating: "No, she will probably want me to take a message to Albert". The Queen sent two wreaths of his favourite flowers, primroses, and although etiquette precluded her attending the funeral she later visited the tomb which was reopened in order that she could place a chaplet of flowers on his coffin.

Of all her Prime Ministers, he was her favourite.

Mount Braddon eventually became a hotel, then a restaurant - Disraeli's - though by the late 1980's planners agreed to its conversion into 21 permanent flats and mews cottages.

RICHARD W. WOLSTON - Brixham's railway pioneer

ANY ENTREPRENEUR in the Victorian age must have been brave but to achieve multiple success in a variety of businesses demanded outstanding talents. Unfortunately, for such a man - a lawyer at that - not to protect himself legally proved foolish almost beyond belief.

ALTHOUGH HAVING FAMILY ORIGINS IN DEVON, Richard Walter Wolston was born in London in 1799. On qualifying as a solicitor he moved to Brixham in 1829, firstly to the centre of the town but soon afterwards building a substantial villa which he called Parkham Wood House, now Saxon Heights, standing in one and a half acres overlooking New Road and Tor Bay.

Wolston was an obsessively secretive man but both visionary and energetic. A wealthy solicitor and public notary, he was appointed clerk to the Harbour and Market Commissioners, became secretary of the Torbay and Brixham Harbour of Refuge & Dock Company, and was made a Commissioner of the Dartmouth and Torquay Turnpike Trust.

His energy, enthusiasm and vision led him to invest in property, which by 1830 even included a windmill, run by tenants, on Furzeham Common.

Realising that some of his land and other sites around Brixham contained iron ore, he ejected the tenants in 1840 and started a mining business producing iron ore, limestone and clay. A manager, John Dennis, a Cornishman, was appointed,

Below: A 19th century view of Brixham with Wolston's house on the extreme left

a tramway was built from the windmill site to the cliffs, and the aptly called Wheal Prosper mine was established.

But in spite of success, Wolston's bank was soon demanding repayments which he could not meet on the mortgage on Wheal Prosper, and it had to be put up for sale. By now shipments of the highly sought after iron ore were being made to the Cyfarthja Iron Works in South Wales and an industrial outlet was found for the clay. It was used to manufacture earthenware jars, sewage pipes, firebricks and tiles; even ochre, a by-product of the process, was being sold to preserve the sails of local fishermen.

Lady luck or a coincidence then intervened. During 1847 John Rendall, a full-time chemist in Torquay, in wanting to help Wolston - his future father-in-law - or perhaps seeing an investment opportunity for himself, discovered that by grinding the unwanted ochre with linseed oil, a substance to prevent rust on cast iron was formed.

The concept was inspirational, and "primer paint" would change the world of heavy metal. With the bank pursuing Wolston, Rendall purchased Wheal Prosper mine in 1849.

With the world's munitions and armaments made of cast iron, as were parts of bridges, railways, aqueducts and, of course, pipes for water and gas, etc, any rust prevention paint was assured of success.

Rendall was already one of the earliest homoeopathic chemists in the South West and after successfully opening dispensaries in Exeter, Plymouth and London, his primer paint would ultimately be a world leader.

With the purchase of Wheal Prosper "in the family" Wolston set up a factory close by the mine, to commence production of the primer paint. It traded as Torbay Iron Paint Works Company with Wolston as its first chairman.

This almost guaranteed success should have been his salvation but, sadly, it was not to be. To meet growing demand for primer, in 1852 a larger factory was built below the cliffs at Oxen Cove, financed by Wolston's brother Arthur, a solicitor based in Exeter.

Now between 1852 and 1864 Wolston, not content with being a successful lawyer and heavily involved in local affairs, and a successful industrialist to boot, still had a further ambition to fulfil.

His vision since 1845 had been the building of a Brixham rail link, to assist the growing fishing industry by ensuring that the landed produce could be sent to market more quickly than by horse-drawn carriage.

Above: The Brixham paint factory which was closed in 1961

He estimated that 1,800 public shares at £2 should be sufficient to build and connect the branch line from Churston, and for an added incentive he was perhaps spurred on by his own mineral and industrial products also needing carriage. In the event he sold 100 shares, leaving him to underwrite 1,700, a flotation disaster.

With the Wheal Prosper mine assisting quarries as far afield as Exeter, Topsham and Barnstaple to compete with imports from South Wales, Wolston was a man refusing to rest on his laurels, even though success was within his grasp.

By 1864 large sales of his products were going to such august names as the Royal Navy and the Great Western Railway. Galvanising metal was impossible with large objects and when Brunel built the Royal Albert Bridge across the Tamar in 1858/1859, even he used the new primer. Like many engineers, he must have realised that the simpler method of painting cast iron to deter rusting had huge potential.

But then enter Samuel Calley. He also owned land in Brixham, and in 1856 had introduced what was called a rust inhibiting oxide, specifically an anti-foulant paint. Unlike Wolston, he immediately patented his product and the process. Rendall and Wolston had never registered their formula, let alone patent the process - a potential legal minefield.

The Genuine Paint Works, founded by Calley in 1864, provided strong rivalry between himself and Wolston, to the extent that within a decade Calley had successfully sold his business.

Brunel's railway line meanwhile passed through Churston en route for Kingswear, Wolston despairing of getting public support, personally financed the building of this branch line. A steam engine, "Queen", was now purchased.

His new company, the Torbay and Brixham Railway Company, opened to passengers on February 28,

1868 and to freight May 1, 1868. Initially 150 tons of fish were delivered to Bristol and other market towns and cities each week - another vision realised.

But the venture cost Wolston £40,000 and spelt financial disaster for him. Just three weeks after the opening, he was obliged to hand over all assets to his bank, and in December, 1870 filed for bankruptcy.

The paint factory, the land at Wheal Prosper and the quarry all went to his brother, Arthur Wolston, who then leased it back to Rendall. The unpatented red primer paint had become commercially worthless.

Though a lawyer, Wolston proved to be no accountant and perhaps had too many fingers in too many pies. He was certainly inept and ignorant of the financial aspects of running a railway, and a less enthusiastic man might have been satisfied with creating the successful manufacturing and mineral factory.

But it was the management of the railway that brought his downfall. He could handle payment of taxes on income but was oblivious of rebates on "parliamentary trains and terminals". Train companies were entitled to various rebates, particularly where the third class fare did not exceed 1d, but the "terminal" rebates were even more complicated.

They involved through traffic connections and it was later proved that the South Devon Railway Company had taken rebates due to Wolston. Having gone to court in 1877 Wolston was awarded £2,000 for their dishonesty but it was all too late; he was already bankrupt.

Both types of Brixham paint achieved world success but the dispute of who had invented what went on long after the death of both protagonists. Interestingly, Wolston died in 1883 leaving £62 10s and when Calley died in 1887 he left £1,271 - hardly a fortune for either man.

Their two companies eventually merged in 1897, and survived until 1961 when Courtaulds finally closed what had become their subsidiary.

Sadly, Wolston and Rendall were long ago forgotten but Kelly's *Directory of Manufacturers* for many years quoted Brixham as "the home of Calley's paint".

After Dr Beeching determined Paignton as the railhead in South Devon, the final passenger train on the Brixham branch line ran in May, 1963 and was then closed 95 years after its inception.

Torbay Civic Society unveiled a plaque to Richard Walter Wolston in 1998 at Saxon Heights, a block of retirement flats on the site of his former home in Brixham, which was also previously a major hotel in the town.

ELIZABETH BARRETT -
A poet's sadness beside the sea

ELIZABETH BARRETT, the eldest of 12 children, was born at her uncle Sam's house in Durham in March, 1806.

IN MODERN PARLANCE SHE WAS in her youth a tomboy. At age 14 her love of sport and climbing resulted in her being thrown from a horse and sustaining a spinal injury that damaged her left lung, which then haemorrhaged, to affect both her breathing and, later, her heart.

Suddenly the enthusiastic tomboy became withdrawn and reclusive, with her doctors prescribing digitalis, opium and an inhaler. She became anorexic and an insomniac, often reading and writing into the early hours.

Elizabeth, who was later to be seriously considered as Wordsworth's successor in the position of Poet Laureate, had a commanding intellect and originality.

In August 1838, having been advised by her doctor that to survive another winter she must leave London's yellow smog and the constant stench from ineffective drainage, the unwell, unhappy and unmarried (at age 32) poet sailed with her maid Elizabeth Crow, her sister Henrietta and brothers George and Edward, from London for Devonport Docks, staying there two nights before joining the local steamer to Torquay.

There they joined an aunt and uncle and their three children at The Braddons on Braddons Hill, not far from Mount Braddon, where the Disraelis often visited their friend Mrs Brydges Willyams.

By October, 1838 the family had moved to No 3 Beacon Terrace, with its attractive balconies overlooking the harbour. From her window Elizabeth could see the steamers Brunswick and Eclipse coming and going on their regular schedule between Plymouth, Portsmouth and Southampton.

A letter of September 27, 1839 says: "In just a few days we move to number one of this Terrace, and there won't be much risk for me in the removal for so short a distance, for my brother means to fold me up in a cloak and carry me".

On October 1 the extended family, including Aunt and Uncle Hedley and seven others, took over No 1 Beacon Terrace, Torquay.

Originally called the Bath House it had for years offered "commodious warm and cold sea baths", and the new incumbents hoped for "a warmer nest".

For Elizabeth, now paying all household expenses out of her income and inheritance, the one guinea (£1.05) per week reduced rent must have helped.

The new home later became Victoria House, then Sea Lawn House, and finally, with annexed properties added, Hotel Regina.

Daily life at No. 1 in 1839 was busy for the family and a household which now comprised two maids, a cook and a young lad doing odd jobs. Elizabeth continued to write, and to a friend, Miss Mitford, she mentions the *Book of Beauty*. She writes: "There was a little poem, a very sweet and touching poem the product of a Miss Garrow, a young woman residing in this town".

The book was actually written by a Theodosia Garrow, aged 15, living at Braddons on Southhill. Theodosia idolised Elizabeth and was soon leaving gifts of flowers and vegetables, and even published a poem, *Presenting a Young Invalid with a Bunch of Violets*. They never met.

As 1838 drew to its close, and even when her widowed father and family members visited, Elizabeth's convalescence brought little happiness. She wrote: "Whenever the steam packet leaves the harbour, or enters it, my bed is shaken by the vibrations" and: "I did most emphatically abominate and nauseate the going downstairs". Apparently most of her time was spent in her bedroom.

By February 1839, with considerable improvement in Elizabeth's health, her father was insisting that brother Edward return home to the West Indies.

The Barretts' fortune had come from a sugar plantation in Jamaica and Edward was now needed there. With Elizabeth

Above: Elizabeth's former Home as pictured on a 1920s postcard
Opposite page: Elizabeth and Robert

improving daily, and Edward enjoying the swimming, boating and nightlife of Torquay, it was Aunt Jane Hedley who wrote to their father asking him to reconsider his request.

During 1840 Elizabeth read and wrote profusely. Her poem *Crown and Wedded* was dedicated to the royal wedding of Victoria to her cousin, Prince Albert, and in a letter to a friend in July she says: "The Bellerophon lay at anchor opposite my bed". It was carrying the remains of Napoleon being returned from St Helena to Britain. Tragically, weeks after this, Elizabeth learned of the death of her brother Sam, from the yellow fever which was rife in the West Indies.

Then came the major tragedy of her life. Her beloved brother Edward, having stayed in Torquay, went sailing on July 11 with three friends. They set course in the boat La Belle Sauvage across Babbacombe Bay and were expected to return that evening. Three days later the family were still waiting at the quayside. The yacht had been seen capsizing and all were presumed lost. On July 22 the harbour pilot found Edward's body washed up on Thatcher Rock.

As she had asked Edward to stay, Elizabeth was mortified. Although they never argued, on that fateful morning they had parted over some stupid "pettish word". Distraught, she immediately wrote a poem, *De Profundis*, in the shadow of Edward's death. It was not published until after her death. The poem perhaps says it all:

The face that, duly as the sun,
Rose up for me with life begun,
To mark all bright hours of the day,
With hourly love, is dimmed away,
And yet my days go on, go on.

The tongue which, like the stream, could run,
Smooth music from the roughest stone,
And every morning with 'Good Day'
Make each day good, is hushed away,
And yet my days go on, go on.

Edward is buried in Torre Churchyard, but no stone marks the place.

Elizabeth remained shut in her room for months, hanging on to life by a thread. When eventually the emotional storm abated, she wrote *The Mask* in an attempt to come to terms with Edward's death for the sake of those around her.

Following the tragedy, regular, enthusiastic and energetic correspondence received from 35-year-old Richard Henry Home, of Grays Inn, had some effect in diverting her grief, and she started working again.

By November, 1840 William Wordsworth had asked her to help in modernising Chaucer's work for publication in 1841.

Christmas that year was memorable, as the whole family were together, including brothers Charles and Octavius from Jamaica.

By July 1841, and now owning a dog called Flush, Elizabeth was able to sit out in the sunshine. Her work on Chaucer was having a positive effect on her health, and the convalescence at Torquay was nearing its end.

She returned to London and Wimpole Street in September, 1841 where a poem *Lady Geraldine's Courtship* was praised by Elizabeth. It was by Robert Browning, then a little known poet. This small gesture resulted in 91 visits, and 600 letters before Elizabeth eventually promised to marry him, provided she survived the winter of 1845/46.

She did, and in spite of her father's disapproval they were secretly married at Marylebone Church in September, 1846.

Leaving from Hodgson's Bookshop in Marylebone High Street, they travelled from Southampton to Le Havre, took a stagecoach to Paris and finally arrived in Italy, where they had decided to live. Elizabeth's father never spoke to her again, and her letters sent but never destroyed were later found unopened in a secret compartment of his bureau many years after both his and Elizabeth's death.

Her dog Flush, although "dog-knapped" for ransom three times, survived until 1854 and like its mistress is buried in Florence. In 1849, three days after her 43rd birthday, the Brownings were blessed with a son, Robert Weidemann Barrett Browning.

After 16 years of marriage, Elizabeth died in her husband's arms on June 29, 1861 at the Florence apartment. Her last words were: "Oh, what a fine steamer and how comfortable".

On being asked how she was feeling, Elizabeth replied: "Beautiful..."

Torbay Civic Society unveiled a plaque at Hotel Regina in 1988, commemorating Elizabeth's stay in Torquay.

TORBAY CIVIC SOCIETY

ELIZABETH
BARRETT BROWNING
1806-1861
POET
LIVED HERE
1838 - 1841

OSCAR WILDE –
Scandal in high society

OSCAR, SECOND SON of Sir William and Lady Jane Wilde, was born Oscar Fingal O'Flahertie Wills on October 16, 1854. At school he was embarrassed by his names, at university proud, and later dismissive, saying: "As one becomes famous, one sheds some of them, just as a balloonist when rising higher sheds unnecessary ballast".

H IS FATHER WAS A surgeon and his mother an Irish nationalist poet. In expecting a girl and having been disappointed, they are said to have dressed Oscar as a girl, thereby affecting his sexuality.

This must be dismissed, as Victorian society saw children of both sexes dressed in frocks and smocks. At age eight, Oscar looks like any other boy of that era. Lady Jane had her wish when their daughter, Isola Emily Francesca, was born in April, 1857.

Sir William and, eventually, Oscar's brother, Willie, both sowed more than their share of "bachelor oats" in years to follow. Sir William sired three illegitimate children, and in 1860 an incident involving a young woman of 19 brought financial hardship to the Wilde family, with a court ruling.

Thirty-one years later, Oscar mirrored this when, following the Queensbury drama, he became bankrupt. It seems men of the Wilde family were true to their surname.

The death of Isola, aged nine, in 1867 had a devastating effect on Oscar, who had been deeply attached to his little sister. He wrote the poem *Requiescat* to her memory.

With brother Willie he boarded at Portora Royal School, Enniskillen, excelling at classics. He took top prize in 1870 and 1871, achieving a Royal School scholarship to Trinity College, Dublin. Oscar's love of matters Greek came from two Trinity Dons, John Pentland Mahaffy and Robert Tyrrell. Interestingly, Mahaffy's book, *Social Life in Greece from Homer to Menander*, involved Oscar correcting the proofs, which included the controversial subject of Greek homosexuality.

The day after his 20th birthday, Oscar, having won a Trinity College Demyship (scholarship), entered Magdalen College, Oxford. Again he excelled, achieving a double first. Later he recalled: "The two great turning points of my life were when my father sent me to Oxford and society sent me to prison".

His intellectual and flamboyant style was born at Oxford, and created an enthusiasm for life that saw him toying with Catholicism, poetry, theory of art and aesthetics. His fascination for quasi-religious rituals and fancy dress led him to freemasonry, to which in February, 1875 he was admitted via the Apollo University Lodge. To produce humanists rather than classicists, he chose to write *Literae Munaniores* for his degree.

By 1879 and desperately short of money, Oscar was sharing rooms with Frank Miles and Frank's mother. It therefore was no surprise that he should jump at the chance to give the Americans a taste of aesthetes. This would earn him international recognition and money. A 50-lecture tour, extended to 140 lectures, taking 260 days from the east coast to west coast and back, saw him returning to London with £1,200 in his pocket.

It was during a lecture tour of Dublin in November, 1883 that he proposed to Constance Lloyd. They married in May, 1884 and Constance, already essentially a romantic, was to become the envy of the world; she talented and beautiful, and her husband the toast of England and America.

After honeymooning in Paris and Dieppe the couple returned to an eagerly awaiting London, to discover what a "professor of aesthetics" might do with his "house beautiful". It took a year to complete, and by then Constance was three months pregnant. Cyril, born in 1885 was followed by a second son, Vyvyan, in 1886. Wilde, now a self-professed "lord of language", was 32 and had a family to support, but no regular income.

Life was to change dramatically. Oscar, although tiring of his wife, was reviewing work for the *Pall Mall Gazette*. He was then approached by a new magazine entitled *The Lady's World*. This publication was struggling to survive financially and Oscar suggested it became more womanly than feminine, and suggested renaming it *Woman's World*. This stroke of genius resolved his lack of regular income.

By 1888 *The Happy Prince* and the *Studies in the History of the Renaissance* were in print and, of course, still to come was the so-called "heathenism" of *A Picture of Dorian Gray*. In 1889

John Gray - poet, dramatist and later Catholic priest - entered Oscar Wilde's life. By 1892 he was replaced by Oscar's own nemesis - his Dorian Gray - in the form of Lord Alfred "Bosie" Douglas, third son of the Marquis of Queensbury.

In 1892, Constance suspecting that Oscar was having an affair, suggested he take the boys to Torquay to stay at Babbacombe Cliff, a property owned by a distant relative, Lady Mount Temple (see No 19). It was available for three months during that winter; he stayed four and the vacation saw Oscar completing his play, *A Woman of No Importance*, and virtually completing *A Florentine Tragedy*, and a historical drama in the vein of *Salome*.

The suspected affair was not with an actress, as suspected by Constance, but with Lord Alfred Douglas, whom he invited to Torquay through the following letter, which was later used as evidence in his trial:

January 1893, Babbacombe Cliff

My Own Boy,

Your sonnet is quite lovely, and it is a marvel that those red-roseleaf lips of yours should be made no less for the madness of music and song than for the madness of kissing. Your slim gilt soul walks between passion and poetry. I know Hyacinthus, whom Apollo loved so madly, was you in Greek days.

Why are you alone in London and when do you go to Salisbury? Do go there to cool your hands in the grey twilight of Gothic things, and come here whenever you like. It is a lovely place and lacks only you; but go to Salisbury first.

Always, with undying love,
Yours, OSCAR.

Douglas (Bosie) and his tutor Campbell Dodgson soon joined Wilde in Torquay. Oscar's note accompanying the rent perhaps says it all: "Babbacombe Cliff is like a college, for Cyril studies French in the nursery, I write my plays in Wonderland and in the drawing room Lord Alfred Douglas - one of Lady Queenbury's sons - studies Plato for his degree in June. He is staying with me for a few days, so I am not lonely in the evenings".

It would not last long; following a lovers tiff "Bosie" was soon departing Babbacombe in a huff.

The rest is history. A small card left by the Marquess of Queensbury on a table at Wilde's club stating "Oscar Wilde posing as a sodomite" resulted in Wilde bringing a libel action against the Marquess.

What followed was one of the most sensational trials of the 19th century, which resulted in Oscar Wilde being convicted of gross indecency and sentenced to prison and hard labour.

The trial proved a social milestone for Victorian values when in court it was heard that Wilde believed pleasure was "the only thing one should live for" and his pleasures, it seemed, included bringing rent boys into hotels as famous as the Savoy. Even Edward Carson, who had been at Trinity College with Wilde, and having now been appointed defence lawyer, is said to have been shocked by the revelations in open court concerning his erstwhile friend. However, it seemed that not even Oscar's brilliance as a wit, orator and writer, nor the public's admiration for his stylistic flamboyance, could save him from what the media now called his "dastardly and heretical views on sex, art, religion and class".

The judge had little alternative but to find in favour of the Marquess and the libel case collapsed. The Government did not have to pursue the matter further but the damage to polite society had been done and Wilde paid the price for his "social rather than sexual crime" by serving two years' hard labour, the sentence being handed down just days before his birthday in May, 1895.

In February, 1896 Lady Jane on her deathbed asked to see her son, still imprisoned, to be told it was "out of the question". Later a petition by Oscar to the Home Secretary for a week's early release to avoid the press was also refused. He was, however, transferred to Pentonville Prison the night before his release in 1897.

Soon re-united with Bosie in Italy, it was all too late and the reunion was an unmitigated disaster. Constance died in 1898, and Oscar's last two years of life were tortuous.

Following a recurrent ear infection picked up in prison, meningitis then set in and Oscar died on November 30, 1900. Destitute, he was given a pauper's burial in a leased grave outside of Paris.

Later, his friend Robbie Ross successfully pursued copyright for Oscar's work and paid off all his debts. This enabled a new resting place at Pere-Lachaise in 1909, but involved Robbie having to assist with the formal identification of his dead friend. This involved the opening of the coffin.

Bosie, later sued for libel by Winston Churchill, also spent two years in prison, at Wormwood Scrubs. Of Oscar's sons, Cyril died in action in the First World War and Vyvyan married, had a son and became a man of letters and a prolific and successful author of fine books.

With "the crime no longer a crime", Oscar's genius as a wordsmith is, of course, still enjoyed by the world today.

Above: The 'house beautiful' in London

RICHARD MALLOCK - Open spaces for the people

THE MANOR of Cockington in 1374 was owned by the Cary family of Torquay, and when they sold the estate in 1654 they had been its been resident owners for 280 years.

PURCHASED THEN BY THE MALLOCK FAMILY, the manor and its 223 acres remained in their ownership for 279 years, before a lease was granted in 1933 to Torquay Corporation, who eventually purchased the freehold, thus ending centuries of private ownership.

Richard Mallock was a second son, born in December, 1843 to Charles Herbert and Maria Mallock. He had seven sisters and an older brother, a second Charles Herbert.

Richard was educated at Harrow and became Lieutenant Mallock of the Royal Artillery, serving in India until 1870.

After his older brother died in 1875, two years after inheriting, Richard resigned his commission, married Mary Jones Dickson in April, 1876 and returned to the family estate the following month.

Once settled at Cockington, he invited the village to tea, with entertainment provided by 200 dancers and the Torquay Rifle Brigade Band.

After just two years at Cockington, his wife died at the age of 22. Though not buried in the family vault, her memorial window comprising three lights depicting the Blessed Virgin was installed in the Mallock family Chapel at Cockington Church. She left two children, Charles Herbert and Helen.

In 1880 Mallock married Elizabeth Emily Maconchy, daughter of G. Maconchy JP of Co. Longford, and then living in Torquay. They were to have two sons, Roger Champernowne and Rawlyn Richard Maconchy.

Torquay in the late 19th century was no longer a fishing port but an established and highly fashionable health resort sporting the Assembly Rooms and the Bath Saloons. The latter was a major meeting place of fashionable society of the era and in the 20th century world became the Marine Spa.

During May, 1882 the Devon County Agricultural Society were having difficulty finding a site large enough for their show in Torquay, when Mallock came to the rescue by providing three fields. These were joined, fences were taken down, and stone walls, a cattle yard, dairy and even a stile and a stream removed, perhaps establishing an early sign of benefactions to follow.

The Redistribution Bill of 1885 created a Torquay Division in 1886, and in the second general election that year, brought about by Gladstone going to the country over Home Rule, Mallock successfully overturned the Liberal Unionist to become Conservative Member of Parliament for Torquay by just 80 votes. He held the seat for nine years, declining to stand in 1895.

A stalwart churchman and churchwarden, he had during these years provided a Wesleyan Church and two mission rooms on the Cockington estate. Already referred to as a "political godfather" he had by 1887 also relinquished the patronage of Torre to the Bishop of Exeter.

Coastal land offered to the authorities by Richard in 1897 was refused but, undeterred, he gifted land at Ashfield Gardens, with provisos that it must "remain an open space forever".

That year also saw him gifting land at Chelston to mark Queen Victoria's Diamond Jubilee, now Victoria Park, and land for a school at Cockington and for St Matthew's Church.

Mallock had many interests, which included being a ruling councillor of the Primrose League at Cockington, a Justice of the Peace, a Deputy Lieutenant of Devon, and president and trustee of Torbay Hospital.

His consistent concern when gifting Mallock land was that it "at all times be used and maintained as open spaces", thus leaving in perpetuity a huge responsibility on the local authority. Perhaps this was why the authorities were cautious in accepting such gifts.

The family trustees would continue his wish to place strict conditions on every piece of gifted land. For instance, the parish rooms at Sherwell Lane, officially opened by the Bishop of Exeter in 1899, were used for 70 years, and even when sold the covenants still held, the rooms going to the Christadelphians.

The year 1900, when Cockington and Chelston became part of Torquay, was also the year of Richard's tragic death at the early age of 56.

He and his wife and son, Roger, were on a three-week summer golfing and cycling holiday in Scotland, when he was seen to stumble and then fall while pushing his bicycle.

He died within minutes and after he was brought home on June 30 his funeral procession involved a posse of police, 80 clergymen, 165 carriages, and 16 bearers alongside the hearse. Thousands turned out, so many that at the grave 18 invalided soldiers from the local convalescent home were ordered to form a protective cordon. His commemorative cross commenced with the words "Richard Mallock, beloved Lord of the Manors of Cockington and Chelston".

Following his death, the son from his first marriage, Charles Herbert Mallock, succeeded to the estate.

Like his father, Charles Herbert was a serving soldier, and saw action in the Boer War. As Captain Mallock he returned to the family estate in 1906 and, again mirroring his father, did so in style. Arriving at Torquay station he was met by 40 mounted horsemen and torch bearers, and escorted home via Walnut Road, pausing only to watch a firework display and an artillery band. On his arrival at Cockington village, adorned with Chinese lanterns and fairy lights, thousands of parishioners escorted his carriage through the manor grounds.

Dismissing the horses at the main gate, they even man-handled the carriage right up the long drive to be met by a fairy light "Welcome Home" across Cockington Court - quite a show for the new Lord of the Manor.

In 1907 the late Richard Mallock's wish that his coastal land at Corbyn Head be assigned to the people of Torquay was finalised by his son - this was land the authorities had refused in 1897. As usual, strict protective covenants were attached.

With the outbreak of the First World War, Charles rejoined the Army and served with distinction, becoming Major Mallock. He met his death by inhaling German mustard

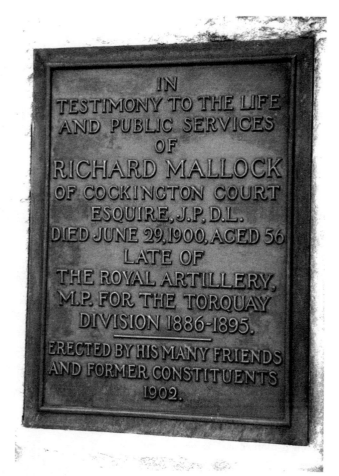

Above: Wording on the clock tower plaque

gas in November, 1917.

His nine-year-old son, a second Richard, was his heir but could not take control of the estates until he "came of age" at 21.

The interim years saw a tenant, Mr J. H. Charlesworth, in residence; he vacated the estate for Richard's return in 1928. Significantly, after centuries of partnership, Richard would be at serious odds with local people, to the point where court action and lawyers became involved in a "rights of access" dispute. After just four years at the manor, he became the last private owner of the estate, when the Court, the meadows and the parkland were sold to the Borough of Torquay for just £50,000.

The first Richard Mallock was not to be forgotten. The foundation stone of a memorial clock tower to his memory, given by friends and 1,700 subscribers, was laid by William Henry Kitson in 1902. The Mallock Memorial Clock Tower still on Torquay's Strand was completed the following year, W. H. Kitson, in his address, concluded that Richard "did his duty in that state of life to which it pleased God to call him; a man who did justice, loved mercy, and walked with his God..."

The memorial itself was finally "gifted" to the local authority, following the long tradition of Mallocks as benefactors.

Torbay Civic Society's plaque to the Squires of Cockington was erected in 1989 and can still be seen at Cockington Court.

AGATHA CHRISTIE - Torquay on the literary Map

AGATHA MILLER, daughter of Frederick and Clarissa Miller, was born at Ashfield, in Barton Road, Torquay on September 15, 1890.

B ROUGHT UP IN AN elegant Tormohun villa standing in two acres of land, Agatha by the age of 11 had seen the death of her father and the end of the Victorian era.

Though money was tight, by renting out Ashfield mother and daughter were able to spend three months in Cairo. In her teens and having "come out", Agatha, with flirtation in vogue, attended at least five dances a week; she received and rejected proposals of marriage from several officers of the British Army in Egypt.

Returning to Devon, Agatha continued her hobby of writing stories and poems, and was soon winning prizes from published work in *The Poetry Review*. She was, however, unsuccessful when writing under the pseudonyms of Mack Miller and Nathaniel Miller (her grandfather) and admitted to her sister Madge the wish to write a detective story, though nothing followed at this time.

In her early twenties Agatha, normally fending off male admirers, became engaged to Reggie Lucy but later wrote to say it was off, as she had met and fallen in love with one Archibald Christie.

They were married on Christmas Eve, 1914 but Archibald, a Captain in the Royal Flying Corps, went to war two days into the marriage, Britain being at war with Germany. Agatha returned home and went to work at Torbay Hospital, to nurse casualties back from the Front.

In her autobiography, she confirms that while working in the hospital dispensary in 1916, she decided to pursue her ambition to write a detective novel.

The first problem was what kind of detective story it should be. The murder weapon was now obvious - poison. But next came every writer's nightmare - the who, what, where, when and why. It was not long before Hercule Poirot emerged.

The first Poirot story involved Agatha seeking the peace of the Moorland Hotel on Dartmoor, to finalise a complicated plot that became *The Mysterious Affair at Styles*. Archie read the novel while on leave and liked it. However, it was rejected by many publishers, though one left it "on the shelf". With the 1914-18 War nearing its end and Archie now a Colonel at the Air Ministry, the Christies moved to St John's Wood, London.

In 1919 daughter Rosalind was born at the family home in Torquay, but with Archie demobilised and still in London, it was time for the family to move to a larger flat in Earls Court. That year saw the shelved manuscript of *The Mysterious Affair at Styles* re-emerging, to be published firstly in the United States and then, in 1920, the UK.

With the Christies in London, and her mother attempting to maintain Ashfield on an inadequate income, the question arose of whether to sell the house.

Horrified, Agatha determined that another novel would be written and the income used to help retain Ashfield. That book became *The Secret Adversary*.

With Archie tiring of London work and a third novel - *The Murder on the Links* - virtually complete, an opportunity arose for a grand tour of the British Empire, all expenses paid. The organiser, Major Belcher, Archie and Agatha set out for Cape Town, Australia, New Zealand, Canada and, finally, a relaxing break in Honolulu.

The fourth book saw Agatha appointing a literary agent, resulting in a lifetime friendship with Edmund Cork. The serial rights for *The Man in the Brown Suit* brought her the first substantial royalties, and a grey bottle-nosed Morris Cowley motor car. Years later Agatha confirmed that the two most exciting things in her life had been the grey car and an invitation to dine with Queen Elizabeth II.

The Christies now moved to Sunningdale in Berkshire but by 1926 it was clear the marriage was far from happy. In December that year, Archie left home to spend a weekend with a mutual friend Miss Neele, confessing to wanting to marry her.

Agatha, having been totally unaware of the liaison, wrote two letters and, with her daughter still asleep upstairs, drove off. After her car was found, the mystery of the infamous "missing 11 days" began.

On being discovered at the Hydro Hotel in Harrogate, registered as Mrs Neele, two doctors, a neurologist and a medical practitioner confirmed Agatha as suffering from an "unquestionable loss of memory". She would later declare that after her illness came "sorrow, despair, and heartbreak, and that there was no need to dwell on it".

With the marriage in ruins, there was now an urgent need for money. In February, 1928 to escape the press which she now reviled, Agatha went on vacation with Rosalind to the Canary Islands where her ninth novel, *The Mystery of the Blue Train*, was completed, and the location of St Mary Mead first emerged.

The divorce proceedings, a tortuous period for Agatha, were not finalised until October 29, 1928 and three weeks later Archie married Nancy Neele.

The following year, Agatha invented a new heroine, a Miss Jane Marple, and unknowingly set in train her destiny with her future husband, Max Mallowan.

In breaking a holiday in 1929 to visit excavations at Ur, near Baghdad in Persia (now Iraq), the beauty and thrill of uncovering history enthralled Agatha. The following year she met Max, a 26-year-old archaeologist, who was immediately smitten and whisked her off on guided tours of Nippur, Nejef, and Kerbala.

Max later came to Torquay, where long hikes and drives across Dartmoor in the Morris Cowley ensued. He proposed while at Ashfield and Agatha, having grave doubts about the age difference, consulted Rosalind. However, they were married in September, 1930 and the following year returned to Torquay for holidays from their London home.

Between 1930 and 1956 Agatha's work also included six romantic novels under the pseudonym Mary Westmacott.

Although still undertaking excavations at Ur in 1933, Max had his own dig in Syria due to sponsorship from the British Museum. These years saw husband and wife happy and content in this work, with Agatha now as on-site photographer while also washing, labelling and mending objects. She was competent and loved the work, and often even contributed to the expenses of the dig.

Surrounded by new building development, Ashfield had lost its sea views by 1938 and so the Mallowans sold it and moved to Greenway, a Georgian mansion set in 33 acres near Galmpton, overlooking the River Dart.

Plays, films, short stories and crime novels continued to flow from Agatha's typewriter but the announcement of the Second World War, heard on the kitchen radio, would see Max in the Home Guard and Greenway becoming a nursery for children evacuated from London.

With life now very different, Max returned to the capital and Agatha to a hospital to renew her expertise on drugs. During this period two novels were put in trust and locked away for publication after Agatha's death; to Rosalind a Poirot story, and to Max a Miss Marple.

When the war was over, the family returned to their pre-war life of working in London and holidaying in Devon until, in 1947, they returned to Baghdad with Max now Professor of Western Asiatic Archaeology, at London University. That year saw confirmation that the royal family had placed a standing order for all Agatha's novels and in 1956 she was awarded the CBE, becoming a Dame of the British Empire, a rare honour, in 1971.

The last Mary Westmacott novel, *The Burden*, completed a total of 81 books by Agatha but now she was able to concentrate on her autobiography, though would not complete this until 1965 at the age of 75. During this period Max was knighted for his services to archaeology.

Home was still Greenway but during a visit to Torquay Agatha went to find her beloved Ashfield and discovered only asphalt and new houses - it had been demolished. Only her beloved monkey puzzle tree had survived.

Dame Agatha died aged 85 on January 12, 1976. Max, who re-married in 1977, died a year later in August, 1978 and is buried with Agatha, to whom he had been married 46 years.

In 1986 Torbay Civic Society created a memorial appeal to furnish an Agatha Christie Room at Torre Abbey and in 1990, to mark her centenary, a bust was unveiled in the pedestrian area close to the new Fleet Walk development. Her daughter Rosalind (Hicks) died in 2005.

Above: A young Agatha plays with a spinning top in the gardens of Ashfield, her Torquay family home.
Below: Dame Agatha at Greenway in the 1970s

FLORA THOMPSON -
Local links with 'Lark Rise'

FLORA JANE TIMMS was born on December 5, 1876, the eldest of 10 children. Her stone-mason father Albert, a sensitive man, had witnessed his own father, a master builder, reduced to labourer status due to his temperament, drink and gambling.

FROM HER MOTHER, FLORA INHERITED a love of traditional songs and stories, and a down to earth, commonsense, dry humour, along with a strong, old-fashioned sense of duty.

In later years she described her childhood as "somewhat harsh and restricted" but bore no malice or grudge, believing this to be part of a life spent in poverty.

Born in the hamlet of Juniper Hill, Brackley, in North Oxfordshire, Flora was to use the characters of her childhood in her writing, like Agatha Christie (See No 14) years later, and she involved her readers in her observed experiences, even though there were few remarkable or significant events of note.

This is what made her different; she would write life as it was, generally from the viewpoint of the poor but always including nature and the countryside.

The annals of the poor are rarely written by them, possibly because they have little opportunity or are incapable. They also have no archival material and may not wish to recall their early life.

In 1897, at the age of 20, Flora moved to Grayshott in Surrey to work at the local post office.

Although she lived first at the post-master's family home, domestic quarrels forced her to move out to private lodgings. Later, in a fit of abnormal violence, the postmaster was to murder his wife and child with a carving knife at that house.

When she was 24 Flora met Post Office worker John Thompson, a sorting clerk at Aldershot, and due to his imminent transfer they married quickly and moved to Bournemouth.

John initially condemned Flora's love of reading and writing as being a waste of time, and her only luxury was the free library reached by walking. Post Office wages, then meagre, ensured that even the 2d (two "old" pennies) return tram fare was beyond her means. Nevertheless, in this way she was at least able to read profusely, and did so.

Their first two children were Winifred and Basil. Flora returned to writing immediately the babies were of an age that they could be left and on entering a competition requiring an essay on Jane Austen, she won top prize and had her first work published.

The women's newspaper running the event gave her another opportunity to send in an article and a short story. Again successful, and having earned a few shillings for her trouble, this was an important turning point. "I had earned the right to use my scanty leisure time as I wished", she said, and now wrote "small sugared love stories" which although artificial would sell.

On reading in 1912 an ode by Ronald Campbell Macfie, a Scottish physician and poet, and being asked by *Literary Monthly* magazine to enter one of its competitions, she submitted an admiring review of the ode, about the sinking of the Titanic. She was again successful and Dr Macfie, especially after writing to her, came to Bournemouth to visit. He became a lifelong friend and her main inspiration to write.

In 1916 John was promoted to sub-postmaster at Liphook in Hampshire and Flora now established the Peverel Postal Association for literary aspirants, ensuring close liaison with other writers, and devoted 18 years to its work. Unfortunately, her brother Edwin was killed in The Great War action the same year and Flora ceased to write until the end of hostilities.

After the war, and when the children were at day school, she started writing again and her first book was published in 1921, a collection of poems called *Bog, Myrtle and Peat*.

But her hunger for walking, nature, and solitude called. Essays on nature published in *The Catholic Fireside* would continue for 20 years, and the *Daily News* and women's magazines also featured her work. In "ghosting" for a game

Above: Flora Thompson's very plain grave at Dartmouth, and, the words which commemorate her son Peter, who was lost at sea during the 1939-45 War.

hunter, Flora saw her work appearing in *Chambers Journal*, the *Scottish Field* and African papers.

Nevertheless, she remained unfulfilled and thought it all too late for serious works. Macfie wrote to her: "Forty - what is forty? I am fifty-one; but if I could have another ten years of opportunity I should be content". He was to have another 13.

Whilst at Liphook, her second son Peter was born but by 1928 John had become restless, requested promotion and was immediately "posted" to Dartmouth.

Flora was left to sell up and make arrangements for her beloved Peverel Association to be transferred, before following on to live at the Outlook above Dartmouth for another 12 years.

Living a quiet, secluded life Flora grew fond of the town and its harbour, but made few friends. Her literary ambitions were encouraged by Dr Macfie until he died in 1931 but thereafter her old childhood feelings, and the need to tell it as it was, sparked off her autobiographical sketches.

The first, a remembrance of the lady beekeeper and lacemaker at Juniper, was published as *Old Queenie* this period also saw Flora unsuccessfully writing a romantic novel. She, however, believed she was neither novelist nor writer of short stories, though posterity deemed otherwise. *The Lady* magazine published *Old Queenie* in the autumn of 1937 and then came *Lark Rise*, a fictitious name for her birthplace of Juniper Hill.

This was the first of what was to become her celebrated trilogy of childhood autobiographical novels. It was published by Oxford University Press in 1939, to be followed two years later by *Over to Candleford*.

In 1940 John retired from the Post Office, and the family moved to Brixham, living at Lauriston in New Road.

Tragically, their son Peter, who had joined the Merchant Navy in the 1939-45 war, was torpedoed and killed in action, as a result of which Flora developed pneumonia. Only her strong will ensured recovery, but it came at a price - a damaged heart.

By 1941 Flora was writing again. *Candleford Green* was published in 1943, and two years later the trilogy, *Lark Rise to Candleford*, appeared.

Her husband was now proud of her work, and *Lark Rise to Candleford* saw Sir Arthur Bryant writing to H. J. Massingham: "It's got an element of real greatness - I put it at least as high as *Cranford*, and I think higher; for under its quiet artistry and truth there's passion and fire".

Later, *The Periodical* asked Sir Humphrey Milford to name the most important book published in his 32 years at Oxford. He chose two - one by Toynbee, the other Flora's *Lark Rise to Candleford*. With 5,000 copies sold in advance of publication in April, 1945 he chose correctly.

This universal praise would have delighted her, though she was now suffering from serious angina; it was her vocation, her sincerity of telling it from the heart, that had made her books so different.

When the war was over, thousands reflected on losses of loved ones and Flora, no exception, grieved long.

More publications included a special edition by Guild Books, a third of which were destined for Australia and the Dominions. With son Basil and family, plus brother Frank in Australia, that would have been an immensely proud time for Flora.

Her daughter, Winifred, now a midwife, called on her from time to time but her sister Betty was the most frequent visitor. They spent hours touring book and curio shops together, especially as Betty had also seen one of her own books published.

Flora's last book, *These Too Were Victorians*, was completed in August, 1946 but not published due to war shortages. It eventually appeared in 1948, a year after her death, with a new title, *Still Glides the Stream*, drawn from a quotation in Wordsworth's *River Duddon*: "Still glides the stream and shall forever glide".

Heatherley - A Country Calendar, published in 1979 and *The Peverel Papers* in 1986 were later adaptations.

With her angina preventing country walks, the garden became her retreat. But the effort of completing her last work had taken its toll and fatigue and a failing heart led to her death in May, 1947.

She was buried in Longcross Cemetery at Dartmouth, where a headstone in the shape of an open book marks her resting place. Words to Flora's beloved son Peter are emblazoned on the stone's open right leaf.

WILLIAM PENGELLY -
'Thorough in all things'

WILLIAM PENGELLY was born in East Looe, Cornwall in 1812, the son of master mariner Richard Pengelly.

He LEFT SCHOOL AT 12 TO GO TO SEA with his father but after the early death of his brother he returned when 16 to stay at home to comfort his mother.

Having been shipwrecked and nearly drowned on three occasions whilst at sea, William chose to become a teacher at the village school, his special subject being maths.

William Pengelly was one of the first to use a blackboard and chalk in the classroom and to further his own knowledge he regularly walked to Plymouth and its library and there learned of far off Torquay. He left Cornwall during the 1830s to establish a day school in Braddons Hill West, Torquay.

He had reorganised the Torquay Mechanics Institute by 1837, and realising the poverty of written material on geology was giving free education to working men, on his free evenings.

In May, 1837 William married Mary Ann Mudge, and they had three children, two of whom died in infancy, and the third while hunting in India. Sadly, after 14 years of marriage Mary also died at a young age, in 1851.

Pengelly, a kind and humorous man, had an addiction to teaching. He undertook lengthy field trips and visits to far off universities and museums in his quest for knowledge of geology and archaeology, and to make up for his lack of formal education or a degree. Although a mathematician, his abiding passion throughout life was natural history.

One of the earliest cave explorations of the era involved T Northmore of Exeter and the Rev John MacEnery, Roman Catholic Chaplain at Torre Abbey. Accessing "Kents Hole" Torquay in 1824, they uncovered bones and teeth of extinct animals and, more significantly, flints - in effect hand axes.

However, MacEnery's report to the British Association was ridiculed. A deeply religious man, but an outspoken sceptic of "the Flood", this may have had a bearing. Certainly, the flints discovered suggested primitive man was around 300,000 years ago, whereas the scriptures showed he only went back to 4004 BC.

Pengelly would much later uncover five entrances to Kents Hole, and then suggested that the extensive ventilation had created an ideal situation for the preservation of fossils in every form. He also noted that Torquay in earlier times would have been 600 feet higher, having primeval forests where we now see beaches.

In 1844, Pengelly and 17 other individuals established a natural history society in Torquay, and by 1846 he had organised a new expedition into Kents Hole, this time to explore far deeper.

Now associating with famous geologists such as Huxley, Lyell and Sedgwick, and wanting to pursue his real passion, Pengelly gave up his school to divide his time between private tuition, lecturing and research.

An early student, Sir Arthur Quiller Couch, recalled: "He was, I think, the most inspiring lecturer I have ever met. He simply compelled one to attend".

With schoolwork behind him, Pengelly the mathematician became Pengelly the geologist and lecturer. Study and scientific papers now flowed, and five years of pioneering work by MacEnery concentrating on "top deposits" would now be swamped by 20 years of deeper exploration, with accurate and detailed recording of finds by Pengelly.

The 1846 report by Edward Vivian, (See No 4) Dr Battersby, Pengelly and others was presented to the Geological Society in 1847. Academics again stuck to their view that the results were incompatible with the Book of Genesis and the creation of man. They believed that the flints and early traces of man that had been found were intrusions washed up, or carried into the caves in some way. The report was rejected.

In 1853 Pengelly was married again, to Lydia Spriggs, and they had two daughters. Although an enthusiastic student of nature, Pengelly also had an unflagging interest on subjects of the day, and was in great demand as a lecturer at institutions and universities. He openly accused educationalists of being mere instructors, and lectured on the merits of an early closing day for shops, to allow more adult workers the time to learn.

His personal interests were extremely diverse and included numismatics, folklore, history, archaeology, politics, astronomy, music and temperance. But a major turning point of his life was imminent.

In January 1858, independent quarrying at Brixham had unearthed an entrance to Windmill Hill caves, exposing layered stalagmite in limestone. This virgin site, hermetically sealed, was a heaven sent opportunity to establish primitive man's antiquity.

The Royal Society and the Geological Society immediately appointed Pengelly to be superintendent of the dig. His detailed report eventually included: "Embedded in the stalagmite, and beneath it, were the bones of cave lion, hyena, mammoth, woolly rhinoceros, and cave bear. And among the bones and below them lay numerous flint tools of undoubted human workmanship".

It was proof at last that man in fact went back further than the scriptures intimated. There was now much to do.

Darwin's (See No 38) theories were meanwhile arousing interest in early man. His book *On the Origin of Species*, not to be published until 1859, ensured an open debate on the antiquity of man. In Aberdeen in 1858 the British Association asked Pengelly, Lyell, Huxley and others to debate their theory, and also arranged for him to visit the Queen at Balmoral, which would eventually lead to royal visits to Torquay.

The Duke of Clarence, Prince George (later King George V), the Queen of Holland, and the Grand Duchess Marie of Russia all eventually came to Pengelly's home, Lamorna in Furze Hill Road, to examine his large collection of fossils and artefacts.

Having worked at the Brixham caves, Pengelly now studied clay and lignites at Bovey Tracey and Heathfield, and discovered an ancient lake. His earlier theories about climate, forests, and conditions in primeval times were also substantiated and rewarded, for he was elected a Fellow of the Royal Society in 1863.

As a president and long-serving secretary of the Torquay Natural History Society, Pengelly was its star lecturer. Always happy at the rostrum, he attended Higher Terrace, the Royal Hotel and rooms at Park Place. But by 1871 it was clear the society needed a permanent museum with a lecture room. The Harveys, prominent local builders, found the land, and the foundation stone was laid on June 6, 1874. The property in Babbacombe Road was completed in 1875.

With Darwin's theories having become acceptable to scientists and academics, Sir Lawrence Palk suggested another expedition into what is now Kents Cavern, using the south, or arched, entrance. The British Association committee in 1865 included John Evans, Sir John Lubbock (Lord

Above: Pengelly's Torquay home, Lamorna, as it was around 1890; it is now a home for the elderly.

Avebury), Sir Charles Lyell, Professor Phillips and Edward Vivian and with its blessing for the next 15 years Pengelly and his team worked five hours a day, exploring and accurately recording the position of every find.

In 1874 an inscription, "Robert Hedges of Ireland Feb. 20 1688", cut into a large boss of stalagmite was uncovered, and was thereafter known as "The Hedges Boss". It was covered by a sixteenth of an inch of growth during 186 years and mathematician Pengelly was able to calculate the 12-foot stalagmite growth as being half a million years in the making. Relics found at Pixies Hole in Chudleigh, Ash Hole and Bench Caverns at Brixham and in caves at Happaway and Stentiford also helped authenticate the many finds at Kents Cavern.

Science undoubtedly owes a great debt to Pengelly, who worked long hours in extremely damp conditions, in candlelight, until the early 1880s. Sadly, his final years were spent as an invalid, and he died from a chest complaint on March 16, 1894.

Torquay Natural History Society built the Pengelly Hall at the museum in his honour, and his old lecture room became the library and reading room.

Pengelly Hall is a lasting memorial to this extraordinary man and his tremendous achievements and his portrait by A. S. Cope, RA, still beams down from the wall for all to see, along with the words: "He was thorough in all things".

His long dedication to geological exploration came at a time when such endeavours enjoyed few comforts and few rewards. Yet the fossils and artefacts he discovered are among the earliest ever found in Britain.

Torbay Civic Society unveiled a plaque at Kents Cavern to honour Pengelly in 1987.

HERBERT WHITLEY - Founder of Paignton Zoo

WHEN SOLICITOR Edward Ewart Whitley died in 1892, his rich widow and five children came from Lancashire to live at Primley in Paignton.

Mrs Whitley had purchased the Belfield estate, at that time comprising a third of the town.

Edward Ewart had been one of the founders - along with a postman and a redundant soap boiler - of what became the famous Greenall-Whitley Brewery.

These unlikely partners brewed the first Warrington Wilderspool Ale, which apparently well suited drinkers of the North and, once established, made a fortune for them.

Once the Whitleys were settled at Primley, only William among the sons immediately sought to farm, he having been honourably discharged from the cavalry after falling from a stable skylight.

However, Herbert, born on January 2, 1886, was always more interested in living creatures than humans, and after an unhappy university life at Cambridge joined his brother as partner to run the estate.

An early story of the shy Herbert, reputedly terrified of women, tells of how he had bred, exhibited and won prizes with his finches, Dutch rabbits, Wyandotte poultry and - the stars of his collection - blue and black cropper pigeons, while in Liverpool. His dream was to fill his first trophy cabinet, which was soon achieved.

With money plentiful in a family made rich from the brewery, he was impatient to develop Primley. He and his brother concocted an innovative plan to create a breeding centre which would offer a home to all pedigree livestock.

The plan was implemented at a breathtaking pace, initially with Primley kennels being extended to supply quality gun dogs, and pedigree Great Danes suitable to grace any luxurious mansion rug.

Although not trained for business, the Lancashire millionaires had quality uppermost in their minds and a good eye for picking staff. This, added to their skill in choosing quality breeding stock and a commitment never to cross breed, virtually ensured success. Existing greenhouses were now expanded to house the thriving propagation side of the business.

The Belfield estate, which dates back to Tudor times, had been purchased from the Belfield family following the mysterious departure of John Finney Belfield, who awoke one morning to state he had "had enough" and left.

The Whitley's now employed Freddy Bowen to be responsible for ensuring that in cattle breeding only native South Devons were seen on Paignton land. Wishing to see conservation of even the world's rarest domestic animals, locals would now see not only sheep, dogs, ponies and horses around the fields, but exotic animals totally unknown in the UK - a zoo in all but name.

The rapid expansion soon saw their farm acreage under pressure and whenever neighbouring land was for sale it was eagerly snapped up.

In 1907 William married, and moved to his new family's home at Barton Pines. Owned by the Whiteheads, the Barton Pines estate with its stables, carriages, coaches, and horses, ensured a different and much more attractive life style.

The brothers' vision of a zoo was now left to Herbert, who became even more reclusive and eccentric.

In 1908 he had a "first" at the Royal Show milking trials, repeated in 1909. With percentages of butter fat now seen as important the early conviction against cross breeding was ensuring the Whitley breeds beat all-comers.

An export business began to fly the flag for Devon. With horses still powering fire engines, foresight had seen the Whitleys establishing an equine stud of nine different breeds. He even purchased a stallion at Tatton Park for £3,700 guineas, then a record sum for a horse.

The investments paid off; horses were sold and at five guineas (£5.25) the "service fee" for Tatton blood gave a quick financial return.

Whitley pigeons gained a new and some said palatial home on the slopes of the present zoo in 1909, and a pigeon manager responsible for 150 varieties was appointed. Compton land was purchased to establish an outstanding herd of rare black pigs and brought more top prizes in 1911 at the Royal Cornwall, Devon County and Bath and West shows.

With a strain of Great Danes already established, collies, whippets, and greyhounds followed. Two greyhounds were appropriately named Primley Pirate and Primley Pinafore to celebrate the historic world premiere of a Gilbert and Sullivan opera at Paignton's Bijou Theatre in 1879.

The Great War years saw Herbert with a reduced staff. Determined to keep the quality of new and old breeds intact, he widened the range of stock. It was said that in ten years he had established a livestock "supermarket" which could deliver multi-bred prize winning stock to anyone, anywhere in the world.

By 1915 the polo stallion Bold Marco had arrived, and a polo ground was created at Marldon to introduce the sport to Paigntonians.

But it was not all easy. The large concentration of mixed livestock was a joy for rats, which had to be culled. Herbert paid "a tanner" (2½p) for every 12 rat tails handed in by locals.

Locals were always suspicious of the crates of all shapes and sizes arriving at Paignton rail head. One story too long to relate here tells of "Beware - Live Bear" stamped on one crate, which was opened on the station.

Primley Gardens were opened to the public, in 1923, initially without charge though sadly a charge soon had to be introduced to keep out troublemakers wishing only to annoy the animals.

In being forced to charge a nominal entrance fee, Herbert came in conflict with the tax authorities. The Revenue demanded an entertainment tax, whereas Herbert maintained the gardens were educational. The courts upheld the demand and, having paid his fines and costs, an incensed Herbert closed the gates.

The 1920s saw Primley's poultry farm prosper. Billy Wilkinson and son Billy Junior became known as "Brass and Brains", offering more than 40 varieties of sitting eggs to buyers. The name "Wilkies" and the "Primley Blue" were soon known worldwide, owing to their stunning quality.

Herbert was by now a member of the Zoological Society of London and similar associations wished to use his expertise to educate others on quality. He had also become a benefactor, for he had given some Clennon Valley land to the town for sports purposes, and was supplying plants for municipal gardens and the public land at Roundham Head.

Primley's gates re-opened in 1927 by which time Herbert had amassed one of the finest bird collections in the world and had created new tropical and sub-tropical houses. He even introduced a circus act - Samson, the strongest man in the world.

These were the halcyon years, with expansion of every species continuing under his watchful eye, through to 1937 when history repeated itself. He clashed with authority again over entrance fees, and a judge summing up in a case that year suggested a society of some sort be formed to resolve the repeating tax dispute. Herbert rejected the thought, and closed the gates again.

What he didn't foresee was the Second World War. Primley Gardens would never reopen again under his sole management.

The end of the war saw a business partnership having to be established, and the gates finally reopened under the name "Paignton Zoological and Botanical Gardens".

Herbert, known to zoologists and naturalists all over the world, had shown that breeding in captivity, even with endangered species, could guarantee high quality if there was no cross breeding. His life at Paignton had been a daily round of interest, learning and excitement with little or no time for relaxation, sleep or eating. Few of his staff or colleagues could keep up his pace. Often intolerant he used harsh language, and had little time for non-working "toy animals" or idle chat.

Despite being a virtual recluse he nevertheless had established botanical and zoological gardens of international renown, and had also created pools, lakes, glades, dens and massive enclosures for his animals.

He also founded the Herbert Whitley Trust, a non-profit making institution for the zoo. His concept of a light railway or cable car to bring visitors from seashore to zoo was a vision he never fulfilled; similar schemes were mooted again towards the end of the century.

He died on September 15, 1955 and was buried in the family grave at St Peter's Church, Buckland in the Moor, where his brother had made a little bit of Dartmoor his own Whitley country.

Torbay Civic Society installed a plaque at Primley House in 1987 to honour the Belfield family and Herbert Whitley.

Below: A late 1920s view of Paignton Zoo entrance.

ARTHUR HYDE DENDY - Bringing progress to Paignton

ARTHUR HYDE DENDY was born in London and became a wealthy lawyer, having practised in Birmingham before his move to Devon. In just 16 years he was to make an indelible mark on Paignton.

HIS FIRST VENTURE IN THE EMERGING SEASIDE town seems to have come in 1870 when he built the Gerston Hotel, in a prominent position by the railway station.

He then acquired land on the Steartfield estate from William Froude and Edward Studdy, and started to develop the Esplanade, firstly with his Esplanade Hotel, now the oldest building on that part of the seafront. Today in extended form it is the Inn on the Green.

His purchase of part of the Steartfield estate also included Parkfield House, where he lived between 1878-1879.

The Esplanade Hotel was followed by the Adelphi and then the Terra Nova properties (now the Park Hotel), and an extension to the Gerston Hotel in 1873, creating the Bijou Theatre.

The theatre was a piece of Victorian extravaganza, being not much larger than a goodly sized drawing room. This was perhaps Dendy's way of becoming a patron of the arts.

A guidebook of the time states: "The Bijou theatre is elegantly - nay, luxuriously - fitted up, where high class theatrical and other entertainments frequently take place".

It was certainly the only building in Paignton licensed to stage plays, and from 1880 a local company regularly performed there for a number of years. To ensure large audiences Dendy ran nightly omnibuses from Torquay as late as 10.30pm.

In 1879 the D'Oyly Carte opera company used his Bijou theatre for the premiere of the comic opera *The Pirates of Penzance* (sub-titled *The Slave of Duty*).

The opera company, interrupting a nightly performance at a Torquay theatre, came to Paignton in *HMS Pinafore* costumes to perform the first production of the new opera anywhere in the world, on December 30 1879, to protect the G & S copyright in Britain.

Dendy's next venture was mobile beach huts or bathing machines. He had established a new business, The Bathing Machine Company, in 1871 and with mixed bathing banned it was not long before one man was prosecuted for being a little too near a ladies' bathing machine.

A Dendy guidebook stated: "Bathing Machines: Of these there is an ample supply, both for ladies and gentlemen. Being drawn by horses, they are available at all times of the tide and the charges are lower than at most other watering places. The bathing season usually commences about the 1st June, & terminates about 1st October. By special arrangement bathers can be accommodated at any time of the year on application to the manager of the Esplanade Hotel".

With the Duchy of Cornwall owning all foreshores, some quieter beaches had nude bathing, but mixed bathing (then "continental" bathing) was strictly forbidden in Paignton up until October, 1900. Public tastes then changed, and Torquay soon followed the Paignton relaxation of rules.

The entrepreneurial risks taken by Dendy ensured that visitors had every type of facility, and this seems to have been his objective. The bathing machines hired on the beach led him to establish a horse-drawn omnibus service in 1872, which allowed travel between Torquay and Paignton by a

Below: Dendy's Esplanade Hotel stands today in extended form as The Inn on the Green. Just to the right of it can be seen the arched entrance to the cycle track.

regular scheduled service, even at night.

Arthur Hyde Dendy's most lasting visible legacy, however, has to be Paignton Pier.

He had originally purchased the Teignmouth Promenade Pier for £1,100 with the intention of dismantling it for use at Paignton but structural difficulties made the idea impracticable. It was instead restored and the new pier reopened for the Teignmouth populace on July 24, 1876.

Having obtained Royal Assent in 1874 to build a Paignton pier, Dendy's flair for "spending money to make more" was never going to see him miss that opportunity, and by 1878, with other businessmen, he floated a Paignton Pier Company, and it commissioned local architect George Soudon Bridgman to complete a new design. The pier was started in 1878, and was open to the public by June 1879. The financial return came from the pier itself, the dance hall and theatre, and from boat trips, across and around the bay. One can guess who owned the boats...

Bridgman, through his many projects, would later be called "The Father of Paignton". For instance, the main road from Paignton's small harbour to Goodrington was called "Lovers Lane" and comprised mainly cabbage fields and cattle grazing land, where we now enjoy Roundham's cliff gardens and beautiful terraces – and it was George Bridgman who laid these out.

With Paignton's growing population, its attractions, and the town being seen as a popular place to work, live, or visit during the 1880s, Dendy's vision, dynamism, promotional skills, commercial nous and entrepreneurship were paying off.

Nevertheless, he failed to reap a second fortune from these ventures, though his imaginative risk-taking made him largely responsible for the new image of Paignton, and perhaps he should rightly have been named "The Maker" of Paignton, mirroring Kitson (See No 7) in Torquay.

He also established a local newspaper and, with the D'Oyly Carte company returning to his pier in July, 1880 for a full company performance of an opera entitled *HMS Pinafore on the Water*, his diverse promotional skills were obvious for all to see.

By 1881, with the pier head enlarged, the complex sported

Below: Dendy's Gerston Hotel, built in 1870

Above: Disaster day in 1919, as the pier theatre burns down

a long walkway, a pavilion theatre, a refreshment room, a billiard room, a roller skating surface, and changing rooms and facilities for bathers. Strangely, mixed bathing was still only allowed until 8am each day, and even on the pier "mixed sexes" were presumably strictly taboo.

By 1883, Dendy had a cycle track laid behind his Esplanade and Palace hotels. This was officially opened on August 15, 1883. A guidebook of the time described the track as "one of the safest, best and most scientific yet constructed in the country".

The track enabled Dendy to create an archery range of some 410 ft by 110 ft in its centre. In season it was used as a rugby ground by Paignton's famous Scarlet Runners XV, being fully equipped with refreshment and dressing rooms, with accommodation for 250 in the grandstand.

A final Dendy promotional guide of 1885 describes Paignton thus: "Every watering place has its own special features and Paignton has its own too. Here you will find no rollicking horseplay and boisterous fun such as you may have been accustomed to on Ramsgate or Margate Sands - Paignton prefers to be select, dignified, and discreet; yet there are not wanting abundant means of enjoyment".

Arthur Hyde Dendy died at Paignton on August 13, 1886 and his wife died in August the following year. His name lives on with roads named after him - Hyde Road and Dendy Road.

After his death, the local council outlined proposals in 1891 for a public park on his marshy land between Hyde Road and Victoria Road, but the trustees refused to sell. Compulsory purchase was enforced in 1894 and Victoria Park gardens and ponds were completed in time for an agricultural show in 1900 which by coincidence commemorated Queen Victoria's death in 1901.

Dendy's pier was the principal attraction of Paignton until 1919, when its theatre was destroyed in a fire. The structure then went into decline and became a blot on the town's landscape through to the Second World War. Adding insult to injury, a piece of the inshore section was then removed as an anti-invasion precaution. The pier and all its facilities were then out-of-bounds to everyone. Happily, the structure has now taken its place once again as a popular family venue.

GEORGINA MOUNT TEMPLE - Champion of the underdog

THE WOMAN who was to become Baroness Georgina Mount Temple was born in 1822, the youngest daughter of Admiral Tollemache and a sister of the first Lord Tollemache of Helmingham.

GEORGINA, DESTINED TO BECOME A great champion of the disadvantaged, married William Francis Cowper, a Liberal parliamentary candidate, in November 1848. William, of Brocket Hall, Hertfordshire was the second son of Peter, fifth Earl Cowper (1778-1837), who through his wife Emily had been connected by marriage to William Lamb, the Prime Minister.

In 1869 William, having inherited the family estates, would assume the name of Cowper Temple following the death of his stepfather, Henry John Temple, better known as Lord Palmerston of Broadlands.

Educated at Eton, William was an enthusiastic supporter of social reform and, more especially, temperance.

Georgina Cowper is recorded as being a strikingly tall, beautiful and stately woman. Besides her faultless looks she exuded "an extra-ordinary dignity of presence and bearing, enhancing a nature noble and elevated".

Georgina was passionately indignant against all cruelty or injustice, and had a genuine love of the outcast and downtrodden. She instinctively allied herself with the weakest in society, often on lost causes or, it was said, impossible beliefs.

She championed those whom the world cast out, and enterprises which some regarded as offensive insanities.

Mr and Mrs Cowper were friends of the Pre-Raphaelites and their circle. The designer of Babbacombe Cliff, their Torquay home, had been John Ruskin, and with Burne-Jones and William Morris having created the

decor, the property was a unique repository of Pre-Raphaelite art. Ruskin, although three years older than Georgina, often turned to her for advice and consolation, and she later became his confidante and intermediary in his unhappy courtship of that time.

In 1866 Dante Gabriel Rosetti confirmed the Cowpers as most appreciative people and in 1876, having stayed with them at Broadlands for a month, wrote to his mother: "Mrs Temple is simply an angel on earth... I must tell you that my bodily state is a very suffering one. Mrs Temple, who is providence of the neighbourhood in all helpful matters, has been herself able to suggest various ideas towards battling the evil. You would simply adore, all must, the noble beauty of Mrs Temple's Christlike character".

In 1871 John Ruskin was taken seriously ill, and it was Georgina who travelled up to Matlock to nurse him. She was a quite special and caring lady. Her husband shared her zeal for social reform, and they lived in an atmosphere where nothing mean or cruel could survive. Within this social state this extra-ordinary lady saw "truth and justice, mercy and self-sacrifice as the vital air". She was called "the soul and the sun" in a strange yet unworldly society.

William represented Hertford as an MP until 1863, and by the time Gladstone made him a Baron in 1880 he had been a Member of Parliament for 13 years.

During that time he had been Lord of the Treasury, and subsequently Under Secretary of State for the Home Department. He had been a President of the Board of Health, Vice-President of the Board of Trade, Paymaster General, Chief Commissioner of Works and had even served as Lord of the Admiralty.

Now elevated to the peerage he left the Commons to become Baron Mount Temple, a title which became extinct on his death, due to there being no heir. The name Mount Temple came from one of his properties in County Sligo, Ireland.

Babbacombe Cliff, just off Babbacombe Downs, was purchased in 1879, and was just one of many homes owned by the Cowpers.

Georgina frequently visited the house during the

next 10 years, and eventually she came to live there permanently. All the bedrooms had names of pretty flowers, with matching wallpapers, except her boudoir named "Wonderland", which had magnificent views of the cliffs and the sea.

In 1888 her husband died, and Georgina, now a widow with no children, saw his death as being "a merciful deliverance to a soul too sensitive to know happiness in a world where others still suffered".

Georgina throughout life supported a number of philanthropic organisations, including the Temperance Society and anti-vivisection crusades. Most particularly there was the Band of Mercy, which had been founded by her husband in association with the RSPCA. She was interested in, and not just a supporter of, the causes she chose to support. She was also passionately fond of birds and flowers and would often be seen feeding her birds on the terrace just off the archway of her Babbacombe home.

Early in 1892 a distant cousin, Constance Wilde (Mrs Oscar Wilde), wrote to Georgina to ask if her family might rent Babbacombe Cliff for the winter. Constance in her youth had been sent to stay there by her father, Sir William Lloyd, probably after a row with her mother. Constance adored her father and like him revelled in beautiful things. She thought him "Bohemian" and his absences merely heightened the romanticism. Sir William, knowing this, thought the house and style of life at Babbacombe would appeal, which it did, as Constance soon thrilled to being with, and travelling with, her aunt Georgina and John Ruskin, and debating the wonderment of the Pre-Raphaelites' mission which embraced art and culture.

In the autumn of 1892 Oscar dutifully visited Torquay with his sons and wrote to Constance then back in London: "The last few days have been wonderfully bright and sunny, and the children are so well and happy here". But to a friend he voiced misgivings: "Are there beautiful people in London? Here there are none; everyone is so unfinished". The word "beautiful" described those richer or more famous than himself.

Wanting to extend his stay in early 1893, Oscar wrote to Lady Mount Temple: "Babbacombe Cliff has become a kind of college or school, for Cyril (Wilde's son) studies French in the nursery, and I write my new play in Wonderland (the bedroom), and in the drawing room Lord Alfred Douglas studies with his tutor".

Douglas was the famous "Bosie" with whom Wilde was having an affair (See No 12).

Baroness Mount Temple was associated with Babbacombe Cliff for more than 40 years, during which time she became an accepted philanthropist and a lady of merciful works.

She died on October 17, 1901 following a five-week illness. Her body was taken from Torquay to Romsey Abbey where she had once worshipped.

Above: The Baroness Mount Temple drinking bowl and statue on Babbacombe Downs.

The funeral was attended by the Mayor of Torquay and representatives of the corporation, 200 children from the Band of Mercy, and representatives from both the Mothers' Meeting and the Women's Total Abstinence Union. Devon floral tributes came from her servants, local traders and the Vicar of Babbacombe.

The memorial on Babbacombe Downs was donated by her friends in October, 1903. It comprises a drinking bowl and fountain, now long neglected, and a statue of the Baroness. It is made from green basalt from Trusham in the Teign Valley, and marble from Ashburton.

Archdeacon Basil Wilberforce, of Westminster, a long standing friend of the Mount Temples, undertook the official unveiling, and in paying tribute to her virtues and gifts said that the provision of a fountain was appropriate "to the memory of a lady who throughout her life did much to quench the intellectual, moral and spiritual thirst of the people".

The statue to her memory is a fine sculptured likeness, and depicts her standing upright holding an injured bird. A simple inscription on the plinth states "Georgina Mount Temple".

Below: Babbacombe Cliff, the Torquay home of Georgina Mount Temple.

ISAAC SINGER –
A 'Wigwam' for Paignton

BORN IN NEW YORK State the eighth child of his German-Dutch immigrant parents, Isaac Merritt Singer left home at the age of 12 when his father remarried.

A DIVERSE NUMBER OF OCCUPATIONS followed for the young Isaac, including ticket taker, scene shifter, lathe worker, cabinet maker, and printing assistant. In those earliest years he also became besotted with the theatre, which would be apparent throughout his life.

Like his father Adam, Issac was a large man with terrific vitality. In 1830, aged 19, he married Catherine Haley, then only 15. They had two children, but after two years he left home for a second time.

He then met Mary Ann Sponsler, of Baltimore, and not admitting to her that he was married, he had a relationship with her over the next 10 years, during which time she gave him 10 children, while he sired a further six by two other women. At age 39 Isaac was penniless, in Illinois.

His engineering experiences now brought a first invention, a mechanical excavator. He sold this idea and made $2,000. The money was used to form The Merritt Players, who toured America but were unsuccessful. Promoting another invention, a carving machine, while on the East Coast led to what proved to be his inspiration, the "shuttle".

This small invention would help to end sweatshop labour and prove a great benefit in the sewing of manufactured clothes by workers then grappling with unreliable machines. With the addition of Isaac's "shuttle" the "Jenny Lind" business, the first real sewing machine, was established. Though he was only one of three partners, Isaac now gave his family name to the new machine, and hey presto, in 1851 the patented Singer Sewing Machine arrived.

During the next nine years, he would amass a personal fortune exceeding $13 million.

The new Singer Sewing Machine business had its up and downs. Rival companies, consumer resistance, trade-ins, cut pricing and legal actions were par for the course.

But Isaac's negotiating and theatrical skills now came into play, and using skilled teachers he demonstrated the advantages of the Singer machine to seamstresses and consumers – "It seams so good" - often on a free basis. Then, aided by a lawyer, he devised a painless payment scheme, "hire purchase", and the Singer multi-millions were virtually guaranteed.

In 1851 the divorced Catherine came to New York and soon Isaac was looking after two mistresses. Mary Ann, however, sued for alimony naming not just Catherine but eight co-respondents. Isaac fled again, this time to France.

Arriving in Paris, he was soon proposing to his landlady's daughter, Isabella Eugenie Boyer. With an English mother and French father she was a highly intelligent and most beautiful 21-year-old, later chosen by the sculptor Bartholdi as his model for New York's Statue of Liberty.

In 1863 Isaac and Isabella went to New York to marry, and did not return to Paris until 1867 for the birth of their third son, whom they named Paris after the city. Isabella gave Isaac two more children, Isabelle Blanche and Franklin Merritt Morse - making his known progeny 24. Over-sexed and seen by some as a fornicator, Isaac was nevertheless a substantial benefactor to the poor, and to his large family. He had, however, been removed from active management of the family firm due to his scandalous affairs.

With the Franco-Prussian War breaking out in the early 1870s the Singers left France for Brown's Hotel in London. With his wife's health failing, Isaac brought the family to Devon to the Victoria and Albert Hotel in Torquay. He was looking for an estate in a cosmopolitan setting and, having failed to purchase the Brunel Estate, he settled for the 20-acre Fernham Estate and lived at its Oldway House (later Little Oldway) while he built a new home, which he always referred to as the "Wigwam".

Local architect George S. Bridgman was commissioned to develop the "Wigwam" - an American-Indian name for home - it was the circular exercise and riding pavilion, the Arena, which came first in 1873. This encompassed a removable floor doubling as a theatre, and had underfloor heating. It is now known as the Rotunda, and is used for offices.

Above: Isaac Singer in the garden at Little Oldway around 1872 with Isabella, and children Winnaretta and Franklin. (From John Wilson's Paris Singer - A Life Portrait, Torquay Natural History Society Transactions and Proceedings, 1997.)

Isaac, unlike his father who lived to 102, did not survive to live in his "Wigwam". He died on July 23, 1875, aged 65, just before its completion. His third son, Paris, would 30 years later return to Paignton to remodel the house in the fashion of the Palace of Versailles when between 1904-1907 it would be transformed into a mansion of 100 rooms.

Paris Singer (See No 29) was also responsible for constructing the Preston sea wall, the Marine Drive and an aircraft hanger on Preston seafront. Through his company he also ensured the infra-structure of Preston, Barcombe and Marldon. But his glittering star was Oldway, with its Hall of Mirrors, Italian styled gardens and miniature box hedges, orangery and grotto.

Like his father, Paris married young. A giant of a giant of a man at 6ft 3ins, he had strong auburn hair, and wooed and won Lily Graham, of Tasmania, at the age 19 in 1887. They soon had five children.

But repeating family history, Paris had a "trial marriage" with Isadora Duncan – she called him "my millionaire". A seven-year liaison with Isadora, a free-spirited American dancer and choreographer who only stayed in Paignton for a matter of weeks in the summer of 1910, saw one more son. However, she opposed marriage and eventually fled the humdrum life and rain of Paignton for the high life and excitement of America.

Paris was a pioneer of aviation in the Westcountry and gave trips over Torbay in his aircraft. But after suffering a suspected stroke in London, and marrying his nurse, Joan Bates, crippling taxation forced them to emigrate to America and then to St Jean Cap Ferrat in France. He continued to maintain two residences in London, but left his brothers Mortimer and Washington to maintain the Singer-Paignton connection. They each had seafront houses, which are now The Inn on the Green and the Palace Hotel on Paignton esplanade.

By 1914 the Singer connection with Oldway and Paignton ceased, though the town is left with many family names in Paris Road, Eugene Road, Steartfield Road, the Merritt flats, Merritt Road, and the Winnaretta, Herbert and Cecil rooms at Oldway Mansion. The Palace Hotel at Paignton retains a Paris Restaurant, a Singer lounge and a Washington bar.

Mortimer was a keen yachtsman, balloonist, and aviator, while Washington enjoyed life as a racehorse owner and Master of Foxhounds, and was president of the Paignton Swimming and Paignton Rowing clubs. As a major shareholder of Steartfield House (Palace Hotel), he added the ballroom, stables and gallops at the rear, in the 1920s. Property purchased at Haytor saw him known locally as Lord of the Manor of Haytor.

Isaac's other three children settled abroad. Winnaretta eventually married Prince Edmond de Polignac, and became Princesse de Polignac, and Franklin became a proficient yachtsman and lived in France until his death in 1939. Isabelle (Blanche) married into one of the "first families of France" but died in 1896 at just 27.

Isaac's will, involving an estate of £15m, left Isabella and her children as principal beneficiaries. His first wife Catherine received nothing, and she contested this in the County Court, which eventually involved the family in an acrimonious and very public battle. The claim by Catherine and her children was judged unlawful due to the divorce, unlike the situation in present day judgments.

Mary Ann and her 10 children, however, received two million dollars and the remaining moneys were put into a family trust.

Isaac's funeral cortege through Torquay was a great spectacle. He lay in black mourning dress on a satin couch on the innermost of three coffins in an American style glass-sided hearse. The main mourners, all men, were in full mourning dress. Led by a large cross the hearse was followed by so many locals that as the leading group passed through The Strand, the rear of the procession was passing Livermead. Isaac was interred at the imposing Singer family vault still to be seen at Torquay cemetery.

In 1988 Torbay Civic Society unveiled a plaque at Oldway Mansion to commemorate the Singer family.

Below: The Singer family tomb in Torquay cemetery.

HENRY PHILLPOTTS - A Bishop in conflict

BORN ON MAY 6, 1778, Henry Phillpotts lived to be 91, and therefore survived well into the Victorian age.

ORDAINED IN 1804 IN NORTH WALES, and consecrated Bishop of Exeter in 1830, "Henry of Exeter" lived at a time of heightening religious conflict but remained bishop until his death in 1869. His long term in office had been exceeded only once, by Bishop Grandison, in the 14th century.

As Lord Bishop of Exeter, Phillpotts was intrinsically linked to that city, but chose not to live there. Soon after his appointment cholera had struck and it seems that in not wanting to expose himself to danger he went to stay in Torquay and Teignmouth.

On returning to the city after the epidemic he met with great hostility. Even the editor of the Western Times criticised his action, which led to the Bishop bringing a lawsuit against the paper. With his diocese stretching from the borders of Somerset and Dorset to the Isles of Scilly, he was always a powerful adversary. A sworn enemy of new Church practices, he had already taken action against the clergy itself, when he felt they were conducting improper doctrinal practices, and was thus recognised as a strong litigant. On this occasion, however, the Western Times was successful and this lawsuit became one of the few the Bishop would ever lose.

Living on the coast could never have been practicable, as it would have taken several hours to travel from Torquay to Exeter. But with his medieval palace at Exeter in poor repair and his undoubted unpopularity, the Bishop commissioned a Torquay architect to build a new home for his wife and their 18 children above Ansteys Cove at Babbacombe. In the meantime they were to live at a villa in Teignmouth.

By 1841 the decision had been taken to build the mansion in the Italianate style, fit to serve as a Bishop's Palace, comprising multiple lounges, nine bedrooms, and 11 servants' bedrooms. The mansion would have a large shed for the washing of his many carriages, and would be built on land 200 ft above Ansteys Cove. To this day one of the main paths nearby is called Bishop's Walk.

Bishopstowe was much extended in 1921 to become the Palace Hotel, originally in the parish of St Marychurch but in 1955 transferred to the parish of Torwood.

Because of the controversy between high and low church running to extremes, Phillpotts was forever regarded by the local clergy as a political turncoat, he having been a controversial rector in Durham.

But with Phillpotts believing himself to have been ordained by God to protect the Church of England, he gave little quarter throughout his life to any ecclesiastical matters which did not agree with his own views.

He hated ritualistic practices, and saw the Church of Rome as the enemy, as unacceptable as Communism was to some in a later age.

With the growing religious fervour of early Victorian times, the gentry were returning to the Church and services were becoming necessary in the mornings and afternoons.

Followers of High Church now saw themselves as restoring Christianity, whereas those in Low Church believed they were keeping the Roman influence at bay.

When summoning candidates to serve the Church, Bishop Phillpotts would at interview provide a questionnaire for immediate completion. Any answers showing Roman sympathies were given short shrift and the candidate was soon hounded out of His Lordship's sight and from his diocese.

The Bishop, being so intolerant of those not accepting his view, spent considerable sums of money bringing legal cases against members of the clergy whom he believed practised improper doctrinal services. He was, though, an efficient administrator, and was also merciless against absentee landlords, expressing the view "Reside or resign", which was somewhat inconsistent with having deserted his diocesan Palace at Exeter.

The most frequently reported example of his intolerance concerned the adornment of flowers decorating a two-foot wooden cross on the altar of St John's Church in Torquay.

The curate, the Rev Park Smith and his large congregation, witnessed the Bishop sweeping the offending ornaments from the altar with his stick, and this resulted in a first "ritual prosecution" in the Diocesan Court. Smith was formally condemned for the offence and soon after left to serve as a chaplain in the Crimean War.

In another incident, in 1847, the Bishop determined to prevent the Rev George Gorham from acting as vicar at Brampton Speke, in Devon. Gorham had expressed the view that the grace of regeneration was not necessarily effected through baptism. The Bishop, however, held that according to the Book of Common Prayer regeneration is always effected in an infant at baptism.

The controversy went to the Court of Arches, who again found in favour of the Bishop but the Judicial Committee of the Privy Council then reversed the decision. The Bishop then went to the Court of the Queen's Bench, the Court of Common Pleas and finally the Court of the Exchequer. He even formally announced that should any Church authority institute Gorham as vicar, they would incur the sin of supporting heretical doctrine.

All these actions did not stop the Archbishop of Canterbury, however, as he installed Gorham - who, strangely, later became reconciled to his furious Bishop.

By 1850 the Bishop had decided the drift towards the Church of Rome had gone too far, and he summoned a synod of the clergy of his diocese. His intention was to use ecclesiastical law to stamp out all "improper practices" in the churches of South West England.

The result was little short of anarchy, and nothing like it had happened since the Reformation; if successful Phillpotts would probably have caused a schism in the Church. Fortunately, his lordship was made to rethink the unthinkable.

During the 1860s a further controversy arose when the Rev Park Smith, now back in Torquay and again at St John's, then obtained permission from Bishop Phillpotts to replace the Georgian chapel of St John with a proper church built in Gothic style.

Smith's supporters had brought in the architect George Edmund Street, known to have sympathy for those in the High Church, and he, in favouring the Early English style,

determined to use the best materials available to build a chapel of beauty. Having warded off objections from all quarters including the trustees, the new chancel building was completed in 18 months. But once again problems arose when Bishop Henry Phillpotts forbad its use.

He was unwilling to approve the new sculptured reredos depicting the crucifixion. But with the addition of the figures of two thieves (in plasterwork) to make it less of a crucifix in the Bishop's eyes, permission to remove the covering sheet was given.

The remaining work and the church tower would not be completed until 1883, after both Street and the Lord Bishop had died. Interestingly, after the Bishop's death the two thieves were removed.

Clearly, Bishop Henry Phillpotts was not greatly loved and he certainly lacked what today would be thought of as Christian values. Nevertheless, he was much admired for his administrative skills, his stalwart defence of churchmen, his high principles - and his philanthropy.

He founded a theological college at Exeter, and donated large sums of money to the restoration of the cathedral and to the building of other churches. His most lasting achievements, however, were the separation of the county of Cornwall from the Diocese of Exeter, and the creation of many new parishes and churches, particularly in Plymouth.

He died at his Torquay home at the grand old age of 91 in 1869. Bishopstowe was later bought by a man christened Sampson, whose family fortune came from a West Midlands brewery. One can only wonder what Henry Phillpotts would have made of that link. The Bishop is buried at the parish church of St Marychurch and its original lofty tower was then built as a memorial to him.

Torbay Civic Society unveiled a blue plaque at the Palace Hotel, Babbacombe, Torquay, to his memory in 1987.

Below: Bishopstowe, from a postcard photograph

HENRY BRUNEL -
Engineering in his pedigree

HENRY BRUNEL may not have enjoyed quite the same stature and importance as his famous father, Isambard Kingdom, but he was nevertheless a significant and distinguished civil engineer.

BORN IN 1842 AND AT THE AGE of 17 losing his father, he was nurtured by another famous local Victorian, William Froude (See No 1), who in effect became his proxy father.

As a young man Froude had worked with Isambard Kingdom Brunel on the Bristol to Exeter railway, until he voluntarily resigned to look after his own father.

As an 18-year-old Henry completed the wooden bridge, started by his father linking the eastern and western areas of the Brunel-Watcombe estate across the main road to Teignmouth.

The well constructed bridge was protected with 30 gallons of creosote and remained in situ even after the turn of the century when the growing height of motor transport determined its demise.

Henry, growing up in an atmosphere of research, innovation and investigation to an exactitude never before attempted, was living at the Froudes' house, Elmsleigh, in Fisher Road, Paignton. There he participated in experiments with pyrotechnics, and planned to build a model railway with the Froudes' son, Eddy, which would have taken over most of the grounds of the house, had it not been for a sea trip on his father's Great Eastern steamship destined for Canada.

Froude, in considering a new home and research centre at Chelston Cross, allowed Henry and Eddy to undertake much of the final design, even though he had employed an architect. The well known "flying staircase" in the main hallway was designed by Henry, but there were more innovations to follow.

By 1857 Froude senior, having worked with Brunel senior on many diverse projects realised there were more experiments he could help with. Henry meanwhile, having served an apprenticeship at Armstrongs in what he termed "bloody Newcastle", associated himself with Froude in many experiments at Torquay, one being for an engine performance indicator, finished just in time for the Great Eastern's trials.

Although using rudimentary materials including "an assortment of elastic bands" this indicator was an early form of the now infamous "black box", and became Torquay's first step towards becoming synonymous with devices of measurement and recording. With an endorsement from the Great Eastern's chief engineer, it became a sensation.

The Froude/Brunel partnership investigated the possibility of flight, and even considered the principles of a jet engine. Henry consulted his mother to ensure his design layout of the grounds at Chelston Cross were practicable, and then employed the nurseryman and gardener from his father's time at Watcombe, Mr Veitch and Mr Elston.

Henry, now an assistant engineer to Sir John Hawkshaw of Severn Tunnel fame, had been given a first assignment, to travel to France to lease sites for trial borings for a Channel tunnel. Having successfully achieved that, he was then asked to take soundings of the proposed route under the Channel.

With no precedents for this work, Henry decided to use his partners William and Eddy Froude and others, to design, make and then test equipment in their research workshops at Torquay.

He required accurate navigational equipment, a dredge anchor, a gravity borer, and a dead reckoning buoy which had to encompass a lantern unaffected by sea spray. And so it was that on the September 25, 1866 a fishing boat called Ethel left Paignton harbour with Henry on board for the purpose of carrying out the first deep water tests to establish boring problems associated with the construction of a channel tunnel. Some design equipment was tested solely at sea, some using Devon's red sandstone on land.

Meanwhile the French were also experimenting. They used a man called de Gamond, an eccentric scientist who decided to investigate their coast by jumping naked into deep water carrying heavy stones for quick descent. With no breathing equipment available, he was then hauled back to his boat by men and ropes, given more stones and thrown in again. Hardly scientific but he got his samples.

By December 1866 Henry, in completing his research, travelled to Dover to undertake the world's first submarine geological survey. Although the whole idea was eventually abandoned, it is true to say that Torquay was the first place in the UK where tests were carried out to establish the feasibility of a cross-Channel tunnel to Calais.

Froude's greatest accomplishment in Torquay was proving that ships did not necessarily have to roll in high seas. He stated that "only about 45 per cent of the power applied by the steam is usefully employed in propelling the ship - there appears to be an ample field for improvement in the propulsion of vessels".

Steamships were subject to roll in high seas, and he realised

Above: The wooden bridge at Maidencombe on the Brunel Estate; it was completed by Henry

that this led to wasted fuel, discomfort for passengers and, in the worst scenario, ships that might actually roll over. Isambard had investigated types of screw propulsion, the optimum number of blades, curvature and so on but it was Froude's earliest experiments in conjunction with Henry that saw the world's first test tank built inside Chelston Cross (now the Manor House Hotel) in an annexe that resembled a domestic chapel. The "sham chapel" can still be seen, externally today.

By 1868 Henry and William had convinced the Admiralty that a 250ft test tank was now required. Permission given, building commenced in June 1870 and was completed by December 1871. Because of work carried out at the 'Admiralty Experimental Tank' in Torquay, ship hull and ship design throughout the world radically changed, and potential disasters at sea were minimised.

In 1886, with 97 experimental projects behind it, the whole research establishment in Torquay was dismantled and taken to Haslar in Hampshire. The local specialists - Froude, Metford, Tower, and Arnulph Mallock, inventor of an optical measuring device, and, of course, Henry Brunel - moved on.

The powers that be, determining that the costs of research establishments must be more accountable, heralded the death knell of ship research in Torquay.

Henry assisted with the transfer of the works to Haslar, near Portsmouth, and soon found – another project - they now required an "accuracy device" to determine square paper.

He solved this with "Mr Brunel's Paper-Ruling Machine" costing the Admiralty £57 29s 4d. It was apparently used until the 1970s, and at the price must have been one of the best investments of the century.

Henry, while undertaking tasks for the Royal Navy, continued to work in Devon. He helped solve the intractable fouling of water pipes, it having been discovered that after several years' use water flow could be restricted by up to 50 percent. An ingenious internal pipe scraper, propelled by the flow of water, had already been invented by a Mr Appold, but it got stuck when stones or debris were present. Henry, in conjunction with Froude, resolved this problem for it to become another "first" for Torquay.

In 1877, as Torquay's engineer for water, Henry supervised the construction of the 194-million gallon Kennock Reservoir, and a ten-inch main pipe to Torquay. Then came secondary pipes from Tottiford and a secondary reservoir built on Warberry Hill, Torquay.

However, Henry Brunel's best remembered construction is the Connell cantilever ferry bridge in Argyll, built in conjunction with Sir John Wolfe Barry. He also assisted with London's Tower Bridge, completed in 1894. By then he was constantly on the move and careless of possessions he would remain a bachelor throughout life.

He was a man who found no resting place, and although he had loved and perhaps should have married Froude's daughter Isy (Elizabeth), her conversion to Roman Catholicism had created tension and opposition from his mother. It was just not to be.

Henry Brunel has remained in the shadow of his father and grandfather and although a brilliant engineer he died in 1903 with no memorial to his name, and sadly no known picture of him can be reproduced here.

Below: The flying staircase at Chelston cross, pictured in it's hotel days

RUDYARD KIPLING - Writer for the Empire

RUDYARD JOSEPH KIPLING had a distinctive ancestry. Both grandfathers were Methodist Ministers and his father, John Lockwood Kipling, was a potter and designer in Staffordshire and also a craftsman mason.

HIS FATHER, HAVING NO MONEY, made Alice Macdonald wait four years until his appointment as an architectural sculptor in 1865 before they married. Then it was off to India, to teach at the Jeejeebhoy School of Art in Bombay.

Rudyard was born in India on December 30, 1865 and by the time he was six doctors were advising that the frail child be taken to live in England.

In writing his autobiography 64 years later, he recalls those first six years in India. "Early morning walks were to the Bombay fruit market with my ayah and later my sister in her perambulator - with Meeta, my Hindu bearer.

"There were Arab dhows on the pearly waters, and gaily dressed Parsees wading out to worship the sunset - and near the house were the Towers of Silence where their dead are exposed to the waiting vultures on the rim of the towers - I do not understand my Mother's distress when she found a child's hand in our garden, and I want to ask questions about it".

Kipling was destined to be a man who worshipped and surprisingly respected all children and their imaginings. Throughout his life, he would happily leave grown-ups to join children at play, and take part in the childish games. As one writer tells us: "This perhaps gives a clue to his magic - a transformation of a small space into a whole world founded in the imaginings of a child".

Arriving in England in 1871, Rudyard and his three-year-old sister Trix (Alice) could not know that six dark years were

looming. The children were not told they were to be left there and without warning they were placed in the care of a retired naval captain and his wife at Southsea.

In fact, they were marooned in a small terraced house smelling of "aridity and emptiness", living as young boarders, with a disagreeable and pious family totally unknown to them.

At school Rudyard showed few outstanding qualities except his passion for reading. Naval Captain Holloway, however, took him for walks around the docks of Portsmouth, and was kind to both children. But after his death in 1875 "The Woman" (Auntie Rosa, an evangelical bigot) and her similarly difficult son were now the Kiplings' guardians. Rudyard, in writing of the house later, recalled it as a "House of Desolation" and "The Woman" taught him of Hell, a concept he was until then completely unaware.

More importantly, his life became a hell on earth, with continual bullying, caning and, worst of all, humiliation. His only joy, the priceless books from his parents in India, avidly read as an escape.

His first six blissful years in the care of his "ayah" (Indian nanny) in Bombay were completely overshadowed by his experiences in Southsea, in the sole care of proxy parents. Years later the beatings and humiliation would surface in *Baa Baa Black Sheep*.

After six years, his mother Alice returned from India to Southsea, having heard from a relative that the children were experiencing problems. Rudyard now went to the United Services College at Westward Ho! in Devon, in 1878. He was happy boarding at college and he now began to develop an extensive knowledge of English literature. Two years later he was to return to India.

Friendships cemented at Westward Ho! would be woven into the adventures of "Stalky" and his friends, and clearly Kipling had a gift for transmuting the commonplace into full drama and a fairy tale world, not unlike Scott and Dickens before him. His exuberance and sense of fun fully emerged in

Brugglesmith (1891) and *My Sunday at Home* (1895), but it was his extra-ordinary perception and recollection that made him a scribe of genius.

This is perhaps why four years later, in 1882, he was asked to join the staff at the Lahore Civil and Military Gazette, and at last in sight of his father; he was soon recognised as a good reporter but a better storyteller and versifier.

Dozens of his famous phrases have survived, such as "East is East and West is West" and sketches, verses, and satiric stories often encompassing a hidden meaning now flowed. The English in India soon noticed their new genius.

Departmental Ditties, Plain Tales from the Hills, Soldiers Three, The Story of the Gadsbus, In Black and White, Under the Deodars, The Strange Ride of Morrowhie Jukes, The Phantom Rickshaw, Wee Willie Winkie (containing 70 stories) and *The Courting of Dinah Shadd* were all were written between 1882-1890. His literary output was staggering, and yet he was rarely satisfied: "A word should fall in its place like a bell in a full chime". He was his own hard task master.

In 1887, the Lahore Gazette's sister newspaper, the great *Punjab Pioneer*, poached him to Allahabad. There he wrote for Hindu rather than Muslim readers, but by 1889 he was off to travel widely across Japan, the United States and eventually London. Hailed as a success in England, his first attempt at a full length novel, *The Light that Failed* (1890) was not so successful. An inveterate traveller, he set off again in 1891 to the Cape, Australia, New Zealand and Columbo, along with what would be his final visit to Lahore.

In January, 1892 Kipling married Caroline Balestier. Their honeymoon took them to the United States and Canada, and they settled at Brattleboro, Vermont. The next four years saw him writing *The Jungle Book, Bandarlog* and *Many Inventions*; their first child, Josephine, arrived on December 29, 1892.

After a tedious publicity lawsuit in 1894, the family returned to Tisbury, Wiltshire, the home of Rudyard's parents,

Below: Rock House at Maidencombe, Torquay

RUDYARD KIPLING LIVED HERE AT ROCK HOUSE FROM 1896 - 1898 ON HIS RETURN FROM AMERICA

TORBAY CIVIC SOCIETY

for a holiday. They decided they would permanently return the following year. Books published now included *The Comforters*, more *Jungle Books* (1894 and 1895) and a moving tribute to Hinduism entitled *The Miracle of Puron Bhagat*, soon followed by *The Brushwood Boy* and a humorous story entitled *My Sunday at Home*, a send up of an over-solemn American doctor in England. But now with two children, Josephine and Elsie, and Queen Victoria's golden jubilee on the horizon, the Kiplings set out for a new life in Torquay, England.

They arrived in the autumn of 1896 and in spite of the mild climate, a wet winter drew the writer's wrath. He penned to a friend: "Bloody British is the only word for it, Torquay is such a place as I do desire acutely to upset by dancing through with nothing on but my spectacles".

Even the newly discovered bicycle-made-for-two tested his patience: "A tandem bicycle, whose double steering-bars made good dependence for continuous domestic quarrel...", he wrote, and after falling off named the cycle "Hell spider" and walked home never to cycle again. Now accepted as a prolific writer and although disliking Torquay, which he left in 1898, important literary work was produced during his time at Rock House, Maidencombe. Included were ten of the "Stalky" stories, nine of which would later be published as *Stalky and Co.*

In August 1897, with the family in Rottingdene, Sussex, son John was born. The death of his "adored" daughter Josephine at age six (recalled in his poem *Merrow Down*) came before the *Just So* books were completed in 1902, and later Rudyard's autobiography confirms he believed these to be his best stories.

Kim, described by many as the best book ever written about India, was published in 1901. *Puck* emerged in 1902 and then in 1907 he was awarded the Nobel Prize. Three times when he was 29 he had refused what others craved, the prized Poet Laureateship.

His son, John, was turned down by the Army due to poor eyesight but his father "pulled strings" to ensure he joined the Irish Guards; he was killed in action in 1915. Rudyard's guilt, sorrow and then his pride comes through in the poem *My Boy Jack*. The sorrow, channelled into a demand that all soldiers, rich or poor, received equal treatment when it came to their gravestones, was met even though his own son's body was not to be found until decades after Kipling's own death.

In 1921 and now aged 45, he found that the style of his writing was losing its appeal among the public. His last books were cruelly noted as "the Kipling nobody reads". His final 20 years saw constant acute pain, accompanied by haemorrhaging through sickness and a duodenal ulcer.

His final work came in 1933, *Souvenir of France*. He died on January 18, 1936 and is buried at Westminster Abbey.

SIR EDWIN LUTYENS - Man of memorials

EDWIN LANDSEER LUTYENS, the man destined to design war memorials for an empire, not to mention a public house in Torquay, was born on March 29, 1869, the 11th child of 14 to Captain Charles Henry Augustus Lutyens and Mary Gallway.

THE INNOVATIVE CAPTAIN HAD CONTRIBUTED to the advancement of musketry and was a well known painter of horses. Like his father, Edwin would be an innovator and eventually an architect of great merit; during his life, his designs made him the best known architect of the period.

Strangely, that great painter and sculptor of London's Trafalgar Square lions, Sir Edwin Landseer, had offered to adopt the Lutyens' 11th child, and although Mary declined she did consent to her child bearing his names.

Educated at home, Edwin would in later life regret not experiencing education at a public school, believing the omission to have accentuated a natural shyness.

Nevertheless, from the start he showed a tendency towards drawing and of "using his eyes", which later helped the elements of his building design. At 16 he went to what is now the Royal College of Art in Kensington, where his early designs for a new church won him his first prize.

While living at Thursley, Surrey in 1888 he designed alterations to the village shop, which led to a commission to design a cottage house, and the establishment of his practice at Grays Inn, London, both before his 20th birthday.

He was to become acquainted with notables like Philip Webb and Gertrude Jekyll, with whom he would collaborate on joint projects for more than 30 years. Gertrude's father, Sir Herbert Jekyll, commissioned Lutyens to design the British Pavilion for the Paris Exhibition. A considerable number of country houses followed, including Orchards at Godalming, Goddards at Abinger, Grey Walls at Gullane, Deanery Garden at Sonning and Marsh Court at Stockbridge. Edwin's obvious skill and innovation were also seen with his restoration of Lindisfarne Castle at Holy Island.

Always an admirer of older women, 25-year-old Edwin had met Gertrude Jekyll in 1894 when she was 52. Her admiration for his skill and her down to earth vision saw a partnership formed. His solid, three-dimensional concepts would clash over the years with her more elastic, visionary outlook but her influential connections and financial resources overcame any differences.

In 1897 Edwin Lutyens married Lady Emily, the third daughter of Lord Lytton, Viceroy of Delhi, despite some family opposition. They would have a son and four daughters but it was an odd marriage.

Lady Emily, besotted with a Mrs Besant and theosophy, would later "go native", clothing herself in Indian dress. Apparently inarticulate in words, Edwin had cultivated a sharp wit as a defensive mannerism early in his career, and although critical of his own work he rarely sketched, preferring to memorise that which interested him.

Designers of the English Renaissance particularly inspired him and he appreciated that to achieve his ambition of undertaking "big work" he had to master classicism. Limited essays in 1902-1904 preceded exercises in the style of the great Wren, which led him to adopt a simplified version of Queen Anne style, relying on dominant roofs and chimneys, fine proportions and mouldings, exemplified by his designs at Middlefield in Cambridgeshire in 1908.

His mastery of religious orders and work at Heathcote, at Ilkley in West Yorkshire, saw him being established as an architect "able to restate first principles".

His professional practice saw many pupils of distinction coming to the fore later in life, two of them connected with Devon - Frederick Harrild and Oswald P Milne. Harrild, articled to Edwin from 1907 to 1910, was commissioned by Horace Pickersgill, son of a Leeds bookmaker, to create Glengorse and its magnificent gardens on Torquay's Lincombe hillside. Today called Castle Tor it is possibly the most magnificent house built in Torquay in modern times; the adjacent plot was purchased in 1930 to prevent further building. Harrild also built Little Tor in the Warberries.

Milne went on to design Coleton Fishacre in 1924 for Rupert D'Oyly Carte, after which Leonard Elmhirst

Above: Lutyens' Drum Inn at Cockington in bygone days.
Picture: David Mason collection.

commissioned him to design the first school buildings and houses on his Dartington Estate.

By 1911 Lutyens was travelling again, this time to Rome to design another British Pavilion and then to South Africa to create the Rand Memorial and the Johannesburg Art Gallery. Widely recognised for his innovative ideas, Lutyens would create a number of buildings for the Viceroy of India, the major work being the Viceroy's House - a dream palace which took 17 years to complete, opening in 1929.

Julius Charles Drewe, founder of the famous Home and Colonial Stores, set the scene for Lutyens' celebrated Castle Drogo at Drewsteignton. He brought Edwin to Devon to design his manor house in 1911. It was to be equipped with a fine collection of furniture, tapestries and china that today can still be seen there. Drogo sits among 586 acres of land on the eastern flank of Dartmoor and in the season is open to visitors.

It was the last castle to be built in England, and its stonework and interior are superb. It allowed Lutyens full reign for his love of vistas and asymmetry. Completed in 1924 and built of granite, it occupies a spectacular site above the wooded gorge where the Teign river cuts its way eastward below Chagford.

The unique site is almost 900 feet above sea level and has fine clipped yew hedges, beautiful gardens and walking areas. The grandson of Julius, Anthony Drewe, eventually presented Castle Drogo to the National Trust and although the family still lives there they still entertain visitors.

In 1917 and appointed architect to the then Imperial (now Commonwealth) War Graves Commission, Lutyens designed many memorials and the massive Stone of Remembrance which is now common to all the larger Commonwealth war cemeteries. Knighted for his work in 1918, numerous other recognitions followed; in 1919 Lloyd George commissioned him to design the temporary catafalque in Whitehall that became the permanent Cenotaph, producing a sketch that same

evening. Made of Portland stone, this national symbol of remembrance stands in Whitehall still.

His works across many continents are too numerous to list but between the years 1919 and 1930 some 90 designs flowed from his practice, all of which he influenced - houses, villas, an abbey and Liverpool Cathedral, which was started in 1933. With the Second World War intervening it was not completed before his death.

Banks, being "palaces of finance" were designed and built for the Midland and the Britannic. His commitment to work was astonishing; memorial structures, embassies, pavilions and even apartments - Grosvenor House flats in Park Lane were finished in 1926.

In 1924 Sir Edwin was awarded a gold medal from the American Institute of Architects, and became a member of the Royal Fine Art Commission. He received an honorary degree of LLD from the University of Liverpool in 1928, and was then appointed an officer of the Legion of Honour in 1932 adding a DCL from Oxford University in 1934.

Towards the end of his career, Sir Edwin came to Torquay to design the Drum Inn (previously the Forge Inn) at Cockington, along with some of the nearby housing on the estate which the Mallock family had sold to the Cockington Trust in 1932; the 223 acres were leased to Torquay Council for 999 years.

Permission had been given for the building of a "new village around a village green" complete with an inn. The village was never built but the inn and its gardens, complete with Lutyens' trademark curved steps, were finished by 1936. The design and furnishings were by Sir Edwin, the Drum Inn sign was by British artist Dame Laura Knight, and in the saloon bar there was an engraved window by Laurence Whistler, well known poet and sculptor. In 2002 the inn was somewhat controversially refurbished.

Sir Edwin's commitment to a neo-Georgian style had by the 1930s been recognised as a bit "old hat" by many, but nevertheless he refused to allow material consideration to coarsen, still less to control, his conceptions.

Throughout life Sir Edwin insisted that art and not science should have the last word. It was claimed by a contemporary, A. S. G. Butler, that Lutyens was "one of the greatest masters of visible proportion and perhaps the greatest artist in building who has practised architecture".

His principal legacy has been described as "applying mathematical ratios to functional designs". Having lived and worked continuously at Bloomsbury between 1897 and 1913 he finally moved to Mansfield Street, where he lived until his death from bronchial sarcoma on New Year's Day in 1944.

Torbay Civic Society unveiled a blue plaque to honour Sir Edwin, at the Drum Inn Cockington Village in December, 2002.

25

LILLIE LANGTRY -
Mistress to the Monarch

EMILIE CHARLOTTE Le Breton was born on the island of Jersey in 1852. Her father, William, was Dean of Jersey and she was the only daughter of a family of seven.

LIFE ON JERSEY WAS HAPPY BUT FOR A TIME the family moved to the English mainland and Torquay, where they lived at Braddons Cliff Mansion for a number of years.

Lillie, intelligent and being her own person, saw society changing and a new, wealthy class arising. She determined that whatever the cost she would have a share of it.

A new class of industrialists, white collar professionals and colonials returning from abroad had wealth and they created a new, "fast set" who saw themselves as having power. This mixing of social classes, dandyism, aestheticism and their attendant freedoms – the relaxation of "knowing your place" - were all strange to Victorians and it was a new social order not acceptable at court, still the sole preserve of the aristocracy.

When Prince Albert died in 1863 the Queen and nation went into deep mourning. But the Prince of Wales married a Danish beauty, Alexandra, set up his court at Marlborough House and soon found that official duties were not sufficient to quell his restlessness.

Restraint, deference and formality were rejected, and boredom was replaced by pleasurable pursuits. The Prince was to be the catalyst who ensured that almost everybody, to use today's parlance, "did their own thing".

At 22 Lillie married Edward (Ned) Langtry, a widower in his 30s, at St Saviour's Church on Jersey. He reputably had three yachts and a stud of hunters. Once married they set sail aboard his yacht Red Gauntlet to honeymoon for a year, returning to live in Torquay at Villa Engadina, in 1875. However, Lillie soon discovered that her husband was not as rich as she supposed and like many Victorians she instinctively craved to be in London.

To explain the path Lillie chose, it is necessary to understand that Christian values and sedate attitudes were being constantly questioned. Informality, immodesty of dress, bawdy conversation, drunkenness and workers in revolt were rife. The "new elite" took lovers and whereas previously in high society a man walking a mistress would never acknowledge a friend or a relative, comment on behaviour was becoming quite normal, in public.

Prostitution and adultery were commonplace, and money gave entry to the holiest of inner sanctums, previously territory reserved for the aristocracy. One sacred London club even pinned a notice on its door: "Members are requested not to bring their mistresses into the club, unless they happen to be wives of other members". And, never forget, it was in this world that Lillie wanted to be a human goddess.

Excitement and change were being demanded in the late 1870s. Obedience, convention, deference and mourning were out. The Queen would dress in black for four decades, but it was the Prince, the aesthetic movement, Lillie Langtry being coached by Oscar Wilde, and the leading socialites that now took centre stage.

Lillie was to become "the Jersey Lily". Her quest for social status started in the art world. Posing at many studios as an aesthetic nude model led to an invitation from the Marquess of Hartington, leader of the Liberal Party.

At this function she officially "came out". Tradition dictated that guests on arrival queued at the marble staircase of Devonshire House, Piccadilly, to ascend and be greeted by the Marquess. The then unknown Lillie made an astonishing entrance and bowled over by her natural beauty the Marquess, ignoring his wife and Ned, took her on a tour of the courtyards and grounds. Pausing at the marble pools full of water lillies, he dived into cold water to retrieve bunches for her. Lillie, not quite 24, discovered her power over men and, at first, she was quite astounded.

Her impact was captured by Bernard Shaw's comment: "I resent Mrs Langtry, she has no right to be intelligent, daring and independent as well as lovely". But now where she led and what she wore other women followed. The painters Millais, Leighton, Poynter, Burne-Jones and Whistler fought for her sittings and even Oscar Wilde spent a night on her doorstep, later immortalising her in the play *Lady Windermere's Fan*. The media adored her, naming her "Venus Annodomini". Many at her feet became lovers, Whistler included, and a painting by Millais gave her the nickname of "Jersey Lily".

Wilde taught her the classics and the ways of society and as a phoenix she emerged to woo society with her adopted attitudes and a style that appealed to men. This mask invented by Oscar ensured that throughout life she hid her true self. He meanwhile saw an opportunity in her deification and in using it taught Lillie to mix, dine and take tea with anyone, there were no limits and this zest for life ensured numerous affairs.

At another function the Prince of Wales had requested to meet the Langtrys. With no knowledge of this Lillie was seated next to HRH. Soon realising what was afoot Lillie made no attempt to impress. She was right to do so as the Prince, though admiring beauty, hated intellectuals. After two decades of mourning, society's lead player finally broke with tradition and in 1877 the Prince of Wales made public he had taken Lillie as his first mistress, and he built her a house at Bournemouth.

She publicly rode with him along Rotten Row in London and hostesses left her name off invitations at their peril. Lillie, through Wilde, had made it - but at a price. Lack of money brought many grey periods. She publicly irritated her Prince by displaying familiarity when Alexandra, his wife, was present, something not done in polite society. Unwelcome at court and in only her second season as an actress she was often desperately lonely. In 1878, when Lillie was just 26, five of her brothers were dead and insolvency threatened her.

Her good times were on stage or in a new romantic liaison. By 1881 her affairs were legion. An early lover, Arthur Jones, was re-instated on a visit to Jersey and when her Prince took another mistress she retaliated by having an affair with his nephew, Prince Louis Battenburg. Later, after Lillie had given birth to a daughter, Jeanne, Ned petitioned for divorce citing the Prince of Wales and two others. The childs father was never confirmed and may not have been known.

Work as an actress took her to America in 1883, and then

Above: Dunstone, the Torquay villa which Lillie is reputed to have once owned as a gift from King Edward VII

to Paris and Australia. An affair with Fred Gebhard, a wealthy American, saw large tracts of Californian land gained. Characteristically, on her return to England she was re-united with her Prince, and with Arthur Jones and others.

She also found time to manage the Imperial Theatre but to little avail, and in 1891 another of her lovers, George Baird, "The Squire", an unsavoury bully and millionaire, was reportedly beating Lillie. Like all her lovers he was rich but he died in New Orleans alone, after a binge.

After Ned's death in 1897 Lillie married Hugo de Bathe in 1899, a man 20 years her junior. He, like Baird was unkind and bragged about his conquests of many chorus girls. Even daughter Jeanne disowned her mother, the grey days were back.

In 1901 the Victorian era ended, and in attending Edward's coronation Lillie sat with Alice Keppel, Daisy Warwick and Sarah Bernhardt in what was termed "the King's Loose Box". Despite the Prince having been crowned Edward VII, he kept his relationship with Lillie intact knowing that she had remarried. Their liaison lasted for over three decades and the King is said to have given Dunstone, a Warberries villa in Torquay to Lillie as a gift, although this is unproven.

She wrote an appropriately titled book, *All at Sea*, in 1909 but her world was changing fast; Wilde and Ned were dead and Lillie was summoned to Buckingham Palace (entering by the customary side door) for the last time in 1910, to be told that her Prince was also dead.

Lillie was still fit and still acted on stage. She was wealthy and even owned racehorses, but was also tired. Her final years were spent in Monte Carlo, not far from her beloved Arthur, now married. She was reunited with Jeanne and her grandchildren, and her memoirs, *The Days I Knew*, were published in 1925. After spending Christmas in England in 1928, Lillie returned to Monte Carlo and died the following February, aged 77. For her burial, however, the Jersey Lily returned to her island home.

JOHN RUSSELL - Dartmouth's sporting parson

JOHN RUSSELL was the eldest son of the rector of North Hill, Callington, in Cornwall and was born at Belam House, Dartmouth, on December 21, 1795.

HE WAS DESCENDED FROM THE KINGSTON RUSSELL FAMILY, whose Devonshire roots date back to 1551. Being born into a hunting family he loved all field sports from an early age, and also participated in sparring and wrestling.

He initially attended grammar school at Plymouth before going to Blundells School, Tiverton, where with friends he established a scratch pack of hunting dogs, for which he bred a fierce, short-legged, smooth coated little dog that came to be known as the "Jack Russell terrier".

When this unusual school project came to the notice of the master, John (now called Jack) was close to getting expelled. Thankfully he survived this first clash with authority and went on to win a Balliol scholarship and matriculated to Exeter College, Oxford, in November, 1814.

At Oxford Russell established friendships with the aristocratic set but unlike them he was often in debt. Nevertheless he continued to enjoy a good deal of sporting pursuits.

His earliest ambition was to excel at hunting and yet on graduating with a BA in 1818 he studied for the clergy, and was ordained in 1819. A year later he entered the priesthood and secured his first curacy at George Nympton, close to South Molton, Devon. Here he made a friend of the Rev John Froude, of Knowstone, whose reputation for a love of hounds and public dismissal of episcopal authority was much famed.

On May 30, 1826 Russell married an heiress, Penelope Incledon Bury, daughter of Admiral Bury of Dennington House, Barnstaple and soon afterwards obtained his second curacy, this time at Iddesleigh. Now an established breeder, he had otter hounds at South Molton and his newly found wealth through marriage brought him the opportunity to fulfil his ambition of establishing a pack of hunting foxhounds at Iddesleigh.

Jack's voice was much envied. It is said it had a stentorian quality and his "view halloo" was famous throughout Exmoor and Dartmoor when out riding with his beloved "wild red rovers of Dartmoor", as he called them.

In 1831 the controversial figure of Henry Phillpotts was consecrated Lord Bishop of Exeter. When being driven away from the service he spotted a passing foxhunt and remarked: "Dear me, what a number of black coats among the hunters — has there been some sort of bereavement in the neighbourhood?" he asked. His chaplain retorted: "My Lord, the only bereavement these black-coated sportsmen suffer from is not being able to appear in pink." The autocratic Phillpotts was known to be no supporter of hunting, and this spelled trouble ahead for the Reverend Russell.

Russell, by now nicknamed "the sporting parson", was a tall, upright man, witty and, with his broad Devon dialect, popular. He enjoyed talking and gave the odd speech, he was an enthusiastic and untiring rider, and an excellent judge of horse and hound.

Some said that he "never needed a whip to turn them" and he "never lost a fox by a false cast". In the pulpit he tried to reform rather than simply preach doctrine and was sternly against foul language, denounced strong drink and the "filthy habit of smoking". For all that he was an enthusiastic imbiber of Devonshire cider and Devonshire clotted cream.

In the hunt Russell had an instinctive knowledge of the line a hunt should take and was masterful in decision. Being abstemious and always early to bed, he had enormous powers of endurance. He was renowned for riding long distances and on one occasion rode 20 miles to Iddesleigh, found and killed a fox, then rode to Ash to dine and dance, before sleeping just two hours and then riding 50 miles to Bodmin, to join another hunt.

He was a friend of the poor in his care and tended carefully to all his pastoral duties. None were left

Above: John Russell was born and brought up in Dartmouth.

During the mid-1850s he then became the catalyst for popularising stag hunting throughout Devonshire, and helped an inaugural tournament at Dulverton to become an annual event. His hunting activities stretched from Torrington in Devon to Bodmin in Cornwall and his phenomenal prowess was much admired.

It was in 1865 that he first met the Prince of Wales, while attending a Royal Agricultural Society meeting at Plymouth. This led to friendship and subsequent meetings at Sandringham, where on one occasion Russell preached at the invitation of the Prince, and where, at the age of 77 when attending a New Year Ball, there he was even allowed to lead the Princess of Wales onto the dance floor — an honour indeed!

On January 1, 1875 his heiress wife, Penelope, died and this ended the seemingly limitless financial resource which had funded his not so reverent lifestyle. Their son, John Bury, also predeceased him and in 1880 he was reluctantly forced to give up his modest income at Swymbridge for a richer living at Black Torrington rectory. He even sold his pack of foxhounds to his friend, Henry Villebois.

Although appreciating the reason for the move from Swymbridge, his parishioners were mortified. They presented him with a testimonial and £800 to help towards his mounting debts as a mark of their appreciation for his incumbency. He had not only restored the local church's interior but had also built two daughter churches at Travellers Inn and Gunn.

Nevertheless, it was not long before Russell, with the support of his parishioners, established a pack of harriers at Torrington. Interestingly, it was almost a century before the links between hunting and the clergy were broken by the Church, which eventually insisted that only those candidates "not interested" in field sports should be ordained.

After serving for three years as rector at Black Torrington, the Rev "Jack" Russell died on April 28, 1883 aged 87 and was returned to his beloved Swymbridge to be buried on May 3, when it was estimated that around 1,000 mourners attended his funeral.

unperformed and this later thwarted Bishop Phillpotts when he tried to discipline his parson. Russell was extremely popular with his parishioners, the hunting fraternity and the gentry, numbering amongst his friends such worthies of the time as Earl Fortescue, the Earl of Portsmouth, George Lane-Fox and Henry Villebois.

Living at Tor Down near Barnstaple, Russell was given a perpetual curacy in 1832 adjoining the parish of Swymbridge. It was here his first major clash with Bishop Phillpotts erupted.

His Lordship, much troubled by the number of hunting parsons in his diocese, ordered Russell to appear before him on charges of neglecting parochial duties, due to his hunting with hounds. Russell refused to give up his pack and refuted the accusation, which was eventually deemed unfounded.

The hunting parson was a much sought after visiting preacher and a successful fund raiser, particularly for the North Devon Hospital where he was a governor, and his efforts in obtaining improvements for the local populace were legion. He worked hard for the rights of agricultural workers and for the Royal Agricultural Society in the region, activities which eventually came to the notice of the Prince of Wales, who became much interested in this extrovert and controversial cleric. In 1845, Russell was instrumental in establishing an annual fox hunting meet at South Molton, and even helped revive the Exmoor stag hunt.

Below: Blundells School near Tiverton, from where 'Jack' Russell came close to being expelled.

JOHN SNELGROVE -
Store owner and benefactor

BORN IN 1815, the year of the Battle of
Waterloo, John Snelgrove spent a lifetime
in business at the drapery emporium that
came to bear his name, and retired
to Torquay to become a major
benefactor to many causes.

IT WAS 31-YEAR-OLD JAMES MARSHALL WHO WITH a partner
had opened a London drapery business named Marshall
and Wilson.

By 1837 the business had been awarded Queen Victoria's
patronage and was thriving but after working with two other
associates Marshall eventually turned to 23-year-old John
Snelgrove and offered him a full working partnership. He then
renamed the store Marshall & Snelgrove.

As an assistant in the store John had already established
himself as an important part of the emporium, having learned
all aspects of this retail business. Now the new partnership
acquired adjoining properties as the leases came up for sale and
by as early as 1851 the Oxford Street site was much enlarged
and now called the "Royal British Warehouse".

John Snelgrove's personal skills centred around looking after
staff, being very much a hands-on partner. He was a hyperactive
and hard-working proprietor, and the staff certainly appreciated
his commitment to the success of the business. When in 1865
half-day closing of the store on Saturdays was introduced,
grateful employees presented him with an illuminated
hand-written plaque which read: "To John Snelgrove esq.
The assistants of Messrs Marshall & Snelgrove desire to express
to you their high appreciation of the valuable aid you have
given in establishing the Half Holiday on Saturday and they
especially wish to establish their grateful thanks for the
generous and able manner in which you, on a recent
occasion, defended the general body of young men against
unjust aspersions…"

John Snelgrove worked long hours and was recognised for
his strong conviction to hard work. Close to the Marshall
family, he eventually married his partner's daughter and in time
they produced two sons and three daughters.

Then as now, successful senior executives would often
volunteer a considerable amount of time to external interests
and Snelgrove was no exception. Throughout his life he
associated himself with charitable work, sometimes connected

with business but often with institutions that had little or no
commercial value to him or the business. Although identified as
a strong supporter of charities in general he was a special friend
of the Linen and Woollen Drapers' Institution, serving as its
president between the years 1869 and 1881. He headed its
appeal committee between 1870 and 1892 and also became
chairman of its Annual Festival Committee, serving this for a
total of 11 years.

One of his pet schemes was to help the institution's
building committee to ensure that cottage homes were built.
He personally defrayed the expenses of four homes at Mill Hill,
and the institution later recorded that no-one "ever possessed a
more warm-hearted friend or generous supporter". The cottage
homes eventually became part of the Retail Trust that
thrives to this day.

When Marshall retired the business passed into the control
of his son, who with Snelgrove ensured the continued progress
of the business. Many smaller stores were purchased, adding to
this expanding giant of the retail store sector.

The gross turnover of the business by 1903 had
reached in excess of £1,000,000 and the emporium was

Below: A store advertisement from the 1920s

employing over 1,100 people, after continual expansion over almost four decades. The joint ownership was successful but in 1885 Snelgrove, aged 70, finally decided to retire and move to Devon.

He remained a trustee of the Linen and Woollen Drapers' Institution, and was also connected with the warehousemen, clerks and -draper schools and was a major supporter and benefactor in the establishment of an orphanage for their members. He remained a trustee and supporter of the General Porters' Benevolent Institution and was involved in the Milliners and Dressmakers' Association. His decades of commitment to causes and charities brought him many accolades but the award he most treasured was a silver vase given on the occasion of his silver wedding. Suitably engraved, it confirmed his long years of work and support for his beloved Linen and Woollen Drapers Institution.

The boardroom of the institution held a handsome portrait of John Snelgrove, beneath which was framed a letter written by him when 87 in April, 1902. From Torquay it confirmed: "My health is satisfactory, suffering principally from 'leg wear' and extreme deafness." Sadly, the portrait and its accompanying letter were lost during the Blitz in World War II.

From the start Snelgrove's retirement in Torquay was not going to quell his zest for philanthropic work. He became an active supporter of a number of institutions and his local church, St Matthias at Wellswood, was an early beneficiary of his generosity; the Gardeners' Association and the Torbay cabmen were also indebted to him.

In helping the cabmen he used his considerable experience to establish a "Sick and Provident Society" for them, which he achieved in conjunction with Mr Taylor, Mr Struben, Mr Ball and Mr Lord. His personal contribution exceeded £300 but not content with that he then invested an additional £500 in Torquay Corporation stock to secure some permanent income for the society. Gifts were also made at Christmas when his "dinner table" collection, dedicated to the society, invariably raised £10 per sitting.

The family home was one of Wellswood's finest mansions, St Elmo, so it was appropriate that Snelgrove remained a major benefactor to St Matthias' Church. After his death an ornate memorial chancel was adorned in his honour and the publication *Criticus* confirms: "Look upwards and discover that the great rood beam is still supported by life-sized sculptured angels, who themselves are looking up in an attitude of intense devotion to the Calvary Cross, and on the beam is carved *To the*

glory of God and in memory of John Snelgrove AD 1815 - 1903'. St Matthias also received a stained glass window dedicated to his memory in May, 1905.

Months before his death the family moved to 23 Kensington Palace Gardens, London where late on the morning of December 1, 1903 Snelgrove died peacefully. He attained the remarkable age of 88, and was survived by his wife, two sons and three daughters. The funeral took place at Frant, near Tunbridge Wells, on December 7, 1903.

The final Torquay connection with the family came when his children erected a fountain at Wellswood in 1905 in memory of their father. Its worn inscription is still readable: "Erected by his children, to the memory of John Snelgrove, once of St. Elmo in this town".

Originally built on the roadside at the junction of Ilsham Road and Babbacombe Road, increasing traffic and the perceived distraction for drivers saw the local authority resiting the memorial in 1967 to its current location abutting the grassed area.

Although the new site gives better visibility to drivers and pedestrians alike, it unfortunately ensured the water receptacle became a depository for rubbish from modern day passers-by. The desecration would have horrified the family but as the Herald Express reported in September, 1967 "the trash of modern society and the need to have disposable packaging accompanying everything we use, is at least kept off the street". As a source of fresh water the fountain is now unusable.

After 137 years in business, during which time it owned Bobby's of Torquay and Spooners of Plymouth, the name of Marshall and Snelgrove disappeared forever in 1974 when it and its Torquay premises became Debenhams.

Top: The Snelgrove memorial fountain at Wellswood
Below: The Oxford Street store of Marshall and Snelgrove.

28

THOMAS NEWCOMEN - Pioneer of steam power

THOMAS NEWCOMEN was born in Lower Street, Dartmouth. The exact date is unknown but parish records confirm that he was baptised at St Saviour's Church on February 28, 1663.

ON MARRIAGE TO HANNAH WAYMOUTH ON JULY 13, 1705 it was recorded that Newcomen, an ironmonger, was also a blacksmith.

How he became interested in steam engines or, as a description of that time says, became "the inventor of that surprising machine for raising water by fire", remains a mystery.

He was certainly in touch with a Dr Hooke towards the end of the 17th century. He wanted news about a proposal by Papin, a French physicist seeking to obtain motive power by exhausting air from a cylinder by the use of a piston. Hooke wrote to Papin asking if it was possible to "make a speedy vacuum under your second piston", but there is no record of any reply.

At the same time that Newcomen was grappling with his steam engine design, another inventor from Devon, Captain Savery, had on June 25, 1698 lodged a patent for a pump engine which he named "The Miner's Friend".

With raw tin being sought after anything that might help to expel water from flooded tin mines was invaluable. On April 25, 1699 Savery, a personal friend of King William III, was granted a 14-year patent for "engines for raising water by the impellant force of water", and this all-encompassing description virtually debarred all similar engines being patented. Newcomen, who had by now built his steam-driven engine, was therefore unable to protect his invention separately.

The situation became even more intolerable when Savery successfully applied to Parliament for a special order to extend his patent by 21 years. This gave him unique and protected rights until 1733. With little choice other than to form a partnership with his rival, Newcomen, in accepting this, at least ensured that his own engine eventually became the standard of the day.

He also befriended a John Calley (the name may have been Cawley), believed to be a native of Brixham, who became the financial backer for Newcomen's early steam engines.

With Savery having published details of his engine in 1702 there is little doubt that Newcomen's engine of 1712 was superior. The London Gazette in 1716 carried an advertisement which confirms the ongoing events.

It states: "Whereas the invention for raising water by the impellant force of fire, authorised by Parliament, is lately brought to the greatest perfection in all sorts of mines etc, which may thereby be drained and water raised to any height with more ease and less charge than by any other methods hitherto used, as is sufficiently demonstrated by diverse engines of this invention now at work in the several counties of Stafford, Warwick, Cornwall and Flint".

All of these engines were Savery/Newcomen creations, one even being constructed at Whitkirk in the parish of Austhorpe, near Leeds, in December 1717, the year Calley died.

Searches of the Public Record Office have failed to discover any patent by Thomas Newcomen and the partnership must have been sufficiently flexible to give protected rights to both inventors as their engine designs slowly developed and improved.

Below: Newcomen's revolutionary steam engine, which pumped water from tin and coal mines (from the 1875 print).

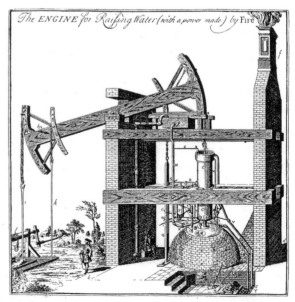

Opposite page: Newcomen's house in Dartmouth is the white building in the centre. It was demolished in 1864.
Above: The inventor's links with Dartmouth are preserved via Newcomen Road.

With Savery's 21-year extension to the patent, the coal industry in Scotland was to become one of the first beneficiaries of a large steam-powered engine for non-tin purposes, at the Edmonstone Colliery, Midlothian. The colliery engine brought an agreement in 1725 that gave a royalty fee of £80 per annum "for and during and until the full end and period of the said John Meres and proprietors aforesaid". The royalty continued until 1733 (by which time Newcomen had died) when the patent expired; Meres was Sir John Meres, FRS (one time Governor of the York Buildings Waterworks), and the engine constructed was Newcomen's improved version incorporating a wooden beam and arch heads.

Writing of this period Dr Allen, a friend of Thomas Newcomen, stated: "It is now more than 30 years since the engine for raising water was at first invented by the famous Captain Savery and upwards of 20 years that it received its great improvement by my good friend the ever memorable Mr Newcomen, whose death I very much regret". The letter is important as it substantially confirms that the two inventors must have been working on different systems of power, yet because of the patent they had worked together.

Further confirmation of the events is drawn from the second volume of Desagulier's book of 1744, entitled *Experimental Philosophy*, which states that "Calley and Newcomen having made several experiments in private and having brought their engine to work with a piston... in 1711 made proposals to draw the water at Griff in Warwickshire".

The book goes on to point out that neither man was sufficiently skilled to understand the actual philosophy or mathematics of the power they required in order to achieve the required condensation, which was eventually discovered by accident.

However, once discovered it was not long before a boy operator named Humphrey Potter attached a set of "self acting" catches and strings to the cross beam which enabled the engine's valves to be more accurately and automatically controlled. But even this story is later repudiated as apocryphal.

It was said that the boy was a misconception and in truth was a "buoy" (a float) which had been used to open the injection cock. Whatever the truth, the beam and its many adaptations certainly improved the engine's overall performance.

A technical account of Newcomen's engine of 1723 at Griff, near Coventry, appears in Desagulier's book, which also contains several plates of note. The British Museum possesses a plate/print engraved in 1725 by Sutton Nicholls, entitled "Description of the Engine for Raising Water by Fire", which pictures the Dudley Castle Engine.

It took until 1876 before a copperplate print of Newcomen's first engine of 1712 came to light. Discovered amongst a collection of scientific material loaned to an unnamed exhibitor at a South Kensington exhibition, the print shows Newcomen's atmospheric engine with wooden beam and arch heads and a plug rod working the tappets which, in turn, work the injection steam valves.

This self-acting ("automatic") engine had a 21-ins diameter cylinder, 7ft 10ins high. The engine was capable of 12 strokes a minute and could raise 50 gallons of water per minute from a depth of 156 feet. Mathematicians today calculate this as being five-and-a-half horse power, derived from just-heated water to achieve steam-driven power.

Two copies of the original copperplate print are known to exist, one privately held, the other lodged at the William Salt Library, Stafford. They prove that the Newcomen steam engine with beam was the standard design and that Savery, although the inventor of a steam pump, was not the designer of the beam engine.

His "Miner's Friend" patent was certainly used to protect Newcomen's beam and valve design, which remained a world leader for three-quarters of a century until the 1760s, when Scottish engineer James Watt introduced the final improvement, a cooling condenser system, patented in 1769. A new era of steam power had finally arrived.

Survived by his wife Hannah and two children, Thomas and Elias, Thomas Newcomen died in August, 1729 aged 66. He is believed to have been living in London at the time, though Letters of Administration regarding his estate were granted at the Court of Canterbury.

Below: The plaque honouring Newcomen, in the Royal Avenue Gardens at Dartmouth, Devon.

29

PARIS EUGENE SINGER – Creator of the 'Versailles' Oldway

PARIS EUGENE SINGER was the third son of Isaac and his second wife Isabella, who had left America in 1867 for France prior to the birth of the child destined to be named after its capital city.

AN HEIR TO THE SINGER FORTUNE, Paris would become an architect and the catalyst behind Florida's Palm Beach resort, after a glittering career around the world and, in Paignton, the completion of his father's "Wigwam" home today known as Oldway Mansion.

Born on November 20, 1867 Paris inherited his father's artistic and physical characteristics. Isaac, for a Victorian, had been tall but Paris was taller at 6ft 3ins. As an Edwardian sporting a beard he was a handsome man of distinction.

When Isaac died Paris was seven, and although in his will Isaac made Isabella the principal legatee, this was strongly contested in protracted litigation by an earlier mistress, Mary Ann Sponsler, who had borne him ten children.

The young Paris and Isabella's other children were to be involved in even more controversy when she returned to her roots in France taking them with her. Remarrying, she put her children's inheritance at risk due to the complicated terms of Isaac's will. On reaching 16 Paris and his brothers fled, on a promise they would be made Wards of Court in England to protect their inheritance from their new stepfather. This amazing legal twist, in an age where travel was difficult, was executed by the Singer family solicitor in Paignton, Mr Yard Eastley.

Paris attended Cambridge University but with a personal tutor left for Australia. In 1887 and under age (as a ward) he married Lily Graham in Hobart, Tasmania. Having married without the British court's consent they were forced to return to France and then England to try and unravel the legal complications that again threatened the inheritance. Lily produced four boys and a girl, Herbert, Cecil, Winnaretta, Paris (Jnr) and George. Later, three reception rooms at Oldway would be named after them.

Paris duly received his inheritance and for his coming of age in 1888 a number of glittering balls were held at the "Wigwam". There was dancing in the specially decorated Arena, illuminated by electricity, then a novelty of the age. Paris purchased a Mowbray organ (£2,000) for St John's Parish Church in Torquay, being an early sign of his becoming a major benefactor of Torbay.

Always impulsive and fastidious, Paris was a businessman with many interests. He was generous and enjoyed undertaking things in a lavish style. His early twenties saw him studying architecture to obtain a degree, though he would become less of a practitioner and more a patron of projects. A notable exception was No 3 Cadogan Gate in London, given to his daughter Winnaretta on her marriage to Sir Reginald Leeds. The building is now the head office of the Incorporated Society of Valuers and Auctioneers.

Paris was a motor vehicle enthusiast and a founder member of the Automobile Club de France in 1895 and the RAC in 1897; he was also a founder member and chairman of the City and Surburban Electric Carriage Company, which pioneered the electric car.

This early enthusiasm for cars saw him departing London for Paignton in an English Napier, and in 1901 having the honour of driving Queen Alexandra in one of his horseless carriages. His social status was such that the Daily Express confirmed him as "rich, clever and successful... and understands the practical part of automobilism... is fond of music, a good musician and one of the chief supporters of Covent Garden Opera".

Back "home" in Devon he formed the Paignton and District Land Development

Company and developed the districts of Preston, Barcombe and Marldon. His father's "Wigwam" was transformed between 1904-1907 into a mansion, sporting it's splendid new triumphal arch on its drive. White, in his *Directory of Devon* said Oldway had one of the finest conservatories in Devon. The transformation was completed when Paris brought Achille Duchene, the French landscape architect, to Paignton to create the Versailles gardens in miniature with an avenue of limes, a grotto, a rock garden and the 18th century-style sphinxes on the south terrace.

The year 1909, when he was 42 and separated from his wife, was an important one. He went to France where he met the celebrated innovative dancer Isadora Duncan. Unknown to him, a clairvoyant had predicted to her that she would soon meet a millionaire who would clear her debts and fulfil all her dreams. Paris was the man. They now embarked upon an eight-year love affair taking them across several continents.

That summer saw them sailing to Italy in his magnificent yacht, the Lady Alicia, with its crew of 50. Meals were eaten daily on "a table set with crystal and silver" and the opulence must have been astounding. The following year they journeyed to Alexandria and the Nile but with Isadora pregnant they returned to France for the birth of Patrick in May, 1910.

Paris now purchased land at St Jean Cap Ferrat, where he would build a "great Italian castle" not completed until 1925. Although he forever wanted to marry Isadora, she annoyingly shunned this.

In an effort to impress her with his mansion they spent some weeks at Oldway Mansion during the autumn of 1910. Sadly, having suffered a stroke prior to the visit he now had a doctor and nurse with him at all times, but Isadora hated the lifestyle of Paignton, particularly it's weather: "In an English summer it rains all day". Noting her increasing despair, Paris arranged parties and entertainment and encouraged her to recommence her inspired dancing utilising Oldway's magnificent ballroom.

It was to no avail; Isadora was determined to dedicate her life to art and although she would remain his mistress for another seven years, she returned to France and then America, where life was not so parochial.

In 1913 Patrick and a half-sister were drowned in the River Seine in France in a tragic car accident. By 1917 the love-union of Paris and Isadora was over, though he financially supported her until her death in a second tragic car accident in 1927, at Nice.

During 1917, despondent and in poor health, Paris arrived in Palm Beach,

Florida. Suffering from general exhaustion and a lung disorder his intention was to recuperate. He soon fell in love with the Florida resort and in 1918 an ambitious dream became reality. Palm Beach, famed for its appeal to the "super rich", was to benefit greatly from the Singer fortune and Joan Bates, the nurse who had tended him in England.

The first project was a convalescent hospital for shell-shocked officers returning from the Great War, the Touchstone Convalescents Club. In 1919 Paris transformed this into the famous Everglades Club. More land was purchased from lakeside to ocean, and his inherited entreprenurial flair rapidly developed hundreds of acres. This period would later be remembered as the "the Golden Age of Palm Beach".

Not everything went as Paris wished. In 1927 he was arrested on charges of alleged fraudulent advertisements, later dismissed, and in 1928 a hurricane brought disaster when his Blue Heron Hotel failed to be completed; it was later known as "Singer's Folly".

The Wall Street Crash of 1929 saw Paris, like many others, becoming bankrupt in the States. With his former nurse Joan now his new wife he returned to Cap Ferrat and never saw Palm Beach again. On visiting Paignton in 1929 he founded the Torbay Country Club at Oldway (1,000 members) and left instructions that after his death Oldway be offered to the local authority.

From 1930, though resident in Cap Ferrat, the couple still travelled widely and it was on one of his visits to his heart specialist in London that Paris died. The date - June 24, 1932; he was 64.

His body was interred in the Singer family vault at Torquay Cemetry and in accordance with his wishes, Oldway was sold to Paignton Urban District Council in December, 1946 for £45,000. Today, much of it is used as Council offices.

Below: Oldway Mansion during construction, in the years during 1904-1907.

30

WILLIAM KEBLE MARTIN - Cleric who painted wild flowers

KEBLE MARTIN, the sixth child of Charles and Dora Martin, was born at Radley, near Oxford, on July 9, 1877. His father was to become Rector of Dartington in 1891.

EVEN IN HIS YOUTH KEBLE showed a keen interest in birds, butterflies and fauna and throughout life was a gentle, kindly and unassuming person but a passionate botanist.

A member of the Natural History Society at Marlborough College, he ultimately went on to Oxford to read Greek philosophy and botany, for which latter subject the tutor encouraged students to draw what they observed under the microscope. Keble's first known drawing was at Dartington in 1899 where he captured snowdrops on ivy leaves. A year later numerous drawings of flora and fauna were sketched in Southern Ireland.

Ordained deacon in December, 1902 and priest a year later, his first religious posting came in the industrial parish of Beeston, near Nottingham. Never much concerned about inconveniences, he thought little of journeying overnight to capture a single drawing of a plant in its native habitat. Once captured, the sketch was then added to his growing collection.

These forays took him to the Derbyshire Peak District, Charnwood Forest, Winchester and even Beer in Devon, where with his brother Arthur he found rock sea lavender.

This period saw him obtaining the London Catalogue of British Plants and in reassembling this into 100 sections he unknowingly created the framework of 100 plates which he was to use in his own famous publication, the *Concise British Flora in Colour*, in later years.

He moved to Derbyshire in 1906, and despite mislaying his bride-to-be's wedding ring, he married Violet Chaworth-Musters on July 8, 1909 at Ashbourne, having between times

taken up a curacy at Lancaster. He then took up the ministry at All Saints, Wath-upon-Dearne, near Sheffield, where his flower drawing was put on hold due to the hard workload of this busy parish.

The Martins were blessed with two children, Patrick and Vivienne, before his posting in the First World War as an Army Chaplain. He learned in 1917 that his parish church had been gutted by fire, at the hand of a boy seeking revenge on an organist who had smacked him.

On demobilisation Martin returned to Wath-on-Dearne, remaining 12 years and today "Keble Martin Way" still exists there in his honour.

With little time for recreation or botany the intervention of Miss Carew in 1921 was a blessing. She offered him the benefice of Haccombe with Coffinswell, near Newton Abbot, Devon, which saw him taking the next step into what was to become the most exciting and rewarding period in his life.

His appointment to Coffinswell, where an earlier incumbent had been his older brother Jack, gave him 12 years in which he could be devoted to his flock whilst also able to pursue his beloved botany. He was also to assist an elderly colleague in the neighbouring community of Milber, which although having no church was undergoing rapid growth. He got to know the needs of his new parishioners and was soon organising the formation of a parochial church council and laying plans to raise money for the construction of a new church there.

Though now tending two flocks of parishioners, Keble was still able to flex his time and was much satisfied to note in his diary that "the flower drawing advanced rapidly". It was to take until 1928 before a local landowner, the Earl of Devon, offered Milber villagers two acres of land for £300, so that a new church might be built there.

Two years later sufficient funds had been raised for Milber's first wooden mission hut, "The Hall", in essence a first church. It comprised a small sanctuary with an altar screened off at one end. It was dedicated by the Bishop of Exeter in 1930, with Martin believing the building necessary if only because "social gatherings have their proper and essential place in church life".

On his return from Perthshire after a hurried visit to "collect" a specimen, Keble was to have an experience that would have an effect on his life for the next 30 years. Even in 1931 hooligans were a problem in urban areas and following some recent local animosity towards the fledgeling church Keble experienced a particularly vivid dream one night in March, 1931, in which there was a disturbance in a church where he was preaching and where trouble makers had to be turned out by the churchwardens.

His "dream" church's architecture was every bit as interesting as the incident within it and next morning he was able to send sketches of the dreamt of building to his brother Arthur, who was an architect and who was then able to create proper drawings from the sketches.

Keble's vision is best expressed in his autobiography, in which he states: "I was preaching in a new church building from the chancel step; the church was full of people and was of a curious pattern. The altar behind was in a round stone apse, in front were three diverging naves, one unfinished."

Arthur's plans not only pleased his brother but also satisfied the diocesan authorities, and ultimately resulted in a church of remarkable symmetry - it was 1000 inches in height, length and breadth.

Sometime during this period Keble Martin had accidentally upset some cobalt-based blue paint on to white paper, which having impregnated some aureolin yellow resulted in a magnificent green being produced. Fortuitously he had invented a new leaf green paint.

In 1928 Keble Martin was elected a Fellow of the Linnean Society and a member of the newly formed botanical section of the Devonshire Association.

The winter of 1932-33 saw him and Violet finally deciding to compile 100 hand-painted plates of flowers from his 1,480 sketches. The task was over complicated because the earliest drawings had been produced on poor paper whereas sketches after 1924 had been on quality paper – the earlier ones had to be redrawn.

Little progress was made in 1933 in botany, drawing or paintings, and in 1934 Keble Martin was appointed Vicar of Torrington. He visited Milber, Newton Abbot in June, 1936 to cut a sod and lay the foundation stone of the church of his dream, though would be another 27 years before the building was completed.

Shortly before the outbreak of the Second World War The Reverend Martin, in conjunction with Gordon T. Fraser, edited the *Flora of Devon*, a scholarly volume but with none of the drawings that would later make his own flora so famous.

After serving as Vicar of Torrington for 10 years until after the end of the Second World War, Rev. Martin returned to his old stamping ground in 1946 to become Rector of Combe-in-Teignhead with Milber, at the age of 69.

Above: Postage stamps issued in 1967, showing some of Keble Martin's drawings of wild flowers.

Three years later he retired to Gidleigh, near Chagford, and became a locum vicar during which time he visited 46 different churches.

In 1957 he and Violet moved to Woodbury, East Devon, and celebrated their golden wedding two years later. In 1963 Martin was devastated when his wife died; they had lost their daughter, Barbara, from leukemia that year and he had already lost his two brothers. The local paper said of Violet that "with a husband who was frequently on another planet, she had loyally and willingly borne the burden of family life".

Also in 1963 the new church of St Luke at Milber was consecrated, 27 years to the day after Martin had laid its foundation stone. He was, of course, present for the occasion.

At 86 he now devoted his time to his flora and after his coloured drawings were exhibited at a Royal Horticultural Society meeting in Vincent Square, London, an appeal was launched to enable their publication. Over 80 botanists supplied further specimens to enable the book to be completed, following which a publisher, George Rainbird, was found.

Living alone at Woodbury, Martin eventually proposed to Florence Lewis in October, 1964. Florence, appropriately known as Flora in her family, initially remarked: "Oh, no - I like the name Lewis", but she still married her 87-year-old suitor in January the following year.

On May 6 they journeyed to Buckingham Palace to meet Prince Philip, who had consented to provide a foreword for Martin's new book.

Much to his surprise this extraordinary cleric became a best selling author in 1965 when 100,000 copies of his book were sold. He received an honorary degree of Doctor of Science from Exeter University, and the Post Office even issued a national wildflower postage stamp issue, based on his drawings.

The Rev William Keble Martin (called after the celebrated clergyman John Keble, a leader of the Oxford Movement) lived to a lively 92 and died on November 26, 1969. His memorial in Woodbury churchyard reads: "He loved God all his life, and served him in the priesthood for 67 years 1902-1969. Artist and author."

31

ROBERT RANKE GRAVES - Wartime interlude at Galmpton

ROBERT RANKE GRAVES, the eldest son among five children, was born at Wimbledon in July, 1895.

HIS MOTHER WAS ELIZABETH SOPHIE (Amy) von Ranke, second wife to Alfred Percival Graves, an inspector of schools.

Robert's ancestry seems littered with writers. His maternal great uncle was historian Leopold von Ranke, and an 18th century Richard Graves wrote *The Spiritual Quixote*. His father wrote poetry, collected folks songs, and even wrote the Irish song *Father O'Flynn*.

Having attended no fewer than six preparatory schools, the young Graves entered Charterhouse in 1914. Just as he was about to go to St John's College at Oxford, the First World War broke out. He was living at Harlech and after being told that some men were receiving automatic commissions rather than serving through the ranks, he reported to his nearest recruiting depot at Wrexham.

Having informed the adjutant that he was attending the Officer Training Corps at Charterhouse (in truth he had resigned) he was given a commission to serve with the Royal Welch Fusiliers, the same regiment as the poet Siegfried Sassoon; his mother meanwhile was said to have commented: "Our race has gone mad - he is already a hero".

Graves was in fact indifferent to the whole idea of an Army career but he was sent to Lancaster and put in charge of new recruits and German prisoners. Next came France and the Western Front as a second lieutenant of a platoon of 40. He came across one 63-year-old conscript (a veteran of the Boer War) who had also bent the rules to get in and hadn't fired a rifle in 30 years. The nightmare of war thus dawned early on Graves and he became an ardent critic, as his poems later reflected.

Promoted to captain he was appalled at the holocaust and witnessed but survived some of the heaviest fighting, being twice mentioned in despatches. He was eventually wounded and returned to Oxford to convalesce.

In 1918 he married Annie Mary Pryde Nicholson (Nancy) and wanting to finance the completion of his education then ran a small grocery shop and lived in a cottage in the garden of the poet John Masefield, while attending St John's, Oxford.

The business was of little consequence and in any case Graves was convinced his career lay in poetry. Some stirring lines of 1922 heralded another turning point:

> I'd die for you, or you for me
> So furious is our jealousy
> And if you doubt this
> Kill me outright, lest I kill you.

He received his degree in 1926, and with Nancy moved to Egypt to take a post as Professor of English at the University of Cairo. A year later they returned and separated. Their last seven years had produced four children but Graves, having lived with the mental stress of war for 10 years, now fled to the Mediterranean and the island of Majorca.

There he met an American poet, Laura Riding, and evolved a new theory of "pure, non-literary and integral" poetry and writing, his usual romanticism style having apparently "boiled dry". By 1929 his most famous book, *Goodbye to All That*, one of the greatest of Western Front autobiographies, was published.

He established a home at Deya, a village in Majorca, with Laura Riding, and with the world accepting him as a writing giant Graves declared: "I write poems for poets, and satires or grotesques for wits. For people in general I write prose, and am content that they should be unaware that I do anything else".

The "anything else" was historical novels, plays, ordinary novels and fictional books. His historical works include *Claudius The God, Count Belisarius, Sergeant Lamb of the Ninth, King Jesus* and, of course, *I, Claudius*, for which the James Tait Black Memorial Prize and the Hawthornden Prize were awarded in 1934.

Goodbye to All That provided sufficient income for Laura and Robert to collaborate on many books and publish these using their own business, the Seizen Press. The "wild love affair" however did not last and when the Spanish Civil War uprooted them from the island home they fled firstly to London in 1936 and to France in 1938, when Laura left Robert for another man.

As Robert's sister, Rosaleen Graves (Dr Cooper), a medical practitioner at Bishopsteignton in Devon would confirm in an interview some 50 years later: "My brother's stable relationships with women have sometimes proved elusive;

Above: Vale House, Galmpton, in the early years on the 20th century.

he was a very sensitive young poet and the war shook him to his foundations, and he needed to write the horror out of himself for quite some time afterwards".

On returning to England Robert met Beryl Hodge, daughter of Sir Harry Pritchard, solicitor and parliamentary agent, and wife of the poet Alan Hodge. With the Second World War perilously near this was a productive time for Robert. The Femina-Vie-Heureuse prize for his novel *Count Belisarius* was won in 1939 and in late autumn, Beryl left her husband for him. The couple visited Devon, saw Rosaleen at Bishopsteignton and then discovered Galmpton.

Vale House in that village became their home from May, 1940 and they remained there throughout the war. Graves, strangely, invited her estranged husband to Galmpton and it seems Alan was happier being a friend to Beryl than a husband. Beryl and Robert's first child, William, was born at Paignton Hospital on July 21, 1940, three days after the poet's 45th birthday.

Then, the business partnership arrangements with Laura became complicated. Besotted with one Schulyer Jackson, Laura was desperate to resolve the Deya business partnership, which was complex; eventually conceding the property to Graves.

Despite there being no opportunity to return there, he lectured Beryl on how island life on Majorca would be idyllic.

Local friends were made in Devon, including the military historian Basil Liddell Hart and Agatha Christie, who dedicated a novel to Graves. *The Golden Fleece* and *The White Goddess* were also written at Vale House, and they are said to be two of his best poems.

The collaborations with Alan Hope, *The Long Weekend* and *The Reader Over Your Shoulder* were published, and in 1942 some 4,000 copies of *Proceed, Sergeant Lamb* were destroyed by the Blitz. Interestingly, his book *I, Claudius* was to be used as a

plotter's code book by those behind the 1944 German coup against Hitler, resulting in Count von Stauffenberg, a distant relative of Graves, eventually being shot.

Having lost his first son David to fighting in the Burma campaign, the end of the war saw Robert even more desperate to return to Spain. After eight months of negotiation regarding currency and visa arrangements the family started to plan and pack for the migration.

A new impression of *The White Goddess* was published on April 5, 1946, and sold a handsome 7,500 copies but Robert remained unmoved and chartered an aircraft. The family left on May 15 and after two forced landings, one to refuel, the other to negotiate permission to land in Spain, they eventually touched down at Palma airport and journeyed to Deya where Graves and Beryl remained for the rest of their lives.

They married in 1950 and had three more children, the last (Tomas) being born in 1953. He was sent to a co-educational school in Hampshire, which seemed odd in the light of William having a public school education in England and Lucia and Juan being educated in Switzerland.

Graves was Professor of Poetry at Oxford between 1961 and 1966 and received his second gold medal for poetry in Mexico in 1968. He had throughout life suffered difficulty in breathing, due to a botched nasal operation in 1916, and three operations during the early 1970s tried to correct this but all failed.

There was a last television interview in 1976 but nothing of note seems to have been written after 1977. Despite his earlier masses of poems and at least 43 fictional books and novels, plus ten translations, little is recorded of the last eight years at Deya. What we do know is that Robert died there on December 7, 1985.

A plaque to honour his memory was unveiled at Vale House, Galmpton on September 19th, 2003.

32

EDGAR WALLACE - Learned angler's skills at Torquay

EDGAR WALLACE WAS born in December, 1875 at 7 Ashburnham Grove, in the Greenwich area of London. He was the unwanted and illegitimate son of Marie Richards (known as Polly) and Richard Horatio Edgar Wallace.

POLLY WAS A DANCER AND PLAYER OF small parts in provincial theatres, and she abandoned her baby after just nine days.

Little Edgar was found by a Billingsgate fish-porter, who took him home to a family of 10, to be brought up as "Dick Freeman".

Wallace turned out to be an affectionate, impudent, and engaging child. As a teenager he sold newspapers on the street and eventually joined a printing firm. He then worked in a shoe shop, and finally went aboard a fishing trawler.

As an errand boy, the young Wallace was able to visit areas of London outside of his adopted Billingsgate and Old Kent Road area, thus greatly widening his knowledge and experiences.

His formal education ended at 12 but he always carried a pocket dictionary and ardently studied it.

Enlisting as a private in the Royal West Kent Regiment in the 1890s, Wallace was sent to the Medical Staff Corps South Africa. Whilst there he contributed to the *Cape Journals* with his Kipling-style poems, which would later be collected in *The Mission That Failed* and *Writ In Barracks*.

On discharge from the Army in South Africa in 1899, he joined Reuters as a journalist, becoming a second correspondent with Lord Methuen's Western Division. By a stroke of luck a female typist in Cape Town sent one of his despatches to the *Daily Mail* offices in London, and it was not long before Alfred Harmsworth, founder and owner of the *Mail*, engaged him as an overseas correspondent (Harmsworth later became Fleet Street's first press baron, Lord Northcliffe).

The typist, Ivy Caldecott, daughter of a Wesleyan missionary, was rewarded in April, 1901 when she became Mrs Edgar Wallace.

On return to London Wallace involved the *Daily Mail* in a £50,000 lawsuit against the massive Lever Brothers' soap manufacturing company, and this, together with a second legal fight pending, saw him sacked. Then came the turning point in his career - his first adventure story, *The Four Just Men,* published in 1905.

Now his new career as writer and dramatist, Wallace would during the next 20 years produce a total of 150 thrillers, 17 plays and undertake script-writing for Hollywood. In the words of his daughter-in-law and biographer, Margaret Lane, he gave his public "suspense, action and excitement, humanised by a deft touch in characterisation and an easy humour".

His principal work prior to visiting Torquay was *Angel Esquire* (1908) and the writing of an early series of stories set in a very different land, West Africa, which included *Sanders of the River* (1911) and *Bones* (1915).

On his first visit to Torquay in 1921, Wallace leased The Grove (later to become the Babbacombe Cliff Hotel) for three months, joining a select stream of visitors to this house (formerly Babbacombe Cliff) who included Dante Gabriel Rossetti, Oscar Wilde, John Ruskin, and Fred Clay and Rosina Vokes, who first took the Gilbert and Sullivan operas on tour.

He now befriended the local postman Mr Varnham, who was to learn that Kipling was Wallace's hero. Kipling apparently gave the budding author his start in the literary world, and by coincidence he had also lived in Torquay some two decades earlier, in 1896.

Knowing his postman was an experienced fisherman and in wanting to learn the angler's skills, Wallace now nurtured this friendship. The postman takes up the story: "He was a very affable, unassuming man, living a free-and-easy life, and I found that he had an amazing thirst for knowledge".

He continues: "As soon as he heard of my dual capacity he wanted to know everything, from fishing for mackerel to fishing for whales - we would yarn for hours. There can be little doubt that he intended to write a fishing story. In 1921 he said he would come to Torquay the following year and he arranged to go fishing with me."

But after returning to London to produce a play that was a failure Wallace never fulfilled his promise to Varnham. The postman concludes: "With regard to the literary value of his work, Edgar Wallace considered himself a commercialist, who gave a certain public what they were willing to pay for".

Varnham, however dispelled the long believed myth that Wallace never used the long black cigarette holder with which he was often photographed, as he witnessed the author leaning against the mantelpiece dictating to his secretary with the "mythical" holder between his teeth.

Wallace also became acquainted with another Torquay resident, Mr Greville Page. Their friendship developed, and the Page family long cherished the connection, through to the author's death.

In 1922 Wallace dedicated *The Clue Of The New Pin* to Greville Page, who said: "His great weakness was for cigarettes and weak tea. At intervals of half an hour or so, a servant would bring him a large cup of tea which was so weak that it was little more than diluted water".

Page often visited Wallace in London and recalls on one occasion witnessing the author being contacted for a special article. Page said that the fee had been mentioned as 150 guineas.

"You will have to buzz off now, old man", said Wallace to his friend.

"How long will it take?" asked Page.

"About half an hour" said Wallace casually.

Even a century later that's not a bad hourly rate...

Publication of *The Green Archer* came in 1924, followed by *A King By Night, The Ringer*, and *The Terrible People* in 1926. Then in 1929 came *The Murder Book of J G Reeder* and *People*, followed in 1931 by *Sanders of the River, Mr Commissioner Reeder*, and *On The Spot*. Thrillers and dramas poured from Wallace's pen and *On The Spot*, based on the life of American gangster Al Capone, was written in four days.

It was said that one out of every four books published in the UK at that time, leaving aside the Bible and school text books, was written by Wallace.

Certainly, by the early thirties he was earning in excess of £50,000 per annum a staggering sum for someone whose formal education ended at age 12.

Wallace's characters were seen as having little depth, and yet his main detective, J. G. Reeder, had great appeal to many. As Wallace once confirmed, it was not his aim to instruct or uplift, merely entertain and make money. Interestingly, he did both without mentioning sex, a subject he always avoided.

Wallace occasionally returned to Torquay, usually staying at the Palace Hotel at Babbacombe.

Greville Page also continued to visit him when in London on business. He visited Wallace's Haymarket office and his flat at Portland Place, where he recalls witnessing another amusing incident.

Wallace's permanent stenographer, Bob Curtis (who once held the world record for speed writing), had requested an urgent manuscript be written, for which Wallace immediately removed an item from a drawer.

Page explained that stories of different types and suitable for all sorts of publications were systematically filed, to be produced at any required moment. "Wallace would sit at his dictating machine for hours on end and tell those ingenious stories which would eventually be read by thousands".

Edgar Wallace died in Hollywood aged 57 on February 10, 1932 while still scriptwriting. Diagnosed as having died from pneumonia and diabetes mellitus, induced by a habit of working in superheated surroundings while drinking copious quantities of heavily sweetened tea.

Lavishly generous but always a jealous man, especially of his second wife nicknamed "Jim" (his former typist), Wallace left her and the children encumbered by debt.

It seems ironic that he should have died impoverished both in health and wealth after such a dazzling career.

Debts of £150,000 were fortunately able to be cleared within two years from book royalties and thereafter the family enjoyed lucrative dividends from Wallace's literary legacy.

Below: The Grove, Wallace's Torquay home, seen in later years as Babbacombe Cliff hotel.

33

FRANK MATCHAM -
Supreme in theatre design

FRANK MATCHAM, second of nine children of Elizabeth and Charles, was born at East Street, Newton Abbot on November 22, 1854.

HIS FATHER, WHO WAS MANAGER OF the Torquay Brewery in Warren Place and the Malt House in Temperance Street, Torquay, eventually moved the family to Torquay in 1864, after which Frank attended school at Babbacombe before leaving to become an office boy with a local architect.

It was Mrs Mary Bridgman, who owned many public houses in Torquay including the Maritime, the Steampacket, the Railway Inn and the Malt house, that first employed Charles Matcham.

Mary's son, George Soudon Bridgman, ran a local architect's and surveyor's office in the town so perhaps it was not surprising that 14-year-old Frank should find himself working at the Bridgman office.

Certainly this was where his interest in architecture was born. The young Bridgman, at only 23, was already leaving his mark on Paignton, having become involved with designs for the water supply, a school, many public buildings, and even the rebuilding of Teignmouth Pier.

But it was not long before Frank accepted an apprenticeship in London to a City quantity surveyor. However, then after qualifying he returned to Bridgman's as a senior architect.

George Bridgman meantime had become chairman of Paignton Urban District Council, with overall responsibility for the growth and planning requirements of the town. This was a powerful position from which to build his business and was not unusual in those days. William Kitson had earlier enjoyed much the same influence in Torquay, through his connection with Lawrence Cary.

However, Torquay and Paignton were never going to retain Frank Matcham for long. When the successful theatre designer J. T. Robinson gave him the opportunity to return to London and Mayfair he was soon off, for ever.

Robinson had already established himself as Britain's leading theatre architect and in 1892 Sir S. Ponsonby-Fane would describe him as "a very clever designer of theatres… intimately acquainted not only with the building but with the working of theatres". Robinson's influence on Frank was now substantial, and their friendship brought a personal relationship when, on July 9, 1877 Frank married his youngest daughter, Maria, at St James Church, Pentonville.

Sadly, Maria's father died at the breakfast table a year later so it was Frank who then took control of the already successful business, with its full order book. With the family's blessing he even finished Robinson's uncompleted work, which included the now famous Elephant and Castle theatre in London.

Maria gave birth to their first daughter, Eveline, in 1878 and a year later a second daughter Constance arrived; she survived only until age eight. Another personal turning point came in the 1880s when the Revill family employed Matcham as their architect for a new theatre at St Helens, in Lancashire.

Media interest in new theatres was now enormous and interviewers were said to be "on the scent" for Mr Matcham — "I'll try not to match 'em — I'll let them Revill for once".

The Revill family now introduced Matcham to Henry Irving. In 1888, while laying the foundation stone of the Theatre Royal, Bolton and using a silver trowel provided by Matcham, Irvine recognised a picture of himself playing Hamlet, cleverly carved on to the ivory handle. A new special friendship was spawned, and now Irvine officiated at most of Matcham's theatre openings.

Two years on, the Theatre Royal at Ashton-under-Lyne became the fourth of the Matcham-Revill partnership, and over the years dozens more followed, the most famous including the Palladium, the Coliseum, the Shepherd's Bush Empire, the Chiswick Empire and perhaps the crowning achievement of all, the Tower Ballroom Theatre, Blackpool, in 1889.

Matcham did not just design complete theatres he also refurbished, redecorated or reconstructed many and, his firm also acted as professional advisors to fire insurance companies. His theatre construction was, however, unique. He used a variety of designs ranging from the renaissance or baroque periods to the naval and military splendour of the Theatre Royal at Portsmouth and the oriental style used at the Elephant and Castle.

The Devon-born designer became world renowned for his specialism. The 19th century heyday of theatre building was immensely challenging and his timing opportune. Styles of materials and appliances were changing, steel was replacing wood, fire curtains and fire precautions were the norm, and backstage innovation was having to keep up with modernism.

The London offices of Frank Matcham and Co at 9 Warwick Court, Holborn sadly kept no record of his huge personal involvement in the prodigious workload. Matcham certainly had to delegate and this perhaps explains why so many latterly august architects wanted to work at his practice. There was undoubtedly high respect, and friendship, between all partners and employees.

Younger employees were even welcomed at Matcham's home. One, F. de Jong, an accepted king of fibrous plaster manufacturing, became a lifelong friend which eventually resulted in him being appointed one of Matcham's executors.

Personal friendships were a recurring theme throughout Matcham's life. Theatre promoters returned to him for friendly help on numerous occasions. When A. J. W. Broughton lost his Theatre Royal at Portsmouth through fire he commissioned Matcham to rebuild it. Later, when asked by Southsea to put that town "on the map", he would only underwrite plans for a new theatre

in the town if Matcham was architect. The King's Theatre at Southampton was the result and Broughton got every penny of his investment repaid.

Matcham had numerous hobbies. He loved travelling, favoured hill areas for holidays, and often went to the Lake District, North Wales, the Isle of Wight and his native Devonshire. He was generally alone, as Maria was a poor traveller.

Not unsurprisingly he was an ardent sketcher and painter of miniatures and travelled widely abroad, visiting Portugal, Spain, Sicily and Italy. He visited the Pyramids and saw the Sphinx and even went to America where his three brothers lived.

He adored motoring and with his chauffeur was often to be seen in his Daimler-Benz sporting the inevitable cigar. He remarked: "One should enjoy work" and he certainly followed that maxim whenever possible. He also liked to attend the opening night of any new theatre and although described as an extrovert, when asked to make a speech would merely ask the audience if they liked his new theatre.

Style seems to be the keyword in this man's life. His companionship, humour and friendship played an important part throughout. The nicknames given to him of "Matchless Matcham" or "Magnificent Matcham" followed him everywhere. It was the notorious actress Lillie Langtry who penned a prologue to him when she opened at the new Cheltenham Theatre and Opera House in 1891, in which she said:

Nay, where (within this house you'll agree),
Not all can sit but all can see,
The architect's arrangements if you'll watch'em,
Like these two rhymes tis hard to match'am…

From then on he was known as "Matchless Matcham".

By 1912, however, the boom in new theatres was in decline and Matcham's workload was falling; war was on the horizon and only a handful of commissions would be completed over the next few years. By now he had designed around 150 theatres - but cinemas were becoming the rage.

In 1919, aged just 55, he decided to retire.

Over many years he had created a special armchair ambience in the opulent seats in the most sumptuous of his theatres, such as the Northern Palace of Varieties in Leeds; he was never to know that, thanks to radio and television, a later era of armchair entertainment would be based in the home.

Matcham was blessed with good health throughout his life but this gifted man died of heart failure at his home in Southend, on May 17, 1920.

Curiously, it was not overwork or a congenital disease that brought his death, but the careless trimming of his finger nails, which led to blood poisoning.

34

WILLIAM SCORESBY – From whaling to holy orders

WILLIAM SCORESBY WAS born in 1789 and brought up at Cropton, near Pickering in Yorkshire. The area just 20 miles from Whitby saw his early years bound up in the sea, ships, ports and particularly whaling.

HIS FATHER, ALSO WILLIAM, HAD BEEN AT SEA since aged 20 and was a noted whaling captain, reputed to have designed and built the first crow's nest on a ship. He had lived through the era of Capt Cook, who by coincidence had been born less than 30 miles from Pickering.

In 1800, at the age of 10, William was showing immense interest in his father's vessel, the Dundee, (later recorded as stating "the activity excited my imagination and interested my feelings"). His father eventually allowed his son to remain aboard and make his first journey to the Arctic.

In 1803 the young William was apprenticed to his father on the Resolution and by age 16 he was appointed chief mate. Now began a lifelong series of voyages to the Arctic and around the world.

Attending Edinburgh University as a student of chemistry, natural history, philosophy and mathematics, Scoresby was to be influenced by the greats of the time: John Playfair, John Leslie, Robert Jameson, and the naturalist Sir Joseph Banks. By 1807 he had a scientific desire to fulfil, and after many voyages this would be reflected in his early meteorological journals, written in the years to 1814.

He wrote of the structure of snow crystals and polar ice, undertook talks and lectures and was in 1809 elected to the Wernian Society of Edinburgh. By age 21 and now captain of the Resolution his first voyage brought a record yield of 30 whales.

Like his father before him Scoresby was recognised as a highly successful whaler but increasingly became aware of the "need for conservation and preservation of natural resources, seeing no conflict between religion and science".

The next decade saw the culmination of his work being recognised as "the foundation stone of Arctic science", with unknown parts of Greenland being charted and published in his *Accounts of the Arctic Regions* (1820) and *Journal of a Voyage to the Northern Whale-Fishery* (1823). Later, after 17 voyages to Spitzbergen or Greenland, he was internationally recognised as the first Arctic geographer. His meteorological journals were unparalleled, with their full accounting of the "atmospherology of Arctic regions" and the physiological effect that cold had on man.

A voyage in 1823 became his last to Greenland. In 1824, after visiting Paris and being elected to the Institute of France, he changed career to be appointed the first chaplain in charge of the new floating church for seamen in Liverpool.

Now a cleric, Scoresby was nevertheless destined to remain a scientist of international repute. He continued to write and defined for the first time terminology such as iceberg, field ice, drift ice, bay ice and floes.

His drawings of what he had seen, and of the apparatus used by whalers, left behind a truly remarkable history to help us to understand those early northern voyages. His theories on ice formation, and on the types and movement of ice, later formed the basis of all theories for glacial geomorphologists. As an explorer, a scientist and a surveyor he believed he had achieved "the nearest approach to the Pole that I conceive has ever been made" and mapped this to show the full extent of formed ice in the sea of Greenland. His publication, entitled *The Edinburgh Encyclopaedia*, (1825) contains the geography of the northern region.

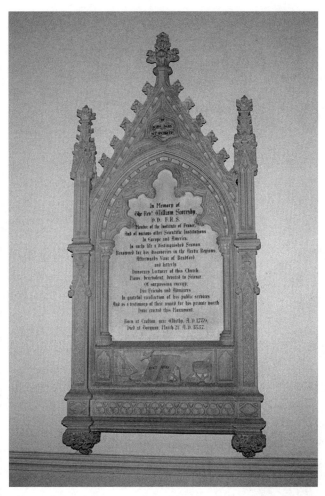

Above: The Scoresby memorial in Upton Parish Church, Torquay.

His remarkable change of career saw him ordained a minister in 1825 and, still finding time to write numerous scientific papers in the intervening years, in 1832 he was appointed chaplain in charge of the Bedford Chapel, Exeter, where he remained for seven years. The chapel was lost in a Second World War blitz in 1942, and perhaps this helps to explain why Scoresby is little remembered in Devon.

Nevertheless, while in Exeter he established a school for poor girls, to enable them to train to be domestic servants. Scoresby married three times during his life and while at Exeter lost his eldest son, who is buried there.

Bearing in mind his great interest in science, the change from whaling to take holy orders was surprising. It may have been explained by his inability to raise formal sponsorship for his Arctic exploits, but even as a priest he still found time to continue scientific work. This would eventually lead to a remarkable invention, the Scoresby Compass Needle, and a publication entitled *Magnetical Investigations*, published in 1839.

During 1839 he moved to the industrial north to become Vicar of Bradford, where he turned his attention to matters of social reform, making an outstanding contribution to public health and working conditions, and the establishment of "model" schools.

Visiting the United States in 1844 led to a further publication, *American Factories and their Female Operatives*, which greatly influenced the working conditions of employees in Bradford.

While Vicar of Bradford his continuing interest in science led him to collaborate with J. P. Joule, then engaged in electro-magnetism. Scoresby's versatility also extended to being interested in hypnotism and later in zoistic magnetism. He was by now a prolific writer with more than 100 publications to his credit, ranging from polar geography, oceanography, natural history, magnetism and, of course, religious works and social reform.

But with failing health he resigned the ministry to return to Devon, this time to Torquay where he arrived in 1846. He was eventually able to assist as a curate at the new church of St Mary Magdalene, Upton Vale, designed by the famous architect Anthony Salvin, and built between 1848-1849.

This period also saw him writing and lecturing on the riddle of the ill-fated expedition of Sir John Franklin in 1845, and publishing *Franklin Expedition* in 1850. That same year saw another book published, *My Father*, in which he recorded those earliest important achievements of both his father and himself.

Nearing the end of his life, and having considered the influence iron hulled ships might have on the standard magnetic compass needle when at sea, he wrote to the British Association in 1855 about his observations.

The evidence convinced them that his plan for a compass held aloft might be more effective to show accurately the direction of a ship's course. And so, in 1855, he set off for what was to be his last voyage, in the iron steamship Royal Charter, to prove or disprove his theory. The long sea voyage involved him in hard work ascending the mizzen rigging in an endeavour to estimate the height of the enormous waves encountered. However, on safe arrival and with every theory proved, he was awarded an Honorary MA by the University of Australia.

With his health failing and exhaustion having set in, he returned to Torquay. On this occasion, however, there was to be no recovery and he died on March 21, 1857.

By public subscription a tablet to his memory was erected at St Mary Magdalene. Similarly, in Liverpool, again by public subscription, residents presented a beautifully carved chair to his widow to honour him. The "Scoresby Chair", made from timber of the vessel Royal Charter, has his initials each side of the central carved compass that crowns the chairback. Other carvings show Dr Scoresby's crest and motto, *Thou, Lord, rulest the raging of the seas*.

His final publication, in 1859, encompassed the years of scientific study and was entitled *Journal of a Voyage to Australia and Around the World for Magnetical Research*.

Those associated with the sea, from sailors and emigrants to traders and even underwriters, undoubtedly owe much to the outstanding work and discoveries of this extraordinary Victorian who deserves his place with the greats such as Hudson, Cook and Brunel.

35

EDWARD, PRINCE OF WALES - Frequent visitor to Torbay

FIVE BRITISH MONARCHS have attained the golden jubilee of their reign, Queen Elizabeth II being the latest to achieve this in 2002, but the monarch with the longest reign of all was Queen Victoria, who served her nation for 63 years from 1837.

HER SON EDWARD, Prince of Wales, was by far the most frequent royal visitor to Torbay.

When a Mrs Whitehead retired from the royal household and came to live at The Glen, Babbicombe (note the old spelling), it was Princess Victoria (not yet Queen) who became the first to visit her, in 1833 in the yacht Emerald. The Glen, situated on the slopes beneath the cliffs of Babbacombe, would 32 years later become the infamous scene of murder, when John Lee, a 20-year-old servant, was convicted of killing his employer, Emma Keyse, by bludgeoning her with an axe.

Aged just 18, Victoria succeeded to the throne in 1837. Two years later she allowed the Torbay Regatta to add "Royal" to its name, having previously admired its trophies on her 1833 visit.

When Victoria married Prince Albert of Saxe-Coburg in 1840, they visited Babbacombe in 1846, when her diary recorded: "It is a beautiful spot, which before we had only passed at a distance. Red cliffs and rocks with wooded hills like Italy, and reminding one of a ballet or play where nymphs appear - such rocks and grottos, with the deepest sea on which there was no ripple".

They came back in 1852, on the steam yacht Victoria and Albert, with their sons Edward, Prince of Wales, and Prince Alfred. Again Mrs Whitehead was visited.

Prince Edward returned alone in 1856 to visit Teignmouth and then Babbacombe, before leaving on the six o'clock train. His brother, Prince Albert, visited on Blackeagle in 1858, and Prince Arthur on Vivid in 1862.

The Villa Syracusa (later the Hydro and then Overmead

hotels) had been built during 1858-59 and, with the Romanoff family and the Grand Duchess Marie of Russia in residence, members of the Russian royal family would often visit.

Returning to Torquay in 1864 Prince Edward brought Princess Hesse (a future Czarina) to visit the Grand Duchess at her holiday residence.

After her beloved Prince Albert's death in 1861 the Queen spent four decades mourning, and during this period Prince Edward became the undoubted head of polite society. He led the so-called modernists, those seeking to break from tradition and formality.

The Victorian period was to experience amazing changes in lifestyle, with innovations in health and education, housing and social improvements, along with hard work, bringing rich rewards.

Religious fervour and formality had little part to play in this brave new world, where the newly rich wanted more leisure and pleasure. The Prince of Wales, their champion, was loved both by the working classes and the wealthy. He was the new star, to follow, read about and emulate.

Prince Edward brought his sons, Albert Victor and George, to the Britannia Naval College at Dartmouth in 1877, and they were frequent visitors to Torquay's Imperial Hotel.

In June that year Prince Edward met Lillie Langtry for the first time. It came at a specially arranged supper party at the house of Sir Allen Young, the famous Arctic explorer. A party of 10 were spending an evening together, and they included Lillie and her husband, Ned.

Sir Allen, who apparently always left his front door open, declaring he could not otherwise breathe (memories of the Arctic, perhaps), was fidgety and there was a cold breeze blowing in.

Lillie's memoirs take up the story: "Suddenly, there was a stir, followed by an expectant hush, a hurried exit of Sir Allen, then a slight commotion outside. Presently, I heard a deep and cheery voice say: 'I am afraid I am a little late'. Sir Allen murmured something in reply and the Prince of Wales, whose face had been previously unfamiliar to me except through photographs, appeared in the doorway of Stratford Place drawing room".

With regalia and the blue ribbon of The Garter adorning his chest the Prince now came into the room. Lillie, at first nervous, was seated next to the Prince. Flattered, she soon appreciated the real purpose of the evening. Her memoirs give us a small insight to the occasion: "Though silent, I was immensely interested in watching the Prince, and soon realised that, while good-natured and pleasant to everyone, he preserved his dignity admirably. In fact I decided that he would have been a brave man who, even at this little intimate supper-party, attempted a familiarity with him".

Ponsonby, a member of the royal household who knew Edward throughout his life, tells us: "I never quite understood why he made so many people frightened of him but there can be no doubt that even his most intimate friends were all terrified of him. "He was by far the biggest man and the most striking personality in Europe... and had a indefinable quality making all his staff devoted. He never posed and never pretended to be any better than he was. The upper and lower classes loved him, although the idle classes were often shocked at his actions".

Now his open, public relationship with Lillie Langtry and others came as a breath of fresh air that blew for three decades.

Vanity Fair, on May 19, 1877 reported: "All male London is going wild about the Beautiful Lady who has come to us from the Channel Islands. She is certainly the most splendid creature that has ever risen upon London from an unknown horizon, and so far beyond the pretty with which we are usually more than content, that it is as though some newer and more perfect creature had risen, like Aphrodite, from the sea. She has a husband to make her happy, but still awaits a poet to make her known." That man who became her teacher was Oscar Wilde.

Around 1878 Prince Edward was regularly on his yacht Hildergarde, and a frequent visitor to Torquay. In 1879 he arrived at Oddicombe beach from where he was rowed to Babbacombe to take tea at the Cary Arms. In 1886 he came to visit the Duchess of Sutherland, and worshipped at All Saints in Babbacombe.

That year, the Princess of Wales and three daughters came to visit the Abbey Road Theatre. The royal box was draped with the royal coat of arms in velvet and blue silk ribbons. It later became the Theatre Royal, but within a year was closed, when its optimistic owner went bankrupt. Today, we know the building as the Odeon cinema.

To commemorate the 60th year of Her Majesty's reign, in 1897, Richard Mallock gifted land in Chelston for the "Victoria" playground/park to be laid and in Torquay emblematic gas illuminations were installed to celebrate the jubilee.

The Prince of Wales visited Torbay on no fewer than 10 occasions before becoming King Edward VII on his mother's death in 1901. His Coronation, officially announced for June 26, 1902 was cancelled when he contracted a serious illness. He fortunately survived and was crowned on August 9.

In Torquay the electric light and gas companies provided illuminations, and at Chelston a memorial states: "This pulpit was placed in the Church of St Matthew by the parishioners of Cockington for remembrance that King Edward VII, being near to death, was spared in answer to a Nation's prayers".

As King, Edward never again visited Torbay. His sudden death was announced on May 6, 1910 and as a permanent memorial to his memory The King's Drive and gardens survive to this day adjacent to Torquay seafront.

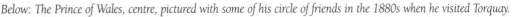

Below: The Prince of Wales, centre, pictured with some of his circle of friends in the 1880s when he visited Torquay.

36

HENRY FORBES JULIAN - Lost on the 'Titanic'

THE JULIAN FAMILY CAN BE TRACED back to the Huguenots of France, and a distinguished line of descendants include an island governor, a canon, a bishop and a judge before Henry and Dorinda Julian of the 19th century.

HENRY FORBES JULIAN WAS THEIR SECOND son among 10 children. He was born on the May 9, 1861, educated at Cork and then from 1870 at Bolton in Lancashire, where the family had settled.

Henry's early childhood gave no indication of the international career that was to follow. It was in his late teens that he started to take an interest in matters of science and would often be in his father's professional workshop.

Choosing to be a self-employed engineer he was fortunate in securing employment in Africa at the age of 25, assisting in mineshaft work, crushing mills and industrial reduction plant.

Henry arrived at Barberton in Africa in 1886 and by luck it was there that gold ore was accidentally discovered in 1887. Within months Barberton's small population had swollen to an estimated 10,000 prospectors. This saw an already inadequate sewage, sanitory and water system making malaria and other diseases rife in the area.

Henry meanwhile had established that a solution of cyanogen (cyanide) could assist with the extraction of gold and silver from its ore, and by 1888 his process was achieving a yield previously thought impossible.

A publication by Forbes and Edgar Smart followed that year, explaining the process. In Britain a similar conclusion was reached and patented by two scientists in Scotland. With the work proven, it became of immense value to future mining operations.

Late 1889 saw Henry experimenting with chlorine, cyanide, an electrical current and sodium amalgam, to evolve a system that ensued an extraction rate of 99 percent in some instances. This time Henry sensibly patented his discovery.

His pioneering work as a metallurgist took him to areas of South and Central Africa and places as far afield as Johannesburg, Kimberley and the Upper Zambesi. Here, having walked 300 miles with natives acting as baggage carriers he was one of the first white men to see the Zambesi falls.

With more research done, Henry announced in 1892 that by using blown air on organic or inorganic oxidisers dissolution was further assisted. Before returning to Britain he lodged a second patent in the Transvaal.

After relaxing happy in the company of his brothers and sisters at home in Lancashire he soon itched to return to foreign parts. Having been appointed technical adviser of mining and metallurgical researches to the Deutsche Gold and Silver Scheide Anstalt of Frankfort in 1893, he now formulated far-reaching improvements in the recovery of precious metals from ores, and was joint author of *Cyaniding Gold and Silver Ores*. His travels during the next years saw him crossing the Atlantic no fewer than 13 times, visiting Canada, the United States, Mexico and the West Indies.

His third patent was established in the Transvaal in 1894, this time concerning cathodes. Widely recognised as an expert in his field Henry was now applauded by chemists, metallurgists and physicists in Germany, Austria, Africa, Eastern Europe and across the Atlantic. But having spent most of his working life away from home and now tired, he returned home in 1895 for Christmas with the family.

Delighted to see him they were, however, concerned at his obvious ill-health. Although wishing to return to Africa, Henry this time took his London doctor's advice and at last resigned from professional work, to look for a quiet place on the coast where he could at least partially retire.

The Isle of Wight, North Wales and many other areas were visited, before he finally settled on South Devon and Shaldon, purchasing the marine residence of the late Lord Clifford. The small country house overlooking the beach was called simply The Ness, named after the nearby headland.

With his father and various sisters around him his health now slowly recovered. Henry, already knowledgeable about horses, dogs and shooting, now added, of all things, motor traffic to his interests. This saw him becoming a founder member of the Royal Automobile Club.

He was also a member of the Royal Horticultural Society and the Institution of Mining and Metallurgy, and yet still found time to create a research laboratory at The Ness.

With the protracted struggle of the Boer War, the turn of the century was an unhappy time for Britain. But for Henry 1901 was a good year; he met Hester Pengelly, daughter of Torquay's famous archaeologist, William Pengelly. Hester, a member of the Geologists' Association, the Royal Anthropological Institute and the Dante Society, like Henry also enjoyed travel.

Both had suffered the loss of their parents and at the age of 42 Henry announced his betrothal to Hester in the spring of 1902. They married at the church of St Mary Magdalene, Upton, in October that year.

Henry now joined the two institutions that his late father-in-law had helped to establish, the Devonshire Association and the Torquay Natural History Society, and became an active volunteer and committee member.

As a member of the British Association for the Advancement of Science, he accumulated friends and alliances across the scientific community world-wide.

Having spent six years at The Ness, Henry moved to Torquay where he and his wife spent the next 10 years at their villa, Redholme.

During these years he was much involved with committees, and in 1905 took Hester on an official British Association trip to South Africa via Tenerife, Santa Cruz, and Las Palmas, reaching Capetown in early August.

They were entertained at functions and visited many of Henry's previous haunts, before the SS Durban Castle took them to Durban. Then it was onwards by train to Pietermaritzburg, the capital of Natal, where he delivered a formal address to the Transvaal Technical Institute entitled "How Oxygen Assists and Retards the Dissolution of Gold in Cyanide Solutions".

After visiting Pretoria, Vereeniging, the Orange Free State, Kimberley, the Zambesi and Capetown, the Forbes Julians came home.

The years between 1905 and 1911 saw the couple entertaining in Torquay and in London. Social and official meetings, and scientific papers, were now par for the course. One cable from America in 1907 resulted in them visiting New York to hear about a "patent vacuum filter" before touring America.

Once back home, Henry was off again in 1908 to visit Mexico, the Californian goldfields and New York. These years brought numerous voyages as far afield as Quebec, Vancouver, Virginia and Bermuda, until what proved to be his last return in 1911.

The maiden voyage of the Titanic, from Southampton, was scheduled to start on April 10, 1912, but with a coal strike affecting the railway, Hester suggested Henry put back embarkation until the 11th to catch the alternative ship, the Celtic, also of the White Star line.

In the event he left Torquay by train on the 9th and after four changes arrived at Southampton and the Titanic on time.

The rest is history. The "unsinkable" liner hit an iceberg and sank in mid-ocean; Henry, reputedly refusing to leave the doomed Titanic while there were still women and children on board, left it too late to board the overcrowded lifeboats and was lost presumed drowned, on April 15, 1912.

Henry had possessed what was described as "a quiet magnetism" by an African friend, a Mr Rinoul of Turffontein.

Being lost at sea, a memorial at St Mary Magdalene remains his only testament. Provided by his many friends and designed and built by Messrs Blacklers of St Marychurch, it was unveiled at the Upton church on February 24, 1914 when Hester was presented with a scroll of the names of subscribers.

She knew that her husband, a man whose intellectual attainments and practical skills had made him a leading metallurgical engineer across three continents, would have been quietly pleased.

Hester's widowhood was to last over 20 years, until her death on February 11, 1934.

Above: Hester Forbes Julian
Below: The Ness at Shaldon, the home of Henry Forbes Julian until he moved to Torquay.

37

WALTER CRANE - Illustrator for Arts and Crafts

WALTER CRANE WAS born on August 15, 1845, the third child of Marie and Thomas Crane.

THE FAMILY WERE LIVING IN THE Mount Pleasant area of Liverpool but three months after Walter's birth, his father's ill health through consumption forced a move to a more temperate climate.

Settling for Torquay, the Crane family family first lived at Laureston Villa, Upton. Already a renowned portrait painter, Thomas had won a gold medal from the Royal Academy in 1824 for his drawing skills and was becoming interested in architectural work and lithography.

There was plenty of work available thanks to the Victorian taste for decorative art and the Crane family were comfortably off. By employing a governess they were able to travel widely, and visited the Great Exhibition of London in 1851.

The expanding family - Walter now had two brothers and two sisters - had by 1854 moved to live at 3 Park Place, St Marychurch.

Devon's idyllic summers led to Thomas's health being much improved but he was unable to find commissions in Devon for the portrait work he desired, and so returned to the North. Fortunately, he had still found time to get a sketching club firmly established in Torquay.

Walter was rarely seen without a pencil even from infancy, and his earliest years saw him sketching and colouring his father's work. He was also attracted to 16th century woodcut pictures in art journals, and was especially fascinated by adventure tales, drawing a battle of the Turks and the Russians in the Crimea on a piece of slate.

Encouraged by his father to sketch, he attended the Page School on Teignmouth Road for a while but because of the harshness of the headmaster (he caned too much) he was soon taken away. His first illustrations of Sir Walter Scott's tales and ballads now emerged, and were given by him to friends. Calculations and mental arithmetic were anathema to the young "Crane minor" (his title at school, presumably

his older brother Thomas being Crane major) and led to a diagnosis by a local doctor that Walter suffered from "congestion of the brain".

He left school for good and with the family moving to London in 1857 he was schooled by his father, and before long was doing his first "oil". At the same time, using pen and ink, he drew illustrations, usually of animals, a passion he never lost. Able to "illuminate" colour borders on important printed work, he also produced sensitive studies of nature, such as barley, corn and poppies, which were then reproduced in calendars and books.

His work so impressed William James Linton, a leading wood engraver, that in 1858 he offered the young 13-year-old an apprenticeship, waiving the usual premium. Wood engraving now greatly expanded Walter's numerous natural talents.

Good wood engraving was always a precursor to good quality printing, and for three years Walter enjoyed learning the art. It was not unsympathetic to his drawing skills when using a 4H pencil.

Meanwhile, Linton was employing a "tint and facsimile person" to do mechanical work which often meant cutting and reducing the standard four-inch wooden blocks to speed the process. But with new techniques and his natural skill Walter discovered he could draw and engrave directly on to the wooden printing blocks.

By the mid-1860s he was accepted as a fine illustrator, and with a little help from Linton obtained his first major commission — the drawings for The New Forest: Its History and Its Scenery, by John R. de Capel Wise.

This work earned him £100, and although pleased with its reception he was peeved to find one reviewer stating that "these exquisitely characteristic bits of foliage and forest life are the productions of a youth of seventeen". Thankfully the reviewer prophesied he nevertheless had "a bright future".

Crane's first submission to the Royal Academy in 1862 was The Lady of Shalott. The Times art critic, Tom Taylor, reported this as "the work of a young and rising artist".

Above: An example of Crane's work, its accompanying artwork, word setting and text.

The next decade saw his reputation growing, particularly as an illustrator of children's books — the sixpenny "yellow backs" published by Evans & Routledge and printed on a yellow enamelled paper. With colour printing in vogue, he produced *The Moors and the Fens* in red and blue with a black key on an off-white paper in 1863. Evans remarked: "Walter Crane was a genius — the only subjects I found he could not draw were figure subjects of everyday life". Crane indeed preferred more imaginative subjects, like the figurative animal drawings he loved to draw for children.

Illustrative work streamed from him. *Chattering Jack, Multiplication Table, Buckle My Shoe, Annie and Jack, Scenes From a Winter's Tale, Sing a Song For Sixpence, The Waddling Frog, The House That Jack Built, The Old Courtier, The Merrie Heart* and many others, all got the Crane treatment.

His work being on sale in a shop owned by a friend in Wigmore Street, led to meetings with Burne-Jones, William Morris, Poynter and other famous contemporaries of the art world.

In 1871 he met and married Mary Frances Andrews, and in time they produced three children — Beatrice, Lionel and Lancelot.

By 1873 Routledges had commissioned a second series of the sixpenny toy books from him and, a year later, a shilling series was ordered which included *Noah's Ark, Mother Hubbard, The Three Bears, Cinderella* and *Puss in Boots*.

These examples of work with nursery rhymes showed his genius when drawing illustrative pictures and their accompanying artwork, word setting and relevant text on all pages and covers. His frontispieces were likened to a facade, leading the reader into a world of fascinating design.

More serious painting was now undertaken and when working on general landscape and cloud study he was meticulous with colour and the time of day being sketched. He did his initial drawings in either pencil or colour wash but with his landscapes finished on site, only the animals, figures and general scene had to be added later. This method was seen by some to lose the "passionate intensity" achieved by the great Ruskin, but that was his preference.

Crane was a member of the RA from 1882 to 1886, and his output of paintings was now enormous, examples being *The Three Paths, Fire, Love Sanctuary, Vietri, Freedom* and *The Triumph of Spring.*

Then, as if drawing, illustration and painting with oil was not sufficient, Crane started organising art exhibitions, lectures and even seminars.

With ever increasing public interest in the Arts and Crafts movement, he assisted the revival of decorative designers at an exhibition in 1888 and joined The Fifteen group, becoming its third Master (chairman) between 1888-1889. He established an Arts and Crafts Exhibition Society becoming its founding president in 1893 and holding that office (with a three year break) until 1912 overseeing the final exhibition prior to World War One. During 1898/99 he was Principal of the R.C.A.

With design and *art nouveau* affecting every sort of material, illustration and design work was abundant. Textiles, tapestries, friezes, wallpaper, pottery, ceramics and tiles, plasterwork, glassware, mosaics, crockery, panels for buildings and even ships' interior decor — all could be enhanced by skilled illustrators and designers.

Crane travelled widely across the continents, and his contemporaries around the world applauded his skills and his seemingly limitless output.

He now began to reflect his political views in cartoons, and designed banners and posters in the socialism cause. He made artistic official trade union seals and many were reproduced by sympathisers abroad.

Accolades were frequent and a visit to Hungary in 1900 was "triumphant". An award was made at the Turin Exhibition in 1902, and in Italy a royal blessing came when he was appointed "Commendatore Crane" and Mary the "Mistress Crane", although she much preferred "Dame Crane".

Mary died in 1915 and after her passing Crane felt "stricken and only half alive" and survived her for little more than two months.

He died on March 14, 1915, at the Horsham Cottage hospital.

38

CHARLES DARWIN -
The dawn of evolution

ERASMUS DARWIN, grandfather to Charles, was a scientist with revolutionary ideas. His son Robert, a doctor, and his wife Susannah, daughter of the famous Josiah Wedgwood of pottery fame, knew their son Charles was destined to be famous.

ERASMUS HAD WRITTEN A BOOK on evolution entitled *Zoonomia* in the 18th century. His ideas on future air and sea travel, and exploration of the sea by submarine, were visionary. Yet his grandson Charles later wrote: "I believe I was considered by all my masters and by my father as a very ordinary boy, rather below common intelligence."

Born on February 12, 1809 he was one of five children. His mother died when he was just eight and he then attended Shrewsbury School and in 1825, Edinburgh Medical School. He was always more interested in rocks, animals and plants than medicine, yet his father reluctantly agreed to pay for him to go to Cambridge to study and become a priest.

Charles retained his independence, gained a Bachelor of Arts degree in 1831 and, not wanting to join the priesthood immediately, started organising a natural history expedition to the Canaries.

Events overtook him, however, when an exciting offer came from the Royal Navy, suggesting he join them as a researcher on HMS Beagle, which was about to sail on a round-the-world trip. With the intervention of Uncle Josiah Wedgwood, Dr Darwin was persuaded to fund his son's passage on Beagle, which sailed on December 27, 1831.

The ship first went to San Salvador in Brazil, then around Cape Horn to the Galapagos Islands, across the Pacific Ocean to New Zealand and Australia, across the Indian Ocean to the Cape of Good Hope, and finally across the Atlantic to Brazil, before returning to England. The expedition gave Charles five years in which to amass an immense collection of plant, rock, fossil and animal specimens.

During the trip he also started to question why various species of animals had died out when there was an abundance of fauna and warm, moist rainforests, normally a paradise for living matter. Why had the giant sloth become extinct when the ordinary one had survived, surely, there must be a link between fossils found and creatures still living.

On the Galapagos Darwin had been struck by the strange nature of all living things. Seemingly unique, each island had its own particular species. Thirteen species of finch were found here but nowhere else in the world. Island inhabitants could even tell the island from which each tortoise came and yet plants and flowers seemingly unique had similarities with those on other islands.

Back in Falmouth by October, 1836 Darwin then spent five years cataloguing his multitude of specimens. He was helped initially by a friend, Sir Richard Owen, who became a strong opponent of Darwin's theories in later years.

Darwin became even closer to the family of his mother when he married his cousin, Emma Wedgwood, in 1838. She was to bear him 10 children and they remained resident at Down House, Bromley, Kent, throughout their life together.

His writing flourished, and books included *Journal of Researches into the Natural History and Geology of the Countries Visited during the Voyage round the World of HMS Beagle* and *The Structure and Distribution of Coral Reefs*. During 1844 came *Geological Observations on Volcanic Islands*, and in 1846 *Geological Observations of South America*.

For eight years Darwin also studied small seashore animals he named barnacles but the 1850s saw him in poor health and although his illness remains a mystery, it may have been the tropical disease chagas, caught during the world voyage.

His most famous work *The Origin of Species*, may never have been completed at all had it not been for a letter he received from Alfred Wallace in 1858.

Wallace, an experienced naturalist even at the age of 24, had published a theory of evolution entitled *On the Tendency of Varieties to Depart Indefinitely from the Original Type*. This work described succinctly what Darwin had desperately been trying to make others understand for 20 years.

Like Darwin, Wallace had been impressed by the theories of Thomas Malthus, a clergyman, mathematician and economist, who in 1798 had written *An Essay on the Principle of Population*, stating that should the human race go on expanding, it would run out of food and living space. Malthus had discovered that the fittest always survived (crucial to later research) and identified three evils of his time - war, famine and disease.

While recovering from fever at a camp in South East Asia, Wallace had a brainwave - could evolution come by natural selection? He wrote: "On the whole, the best fitted live. From the effects of disease the most healthy escape; from enemies the strongest, the swiftest or the most cunning escape; and from famine the best hunters or those with the best digestion... and so on."

By July, 1858 friends and fellow scientists Lyell and Hooker were imploring Darwin to allow them to present his findings and work to the Linnean Society in London that very month. Once agreed, they then insisted that Darwin must finalise his theories, as he had much greater evidence than Wallace. This resulted in *The Origin of Species* being published on November 24, 1859. It's full title was *On the Origin of Species by Means of Natural Selection or the Preservaion of Favoured Races in the Struggle for Life.*

For a short time in 1861 the Darwin family came to Torquay where Darwin convalesced at No 2 Meadfoot House, Hesketh Crescent. The four-storey houses were leased for a minimum of three months and were ideal for large families. His neighbour at No 1 was Angela Burdett Coutts (later Baroness Coutts). Being in poor health he worked only for a few hours each day, preferring to walk and carriage ride later he was proved to still be writing.

It took another 143 years before modern day scientists discovered Darwin's starting point. Scientific efforts to understand the relationship between bio-diversity and how

Below: Visiting students admire the Charles Darwin bust in Torquay Museum.

Below: Hesketh Crescent in the late 19th century - Darwin lived at No 2, next to the end nearest the camera.

eco-systems function had apparently been a priority subject for modern day ecologists. They likened the loss of any species as important as "the loss of rivets from an aeroplane".

The January, 2002 edition of *The Scientist* confirmed the long sought-after answer to the mystery of Darwin's starting point. Dr Andy Hector, of Imperial College, London, and Dr Rowan Hooper, of the National Institute for Environmental Studies, Japan, in becoming modern day "eco-detectives" found the key clue in an incomplete but referenced manuscript for a book by Darwin, *Natural Selection*.

The clue led them to the British Library where they discovered a 19th century book by a George Sinclair, head gardener to the Duke of Bedford. Encompassing perfect dried plant specimens, Sinclair had proved that transplanted turf produced more diverse plant life, which was more productive than lesser communities of species. Darwin had seen the link and had set off on a lifelong quest to prove the point. Our latter day detectives believe Sinclair that was the true "godfather of ecology".

But Darwin's struggle against his opponents took a long time. As late as April, 1871 many scientists and cartoonists were ridiculing his theories. They linked his ideas to men being descended from apes as heresy, they being mainly advocates for God and holy intervention.

Eventually, Darwin's book *Descent of Man and Selection in Relation to Sex*, published in 1871, brought convincing evidence that humans are not the result of intervention but, like other species, merely evolve. He was at last applauded and six years later was awarded a special Cambridge degree.

He continued his researches and concentrated on mould and earthworms (nature's first gardeners), and insect eating (meat eating) plants. Having suffered a mild heart attack in December, 1881 Darwin died peacefully at Down House on April 19, 1882 aged 73.

This controversial theorist had become one of the world's most important men of history, and is interred at Westminster Abbey next to another such giant, Isaac Newton.

Torbay Civic Society unveiled the Blue Plaque (above) at No. 2 Meadfoot House, Hesketh Crescent in September, 2004.

39

HRH QUEEN VICTORIA -
Visitor to Babbacombe Bay

BORN AT KENSINGTON PALACE on May 24, 1819, the only child of Edward, Duke of Kent (fourth son of George III), the Princess Victoria was destined to become Queen and reign for 63 years, the longest in British history.

Wᴴᴇɴ ᴛʜᴇ ʏᴏᴜɴɢ Pʀɪɴᴄᴇss sᴜᴄᴄᴇᴇᴅᴇᴅ her uncle, William IV, in 1837 the monarchy was in a pretty poor state. Her great-grandfather, George II, had ruled for 33 years, during which time his victory at Dettingen in 1743 would be the last battle ever commanded by a British monarch.

When his son, George III, succeeded in 1760, he supported his political ministers in their hard line towards the American colonies but he sadly suffered from repeated attacks of insanity, which became permanent in 1811.

His son, the Prince Regent, succeeded to the throne as George IV in 1820. He reacted against his strict upbringing by leading a life of debauchery and in 1785 married a Catholic widow, Mrs Fitzherbert. He eventually divorced her and then, in return for the clearance of debt, married Princess Caroline of Brunswick in 1795.

He was succeeded in 1830 by William IV, who created new peers to combat a hostile majority in the House of Lords, becoming known as "Silly Billy" for his rambling speeches, a nickname hardly conducive to a monarchy seeking respect.

By his death in 1837 he had sired nine illegitimate children, and it was to be his niece, the Princess Victoria, who succeeded to the throne.

Victoria, who had lost her father at the age of eight, became sovereign at 18 and had the indignity of seeing an over-protective mother, the Duchess of Kent, sleeping in her room each night prior to her Coronation, the arrangements for which also left much to be desired.

It was almost beyond belief, for instance, that the Archbishop of Canterbury would put the Coronation ring on her wrong finger, and that Lord Rolle,

an overweight and elderly peer, in seeking to pay homage to his Queen, repeatedly failed to negotiate the steps leading to the throne. Tiring of the spectacle, the young Victoria left her throne to go down to him.

Even after the ceremony more unplanned mishaps occurred. On removing to the side chapel the dignitaries, while being lined up before proceeding out of Westminster Abbey, found the room they were in littered with uneaten sandwiches and left over wine bottles.

With the Coronation over and back in Buckingham Palace, Queen Victoria now made sure her mother's suite of rooms were at the other end of the Palace.

Having always been sheltered from the squalor and austerity of her people Victoria knew little of the workhouses where the nation's able-bodied unemployed were housed.

Each workhouse had separate dormitories for males and females, and separate exercise yards, so although there was a little leisure there was also little pleasure. These feared places saw the paupers who entered them having to be searched, bathed and then given a uniform. Sadly, the workhouses would survive throughout Her Majesty's reign.

The young Victoria had first visited Torbay in 1833 as Princess, when the yacht Emerald landed the Duchess of Kent and her daughter on Torquay's harbour steps. The opportunity was used to visit a Mrs Whitehead, who having recently retired from the royal household had made her home at Glen Cottage, on the wooded hillside at Babbacombe Beach.

The young Princess had admired the Torquay Regatta trophies she presented during her visit and in 1839, as Queen, she graciously remembered the occasion and allowed the regatta to be renamed the Torquay Royal Regatta from that date. The royal visitors stayed for one night at the Poulton Hotel (later the Royal Poulton and then the Royal) on the Strand and the occasion resulted in Victoria Parade being named after her.

An unfortunate incident occurred during the visit. A local boot-maker named Dart, in trying to break through the secure cordon protecting the Royal party to present the Princess with a pair of

Above: The royal yacht Victoria and Albert, the right of the three vessels, off Babbacombe beach in 1846.

specially made boots, was accidentally stabbed and blinded by a coastguard's bayonet. The Duchess immediately despatched him to the hospital, all expenses defrayed, and later would grant him a lifelong annuity.

It was on February 10, 1840 that Queen Victoria married Albert of Saxe-Coburg and Gotha. A serious man with high principles, Albert was allowed to take on increasing state responsibilities and in 1857 was titled Prince Consort.

Prince Albert undoubtedly helped restore the monarchy to its rightful place in Britain and thus diminished the threat of republicanism. The Queen and "her beloved Albert" travelled widely and even acquired a new home at Balmoral, in Scotland, which was rebuilt under Albert's direction. They also purchased Osborne on the Isle of Wight, another Royal home.

In 1846 the Queen returned to Torbay by yacht, to lay off Babbacombe, and although she and Albert stayed an hour, they did not land. Her diary records: "It is a beautiful spot which before we had only passed at a distance. Red cliffs and rocks with wooded hills like Italy and reminding one of a ballet or play where nymphs appear - such rocks and grottos, with the deepest sea on which there was no ripple."

On a visit to St Michael's Mount in Cornwall in 1846, Her Majesty allowed her foot imprint to be left on the landing steps, which apparently can still be seen. Then in 1852 the Queen and Prince Albert returned to Babbacombe Bay, this time on the steam yacht Victoria and Albert. On this occasion, although they remained on board, Prince Edward and Prince Alfred came ashore to visit Mrs Whitehead.

Finally, in 1856 the Queen's ship was escorted into Torbay by a flotilla of nine vessels before moving on to Dartmouth, where she joined the steamer Derwent to go up river and land at Totnes. The Prince of Wales used this opportunity to revisit Torquay, Babbacombe and Teignmouth, on his own.

When Albert died of typhoid in 1861 Victoria took back sole control of the nation's affairs and refused to give her eldest son Edward, Prince of Wales, any major role in state matters, in spite of him taking a keen interest in public affairs. Nevertheless, he eventually become the people's champion for social change.

The Queen never returned to Devon and in fact remained in mourning until her death. With her husband's passing Victoria had said: "The world is gone for me" - and yet she was to reign for 40 more years.

Throughout that time she continually wore black and for many years refused to attend any state occasions, preferring to reside either at Balmoral or at Osborne rather than Buckingham Palace. She agreed to attend Prince Albert's (Bertie's) wedding to his bride, Princess Alexandria of Denmark, in 1863 but even then she was unable to face the reception and ate alone.

In 1875 Victoria at last conferred royal status on the Torbay Yacht Club.

In 1876, Prime Minister Disraeli successfully passed a Bill to make Victoria "Empress of India" and from then on Victoria RI - R for Regina (Queen) and I for Imperatrice (Empress) - was used on all her kingdom's red pillar boxes.

Hearing of an attempt on the Queen's life in 1882, the Torquay Local Board, like many others sent a letter expressing their abhorrence of the dreadful act.

At national celebrations to mark the golden jubilee of her reign, in 1887, the Queen still insisted on wearing her bonnet, having ordained that after the death of Albert she would never again wear her Crown or royal robes, and never did. Locally, the Royal Salute was given at 8am and thanksgiving services were held in all Torquay churches. By public subscription the Vivian Institute was eventually extended in celebration of her jubilee year.

Another decade brought her diamond jubilee in 1897, and now Victoria Playground in Chelston and Cary Park in Babbacombe became memorials to the occasion.

Her Majesty died at Osborne House on January 22, 1901 and her body was returned to London to be buried at Westminster Abbey. Having had nine children, she left behind 40 grandchildren and 29 great-grandchildren.

Torquay's final telegram of the Victorian era, sent to the new King, Edward VII, at Buckingham Palace, read: "The inhabitants of Torquay, deeply mourning the loss of their beloved Queen, send their tribute of sorrow and most heartfelt and respectful sympathy with your Majesty and the Royal mourners".

ROBERT SHEDDEN CARY - Family life at Torre Abbey

BORN ON JUNE 22, 1828 Robert Shedden Sulyarde Cary was the eldest son of Henry George Cary and Emily Munro, the only daughter of Robert Shedden of Brooklands, Hampshire. His parents had married on July 12, 1827; his father died before the age of 40.

THE CARY ANCESTRY CAN BE TRACED back to "Otho", a powerful English baron of Anglo-Saxon times, when Edward the Confessor ruled. The Torre Abbey branch of the family descend from Sir Edward Cary of Stantor and Cockington, a favourite nephew and Secretary to the Lord Deputy. Sir Edward died in 1654 and was succeeded by George Cary, of New Parke, Hampshire.

He purchased the Abbey from a John Stowell in December, 1662 and this Catholic arm of the family then retained the property for almost 270 years until the cost of upkeep and death duties finally took their toll in 1930.

In 1662, although a century had passed since the reign of Henry VIII and the dissolution of the monasteries, there was still great religious intolerance. For devout Catholics the times were far from easy and during the next two centuries it was still deemed heresy to be discovered attending Mass.

By the time of Henry George Cary's death in 1840, however, sweeping political changes had brought much easier times and the Abbey was extended and converted into a fine residence befitting one of the leading families of Torquay.

The idea of a promenade road in front of his house was strongly resisted by Henry, who preferred to see any new road built behind the Abbey. But he eventually lost the argument, and the local authority gave permission for the building of todays coastal road across his estate in 1840 - by coincidence the year he died.

With the death of his father, Robert, the eldest son, inherited at the age of 12 although until he reached his majority in 1849, the administration of his estate was left in the hands of his mother and her brother as trustees. They would always be in a difficult position until Robert became of age and few major changes were undertaken at that time.

On the eve of his "coming of age" Robert returned to Torre Abbey to take up his responsibility for the Manors of Torre Abbey and St Marychurch. His estate was now so impoverished he was unable to live at the Abbey, but returned there to join hundreds of guests to celebrate his birthday.

The fun and festivities lasted two days, and included a wooden ship on wheels being drawn through the town to the Abbey gardens, where all forms of amusements took place including sports in the grounds and meadows, donkey races, jumping for buns, individuals grinning through horses' collars, and women running for gown pieces. The game was the last occasion on which this sport was ever publicly played at Torquay.

In order that guests could be comfortably fed on "a baron of beef" on the

Above: Torre Abbey mansion - venue for Robert's coming-of-age party.

lawn, a 200ft tent was erected, and the Abbey house thrown open for use by all.

It was probably the arrival of the Brunel railway at Torre on December 18, 1848 that brought the start of major developments at Torquay, the Abbey and the Cary estate.

Certainly by 1860 Waldon Hill, Abbey Road and Belgrave Road were displaying a great number of properties, and around the edge of the Cary estate trees were planted in profusion to screen off the house. The estate was far more extensive than we see today, as the Manor of Torre encompassed all of the Belgravia area from Mill Lane across to Belgrave Road and Elm Avenue, with the front grounds reaching down to the seashore.

At first Cary showed some interest in local affairs, and as owner of the Manor he was elected a member of the powerful Local Board in 1850. But having served for less than two years he resigned, and took no further active interest in public work.

However, he understood the significance of the new railway and its potential for change. With the main station situated on the periphery of his estate and in wanting to assist rather than hold back development of the town he started to offer land on lease from 1851.

One site ensured the building of the old Torquay Town Hall in Lower Union Street, for a nominal rent of four shillings per annum on a 99-year lease. In 1854 another site was provided for the Church of the Assumption in Abbey Road, with added financial support to provide a handsome stained glass chancel window. He was always charitable towards the Roman Catholic

Church and a window carrying an inscription to his memory can still be viewed.

He gave or leased large tranches of land for sites to build at Abbey Crescent, completed in 1858, and the terraces and gardens at the foot of Shedden Hill, Falkland Road and Lucius Street. Sites for the Torquay Museum and even Cary Green, which was later named in his honour, were also given.

The development of Babbacombe and St Marychurch was speeded by gifts of land at Cary Park at the rear of Manor Road, and by the provision of money for the building of the breakwater at Babbacombe beach.

Cary married Margaret Mary Stockman at the Catholic Church, Spanish Place, in London on December 15, 1866.

By 1874 the turnpike trustees controlling the gates of Union Street and at Rock Walk (previously Fisherman's Walk) toll house finally stopped the collection of cash tolls. The toll house became Dyer's Cottage, a gardener's home and later a public toilet. The Land Registry of that time confirms the Carys still owned 430 acres in Torquay, providing them with a rental income of £51,555pa.

Cary was elected president of the Torquay Amateur Boating Club in April, 1876 and with no children of his own, he seems also to have worked with the Sisters of St Vincent's Boy's Home.

After a long and painful illness, he died of cancer of the tongue at his home on September 2, 1898.

A white marble memorial to his memory, set on a black marble base, can still be viewed on the North Wall of the Torre Abbey Chapel. Its inscription reads:

Pray for the soul of Robert Shedden Sulyarde Cary, of Torre Abbey, who died 2nd September 1898, in his 71st year. This memorial is erected to his memory by his loving wife Margaret Mary.

His mother Emily outlived her husband by an amazing 52 years died at Strathmore, Belgrave Terrace, on January 10, 1892 and was buried alongside Henry in the family vault at St Marychurch, Torquay.

The family sold the park grounds and the Abbey to the Torquay Borough for £40,000 in 1930 when it became a home for the local authority's collection of art treasures. A refurbishment was authorised in 1970 and it took another 25 years before that work was complete, when with its new galleries the building returned to its former glory. One of its 25 new display rooms was a memorial to Dame Agatha Christie, established by Torbay Civic Society at which time family items were given by her daughter, Mrs Rosalind Hicks.

Lucius Falkland Brancaleone Cary was succeeded by Robert, whose two older brothers, Henry Fraser Lovat Cary and Lionel Stuart Traquair Munro Cary had died.

Henry had died aged four and Lionel, serving as a lieutenant in the Crimea, had died of injuries sustained at the battle of Sebastopol. Lucius, served his country for the next 36 honourable years in the Royal Navy and then the Army.

TORBAY CIVIC SOCIETY

TORRE ABBEY
FOUNDED 1196
AS A MONASTERY
FOR PREMONSTRATENSIAN CANONS

AFTER 1539
ADAPTED AS A PRIVATE RESIDENCE

HOME OF

THE CARY FAMILY

1662 ~ 1930

COLONEL ROBERT SMITH -
Local landmark was his home

ROBERT Smith, designer and builder of what is now the Redcliffe Hotel in Paignton, was born in France and lived in Italy - but it was the continent of India that had the greatest influence on his life.

HIS FAMILY LIVED AT BIDEFORD IN North Devon and Robert was born there in 1787. At 13 he was already showing artistic promise and two of his series of watercolours commissioned by the Earl of Fortescue are now at Exeter's Royal Albert Memorial Museum. However, financial pressures meant he had to find employment more lucrative than art.

In 1803 Robert become a cadet at the East India Company's College at Marlow, where he probably took drawing instruction for surveying. At 16, he followed his two older brothers to India and later his younger brother would follow; all except Robert died there.

In 1805 Robert arrived in Calcutta to join the Bengal Engineers, and started what would become an astonishing career encompassing engineering and architectural skills in the building of roads, bridges, a lighthouse, and even working on a classical palace for the Rajah of Murshidabad.

By luck he joined a small coterie of gifted amateurs in the circle of a famous artist George Chinnery.

In 1814 Smith was chosen to accompany the Marquis of Hastings (later Lord Moira, the first and only Grand Master of India) on a military tour of duty. But illness began to take its toll, and he requested to go instead to the convalescent island of Penang and then China.

However, during the intervening Nepal War he was seconded as field engineer until 1816, when he finally arrived at the Prince of Wales Island (Penang) as a superintending officer. He now designed defences for the beautiful island, while producing some of his most impressive artwork. His designs for houses for the rich spice plantation landowners ensured he prospered from this time.

By 1819 Smith had returned to London and had given some of his Penang watercolours, which required aquatinting, to the famous artist William Daviell. This resulted in the only public recognition that Smith ever received for his art, as after aquatinting the pictures were so beautiful they were published as a series entitled *Views of Prince of Wales Island* (1820).

During the next decade Smith achieved great prominence. He returned to Delhi, 1,000 miles and three months' travel from Calcutta, and it is easy to imagine he would have succumbed to the European habit of adopting an Indian dress code and may even have converted to a hybrid form of Christianity.

But once in Delhi in 1822 he went to work on the Doab Canal, St James's Church and assisted with the restoration of many historic monuments in Delhi. He then married an Indian woman, whom he later divorced. Appointed garrison engineer of Delhi; sadly, he fell ill again due to having been severely wounded at the siege of Bharatpur (1825-26). Nevertheless, he was specially commended, promoted to Major and sent to convalesce, which gave him an opportunity to paint again. In 1832 he was formally retired with the rank of Lieutenant Colonel and was made a Commander of the Bath for his achievements in India.

In 1854, and with the Ganges Canal officially opened, his pioneering work was again recognised when he was made an Honorary Colonel. He then lived in Italy, eventually returning to England following the death of his second wife, a French woman called Julia, in 1850. She had

Above: Redcliffe castle, circa 1858 (today Redcliffe Hotel).

borne him a son, and a daughter who had died aged 13. On the death of his wife he inherited a substantial fortune.

At 63 years old and with a young son of six, Robert Claude, Colonel Smith came to Torquay to live with his unmarried sister Mary, the only other surviving member of his family, who had recently moved to Florence Villa, Warren Road, Torquay from Teignmouth further along the coast. At the time, Paignton was an undeveloped and little frequented area but when in 1852 Colonel Smith decided to live here he designed his home, called Redcliffe. Work on the building started in 1855, at which time it was rated by the local authority at £9 15s.

It was situated on an outcrop of red sandstone and the only houses nearby would have been at the end of Polsham Road. The surrounding hills were wooded, there was no railway, and perhaps it was to be the building of Redcliffe that helped establish Paignton as a resort. By 1858 the house was being described locally as "Redcliffe Castle" because of its many "towers, minarets and oriental windows".

Together with its driveway, which approached the house via "handsome gates with a lodge" from Paignton Green, it was finally completed in 1864, by which time the rate charge had increased to a staggering £87 10s, a very large sum of money for those days.

The property enjoyed five acres of pleasure gardens, with stone steps to a drawing room and a large dining room, with picture galleries, a conservatory, a billiard room via an octagon annexe, and 23 bed and dressing rooms as well as servants' quarters, outbuildings and stables.

The large complex of buildings also included a novelty feature, a glass-domed plunge bath on the seaward side, approached by a tunnel which is still in use today. It was filled by the sea every day at high tide, Victorians apparently considering salt water baths to be very efficacious. Sadly, the plunge-bath disappeared during a raging storm in the 1880s.

Later in life, the Colonel decided to build himself yet another house in a similar Anglo-Indian style, on a pristine site at Nice, in the south of France. It was known as Chateau Smith but is now the Chateau de l'Anglais, and is apparently even more fantastic than its Paignton predecessor.

In 1872 the Colonel's sister Mary died, and for the last year before his death, in September 1873, he lived at her house in Warren Road, Torquay. The family grave is at Teignmouth.

His heir, Robert Claude, sold Redcliffe due to mounting debt and it was purchased by a Mr J. Prendergast of Middlesex, coincidentally a man with Indian connections. After his death in 1893 the house was later sold to Paignton's branch of the famous Singer family, who already owned and occupied a number of properties on the nearby Esplanade. It was to be the Singer family who renamed the property "Redcliffe Towers". Eventually the house became a convalescent home and in 1902, the "Towers" was finally converted into a hotel.

Although on the Colonels death some 300 "lots" of paintings were advertised for sale, less than one 10th have ever been discovered.

Torbay Civic Society honoured the achievements of Colonel Smith with the installation and unveiling of a blue commemorative plaque at the Redcliffe Hotel on October 22, 2001.

TORBAY CIVIC SOCIETY

COLONEL ROBERT SMITH
(1787-1873)
EMINENT ENGINEER,
ARTIST AND ARCHITECT
IN INDIA
DESIGNED "REDCLIFFE"
IN 1852
AS HIS HOME

EDEN PHILLPOTTS - Devon's forgotton author

BORN IN RAJPUTANA, upon Mount Abu, "The Hill of Wisdom", in India in November 1862, Eden Phillpotts once remarked that "it may be that an Indian foster-mother's milk by nurture influenced my nature".

BEING 4,500 FEET ABOVE SEA LEVEL the outstanding scene of lakes and mountains, encompassing a stronghold of Jainism (a creed that apparently differs from the Buddhist in putting greater demands on its followers), created an unusual beginning for the son of Captain Henry Phillpotts, a civil servant with the Indian Army.

Returning to Britain, Eden and his widowed mother came to live at Dawlish not far from his great uncle, the famous Henry Phillpotts, then Lord Bishop of Exeter. They also had relatives connected with the Church in Cornwall, while in Torquay Commander Phillpotts was its Member of Parliament.

Educated at Mannamead School in Plymouth, Eden's school years were happy times. Then at 17 he moved to London to work as a clerk at the Sun Insurance offices, returning to Devon 10 years later.

In London Eden dressed in a clerk's conventional long coat and top hat and earned £50 per annum, sufficient to allow him to undertake his real calling — writing. Always a keen playgoer he toyed with the idea of becoming an actor but soon realised he lacked the talent. His aspirations for fame, however, would be realised through his 80 years of prolific writing.

The early 1890s saw him widening his experiences and knowledge by choosing to sail to the West Indies; this and other voyages saw him produce many travel books. However, his return to the Westcountry soon saw him drawing upon local lifestyles, scenes and characters in writing about his beloved Devon and Cornwall.

His first novel, published in 1891, was the thriller *The End of Life*, but his public were more attracted to *Lying Prophets*, a story about the fisherfolk of Cornwall issued in 1897.

A year later came *Children of the Mist*, set around Chagford, followed by a plethora of books concerned with scenes and images of Dartmoor. His most famous, *Secret Women*, a tale of adultery and murder, was subsequently dramatised for the theatre in 1912 and was seen by some as his best story, although his own favourite was apparently *The Thief of Virtue*.

His *Widecombe Fair* was transformed to a humorous stage play, *The Farmers Wife*, and became the 14th of his Devon tales. These finally became a complement of 18 stories, all dwelling on the geographical area of Dartmoor and its many characters.

Eden spent the greatest part of his working life in Torquay, and initially chose to live at Eltham, in Oak Hill Road, and so was a near neighbour of the young Agatha Miller (Christie), born nearby in 1910.

He arrived in Torquay in 1901, was made a Freeman in 1921, and remained a resident until 1929 when he moved on to Broadclyst, near Exeter.

Throughout a long life he totally shunned publicity, preferring his own company and hard work every day year in, year out. Work totally dominated his life. He rose early, each day being a writing day, with a routine most authors would find hard to match. Politically, he remained a Liberal throughout life.

Eden made only two public appearances in his 98 years. The first was in 1904 when he unveiled a memorial plaque in Exeter Cathedral to R. D. Blackmore, author of *Lorna Doone*, and the second, over half a century later in 1958 when he appeared in a television interview with the great John Betjeman.

During 1911 Phillpotts learned that John Galsworthy was in Devon at Manaton and he was able to persuade him to ride horseback to Torquay. He found him a man with no humour and their talk apparently centred on the uneven balance between wealth and poverty, and grievances of social injustice and discord, which much depressed Galsworthy.

Always a philosopher, Phillpotts often included his poems in the novels he wrote, but his plays were specifically written for the stage. *The Prude's Progress* and *My Laughing Philosopher* were, however,

Above: Illustrations from My Devon Year

featured in the journal *Black and White*, and its management soon appointed him an assistant editor.

An interesting insight into his extraordinary stubbornness came in 1912 when Britain's national censor refused to license the performance of a play written by him unless two sentences were removed from the script. To Phillpotts, the offending words were immaterial, the principle was all. He refused to budge, and one by one dozens of fellow writers came to his support — all sadly to no avail.

The play was eventually staged, when he allowed free admittance, a quirky but legal way around the problem.

Wonderful stories of this incident abound. J. M. Barrie wrote of the censor: "Clearly the man has no mother, or he could not be so heedless; be that as it may, this pure Devonshire body has been roughly handled".

And Maurice Hewlett wrote: "As to the plot, a murrain on it. That's naught. The crux is this. Should men of genius — or approximately so — be censured by a Jack-in-office? There's the rub. Dramatic art's the lady; no wanton she".

The play was a resounding success probably because of the furore. George Bernard Shaw heard one man remark: "I came to be shocked, but have only been bored" - but then GBS hated Dartmoor, Devon cream and the Eden Phillpotts characters, so perhaps it was natural he would recall the critical verdict.

In wishing to assist the Red Cross fundraising in the First World War, Phillpotts donated an ebony walking stick given to him by kindly kinsfolk. Astonished to find the auctioneer's estimate failed to recognise its value. Eden eventually stated that "along with their diamonds and rubies the walking stick should go", which proved to be the case. A handsome sum being the result and the author was much pleased the auctioneers had got it so wrong.

He never attended any performance of his plays at theatres, and although some of his books were seen by some as classics he dubbed himself a "rank and file writer". The sheer volume and diversity of his writing made it extraordinarily difficult for even his public to follow all his work.

Detective stories, travel books and poetry were hardly similar reading, and when short stories, essays, philosophy and stage plays were added, it is perhaps understandable how challenging his writing was for the most ardent of his followers.

He is best remembered for his five volumes of *Adolescence* and *Old Delabole*, all published before the plethora of books about Dartmoor. Visiting the Amazon website confirms they still list 33 publications by Eden Phillpotts in the 1862-1960 period.

As an assistant editor of *Black and White* his connections with the literary world continued, and in 1955 he was invited to the prestigious Westcountry Writers' Association conference lunch held in Torquay. As usual, he declined but his wife attended and after a toast to Eden's good health she read out a message from him.

To celebrate his 90th birthday the Authors' Club held a cocktail party in London in his honour. Again not present, he sent another message: "In some cases a man's work is all we want to remember about him. In others his work may be the first thing we want to forget. For me to know myself still in the memory of the rising generation awakens great pride and makes of this birthday a red-letter occasion".

This prolific writer also told how to hasten sleep - he "often enumerates famous names and generally chooses those eminent in the arts. Tonight I might bring great painters to my mind, tomorrow summon a regiment of composers, or poets, or novelists, and so call a hundred and more of the illustrious to recollection".

Eden Phillpotts died in his 98th year on December 29, 1960 at his home in Broadclyst, having left his first editions to the Torquay public library.

Above: To commemorate Eden Phillpotts life in Torbay, a Blue Plaque will be unveiled at the site of his home 'Eltham' on November 4th, 2007

43

LOUISA ISABEL SOPHIA CARY -
Benefactor of Torbay Hospital

THE DAUGHTER OF MAJOR George Rowley and granddaughter of Admiral Sir Charles Rowley, Louisa Isabel Sophia became the second wife of Colonel Lucius Falkland Brancaleone Cary, of the celebrated Torquay family.

HER MARRIAGE IN OCTOBER, 1878 TO Lucius Cary was commemorated by the naming of Rowley Road in St Marychurch.

Forbears of Louisa had very distinguished careers. William K. B. had fought the French as Rear-Admiral Rowley at Toulon in 1744, and Major Charles was the first Baronet of his line.

Colonel L. F. B. Cary was born at Torre Abbey on February 1, 1839, his Christian names coming from his father — Lucius Viscount Falkland — and his godmother, an Italian princess.

He had served in the Navy from 1851-1856, joined the Army as an ensign and rose to the rank of colonel. He remained in the Army for 31 years during which time his first wife, Bertha Elizabeth Phillips (whom he married in 1868), died on November 3, 1875. From that marriage there was one son, Henry J. L. Cary, and three daughters, Edith, Bertha and Adelaide Camilla.

From his marriage to Louisa, a further two sons were produced, but Arminel died in January, 1883 before he was four, and his brother Lionel survived only one month longer.

Louisa left us a memorial tablet on the south wall of the chapel at Torre Abbey, which states: "For I sent you out with mourning and weeping, but God will give you to me again with joy and gladness forever". Louisa was to become a major benefactor to Torbay and a Freeman of Torquay.

Lucius and Louisa lived at The Quinta in Reddenhill Road, Babbacombe until the death of Mrs Robert Shedden Sulyard Cary in 1907. This Mrs Cary, the daughter of a local fisherman, was deemed by society to have married above her station and in later life turned to drink. It was not a happy marriage and on her husband's death Mrs Cary, known as "Rose of Devon", was expected to vacate the Cary family seat at Torre Abbey in favour of Colonel Lucius, but flatly refused to do so.

Meanwhile as a memorial to her stepson who died in the Boer War, Louisa added a south aisle to the Church of the Assumption and a side chapel of the Sacred Heart and sacristies for priests and boys, as well as a stained glass window in the aisle. The recumbent figure of Lieutenant Cary in full regimental dress is depicted, with the words: "In loving memory of Lieutenant Henry James Lucius Cary, Devonshire Regt. Erected by his stepmother, Louisa Cary RIP."

The first general hospital in Torquay was established in Higher Union Street (today Castle Chambers), in 1851. It was soon full and thus required more beds and additional wards. With constant expansion, a new lift and a new theatre were installed and by 1903 public benefactors' names were being used to identify new wards. 1903 saw Louisa taking full responsibility for managing a public appeal to raise money to construct and maintain a children's ward within the hospital.

Rosehill, a small external hospital situated at Babbacombe and founded in 1888, was the only child facility, taking up to six patients, generally those suffering from either a chronic or incurable disease.

By 1904 Louisa had made arrangements for a larger Rosehill children's hospital to be built on the site of Goldilea in Lower Warberry Road, Torquay, where eventually it could treat up to 30 children.

The new Rosehill was dedicated in memory of Henry Cary and Louisa, as president of the Torbay General Hospital at Higher Union Street (a role she retained for 12 years), Louisa now spent five years raising funds to underwrite and complete the children's ward project.

On the death of Mrs R. S. S. Cary in 1907, Louisa and Lucius, after nine years of waiting, were at last able to take up residence at Torre Abbey. So delighted were the 500 lessees and tenants to see the "rightful" Lord of the Manor in residence gifts of a silver salver and a silver jardiniere, both carrying Cary Arms, were presented.

An inscription on the salver stated: "This salver was presented by the tenants of the Manor of Tormohun and St Marychurch to Colonel Lucius Cary and Mrs Cary as a mark of respect and esteeem on their coming to reside at Torre Abbey, the ancestral home of the Carys, 31st July 1907".

Lucius, now a Devon Justice of the Peace and Vice-Commodore of the Royal Torbay Yacht Club, was also a great supporter of the Torbay general hospital. To assist his wife's appeal he opened the grounds of the Cary estate to the public each summer, raising between £50 - £60 on each occasion.

In 1909 Louisa at last oversaw the completion of her new children's ward and officially opened it in April of that year. It was endowed with her name and remains the "Louisa Cary Ward" at the modern Torbay Hospital to this day.

Hospitals were a vital asset to a growing population. At that time they had to be run locally on a voluntarily basis and therefore needed funds from benefactors, subscribers and patients or through some locally devised contribution scheme.

Alternatively, they could be underwritten by local rates through the Town Council, but this was generally only done for hospitals specialising in maternity, chronic diseases or fever cases.

In Torbay residents were encouraged to contribute to a voluntary scheme to protect them at times of illness, those over the age of 14 being required to pay 1d (240d equalled £1) per week as insurance. The parents of children under that age were asked to pay a half-penny per child per week.

The restoration of the parish church of Tormohun had taken place between 1849 and 1852, and benefactors for bells there and at Cockington Church were being sought in the early 20th century and the Carys again responded to both pleas. At Tormohun there were six bells but only two were perfect — one dating back to the reign of James I and a second which had

been cast in 1754. A third bell had been restored in 1911, leaving three for replacement.

Colonel and Mrs Cary underwrote the provision of one, the second was paid for by John Kitson and the last via the churchwardens. Each bell cast bore the donor's name, but the Cary name was wrongly spelled "Carey". The surplus "E" had to be filed off leaving forever a space between the letters still visible today.

To mark the centenary year of Torquay's Regatta Mrs Cary and a Mrs Towell raised £134 to provide a ladies' silver trophy for presentation to the female winner. Mrs Cary then arranged a garden party followed by a centenary ball at Torquay's new Town Hall to complete the celebrations of August 27, 1913.

Colonel Lucius Cary died on July 1, 1916 and as a memorial his widow erected a tablet in the Church of the Assumption which reads: "To the glory of God and the memory of my loved and loving husband Col. Lucius Cary, Rifle Brigade, born February 1st 1839, died July 1st 1916. 'Thy prayers and thy arms are ascended for a memorial in the sight of God'".

As a major benefactor of the town Mrs Cary was made a Freeman of the Borough of Torquay on July 13, 1921 and in memory of Lancelot S. R. Cary she left a final memorial, a shrine, at the corner of Old Mill Road with Bamfylde Road, dedicated on November 1, 1927.

Mrs Cary died at Kelvedon in Upper Norwood, West Sussex, on July 3, 1934. Having requested no flowers or mourning even the Bay's local newspapers recorded nothing more than a death notice.

With there never having been an official local obituary, perhaps these pages will bring part of Mrs Cary's life's work and story to those who still benefit locally from her many generous benefactions.

Below: Early days in the Louisa Cary ward in Higher Union Street – on the wall are some of the tile pictures which were moved to the modern hospital.

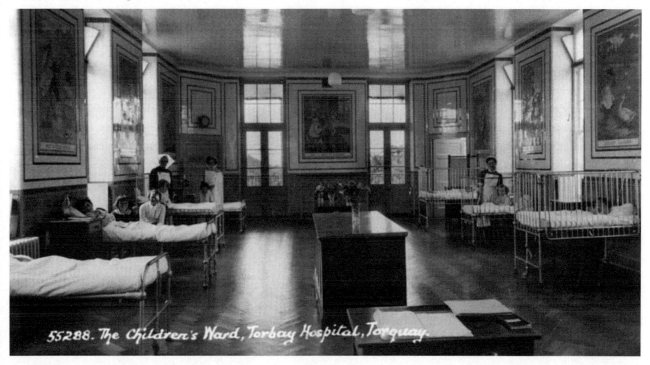

44

WILLIAM HENRY GRANT -
Making Watcombe marble famous

JOSEPH GRANT WORKED in the quarries at Petitor after valuable deposits of marble were discovered in the surrounding hills.

BORN IN 1777 and living at Broadhempston, Joseph worked with Daniel Woodley who was appointed by a London firm to exploit the new marble, and set up a workshop to manufacture architectural items chiefly for noblemen's houses.

The firm survived until 1865 but during that period Joseph's son Henry, having been apprenticed to Messrs D. & J. Woodley, decided to set up his own marble business at St Marychurch.

Working initially with Petitor stone and black marble before progressing to semi-precious stones, Henry's small factory produced a wide variety of items including pendants, crosses and personal seals.

Although Joseph would live to 90, it was to be Henry who in 1847 established the "Watcombe Marble and Mosaic Works" on the Teignmouth road. Then Henry's eldest son, William Henry Grant in following the family tradition started to develop and promote the marble business more widely.

William Henry Grant was born on the April 23, 1836 in a thatched cottage opposite the Palk Arms. Here he saw his first velocipede (bicycle) and an amusing recollection recalled in his autobiography tells: "One day two gentlemen stopped at the inn, having arrived on their machines, one of which had four wheels, with treadle, whilst the other was worked by the hands pushing backward and forward levers".

Having harnessed the machines to a donkey to get an easier "ride" all apparently went well until one cycle touched the donkey's heels and it fled down steep steps pulling the two unfortunates behind. The outcome was despair and the destruction of both velocipedes.

From another incident, when he was 10,

William recalled that when accompanying his father down to Babbacombe beach one day, they witnessed a flotilla of ships arrive with Queen Victoria aboard.

They watched as a red carpet was laid across the beach, due to a local dignitary believing the royal party would land to visit a Miss Keyes at Glen Cottage. She was a cousin of Mrs Whitehead, a retired lady of the royal household who had previously owned the cottage. In fact, the royal visitors did not land that day. Miss Keyes, however, would years later be in the news again when murdered at this same cottage, or so the court ruled, by John "Babbacombe" Lee, known as "the man they could not hang".

In 1851 William attended the Great Exhibition held at the Crystal Palace, Hyde Park and in 1862, with a friend, visited the second Great Exhibition at Chelsea - good grounding for a future marble factory owner and businessman intent on international success.

By 1870 the Watcombe marble factory was renamed Harry Grant & Sons and had 20 employees. It manufactured a wide range of ornaments including inkstands, paperweights, vases, brooches, trays and small caskets, and was known in the trade as the "Art Marble Works".

Henry and William went on to establish the works as British specialists in fine quality marble and stonework. Over the years much larger items were manufactured and a new material became particularly significant — malachite. Although costly it was beautiful and Messrs Edwin Bradford, the Torquay jewellers, with their large staff of in-house craftsmen, became Grants' first major customer.

By 1880 Harry Grant and Sons had opened a retail shop, at 29 Torwood Street, followed by a second shop at 10 The Strand. Here they displayed inlaid marble table ornaments and stone jewellery mounted in silver or gold. The shop existed for 40 years but eventually closed in order that the manufacturing work at the factory could survive.

With the death in 1880 of Mr Potts Chatto, chairman of the Local Board, William, now a successful businessman, was asked to fill the vacancy.

TORBAY CIVIC SOCIETY
THE
TOWN HALL
OF
ST. MARYCHURCH
1883-1900
DESIGNED BY
GEORGE BRIDGEMAN
ARCHITECT
40

Below: The marble works interior in 1985. Note belt driven power.

The board had been established in 1866, at which time annual elections had to be held. By the time an Act of Parliament turned the board into a district council William, was serving as chairman of the Gasworks Committee, and had been responsible for the extension of the Temperance Street gas supply to serve the more heavily populated district of St Marychurch.

With the marble works flourishing, William's father, Henry, died at a relatively early age in 1871, only three years after his father Joseph. William meanwhile was still on the local council, and now supported a massive sewerage scheme for the whole district and created new footpaths, the laying out of Babbacombe Downs and saw through the building of a new Town Hall at St Marychurch. He also witnessed the Devon Agricultural Show being hosted at Chelston in 1882 and saw it brought to St Marychurch in 1893.

In 1896 at the age of 60 William retired from the business and conditionally assigned it to his two sons. They successfully carried it on for a number of years before turning it into a limited company, by which time it had over 50 employees.

Having been on the council for 20 years William was elected its chairman in 1900, and through this obtained a seat by right on the County Magistrates' Bench. One of the first of three councillors to be elected to serve on the district council when the new ward of St Marychurch was established, he lost his seat when local elections became embroiled in politics. Although asked to stand for re-election, he never did.

In 1901 William saw his beloved area of Babbacombe and St Marychurch hosting the return of the Devon

Agricultural Show at Cary Park. The Grant marble factory, renowned internationally, was by now one of only a few British firms still producing specialist stonework.

The family continued their apprenticeship scheme to ensure almost everything produced was crafted by hand. The factory was still lit by gas, and it would not be until the 1970s that electric power would replace gas and gas lamps, by which time most businesses in the country saw electricity as essential to a manufacturer. At Harry Grant and Sons Ltd the gas powered belt-driven lathes were still used when working with some of the rarest semi-precious stones in the world - opal, malachite, lapis lazuli, carnelian, tigereye or turquoise, some of which were often worth more than gold – and the only electric power in the factory came from a six-volt battery until 1978 when cables were finally laid and electricity was fully utilised.

William's wife died on April 25, 1910 after which he lived with his daughter for nearly 10 years. Sadly, he was to lose her when she died after an accident in July, 1920. He then went to live with his eldest son although retaining the housekeeper who for many years had tended the family.

His three other children were Eva Jane, who became Mrs Crabb, William Henry Godfrey, the next managing director, and Harry Frank, whose home he shared.

Having lived and worked in the parish of St Marychurch for 88 years, having had one of the largest businesses of the area and having served in high public office for more than 20 years, William Henry Grant died at age 89 in March, 1924. The era of "the Grand Old Man of St Marychurch", as he was affectionately known, had ended.

The last of the working Grants was Joseph's great-great-grandson, Godfrey Grant, who on the advice of his doctor sold the factory in 1975. Throughout almost 150 years the business supplied major national firms like Asprey's of Bond Street, Tiffany's and, of course, members of the Royal Family which during Joseph's lifetime included no fewer than six monarchs.

Godfrey died in 1979 at age 79 and so ended a family history of commerce and craftsmanship which had taken the name of St Marychurch to the furthest corners of the world.

Below: The old marble works building at Watcombe photographed in 1994. The site was eventually cleared for housing.

45

JOHN CALLCOTT HORSLEY -
He gave us the Christmas card

JOHN CALLCOTT HORSLEY was born on January 29, 1817. He married Mary, the sister of engineering genius Isambard Kingdom Brunel, and although the two brothers-in-law led very different lives they became firm friends and were soon together on a walking holiday through Italy.

BOTH WERE HIGHLY MOTIVATED AND energetic Victorians. Horsley thought nothing of travelling overnight by train and then walking 20 miles to sketch an old church or manor. As a competent artist he would later be recognised as a skilled English painter, particularly of domestic scenes.

His first picture, *Rent Day at Haddon Hall in the Days of Queen Elizabeth*, was exhibited at the Royal Academy in 1839, launching what was to be a successful career.

During the early 1840s, Brunel had seen his proposals for the South Devon Railway fulfilled, and as chief engineer to the Great Western Railway he had started the first ever survey for a rail link to Torquay. Once the Exeter to Newton Abbot line was opened in 1846, it took him only another two years before the Torquay branch line to Torre was complete.

The year 1846 was also a milestone in Horsley's life and in the life of the nation, for he was asked to design what would be the world's first Christmas card. His innovative drawing was printed using lithography and a hand-colouring process, to produce 1,000 cards.

Printed by Messrs Jobbins of London, and published and sold by Summerleys Home Treasury Office at one shilling (5p) each, the cards soon sold out and quickly established the concept of annual greeting cards.

Upper class Victorians bought the cards in huge numbers but it took until 1870 for the cost of national postage to be reduced sufficiently for all British citizens to be able to afford and send Christmas greetings to friends every year.

Within the obviously strong bond of friendship it is interesting that the two mens temperaments were so very different. It was perhaps Horsley's exuberance for life that first attracted Brunel to his brother-in-law but Horsley, beneath this exterior image, nurtured a deep solemnity and very strong convictions. Isambard, on the other hand, suffered bouts of unrelenting melancholy throughout life.

Horsley's paintings initially were of historic aspects but soon he turned towards more contemporary subjects and, as the great Reynolds stated, "scenes of flirtation set in the countryside" with pictures like *Blossom Time* and *Sunshine and pretty women*.

Isambard, meanwhile, was toying with retirement in Torquay. He had been contemplating this for some time, with his wife living firstly at Watcombe Villa and then at Portland Villa, later the Maidencombe House Hotel, now demolished.

As a young man Horsley suffered the tragedy of losing Mary and their two children from scarlet fever. He had predicted and had expected to die early himself but nevertheless married again and with his second wife, Rosamund, produced five children; in spite of his early concerns, he would outlive his brother-in-law by more than 44 years.

By mid-1857 Brunel was quite unwell and he invited Horsley and his new wife to come to Devon and stay for the summer at Orestone House, Maidencombe, now the Orestone Manor Hotel.

Renting Orestone for a year the two families enjoyed typical Victorian pursuits of croquet on the lawn, outings by day and social discourse in the evening, with candlelit dinners and party games.

Rosamund, having inherited a fortune, was enabling the Horsleys to consider a new home at Cranbrook, Kent, where they currently lived. However, they were unable to proceed due to her inheritance being subject to a trust.

By one of those strange quirks of life the Brunels were also ready to build a home, on the Watcombe estate, and they were mulling over plans for a gentleman's mansion on the hilltop. They were similarly having to be patient, as Isambard wanted to see the official launch of his new vessel, The Great Eastern, before moving on. Later he would confirm that the days and weeks at Watcombe were "the happiest hours of his life".

Horsley, however, being much concerned about the stressful pressures of Isambard's life, had written an emotional letter to his brother-in-law and friend imploring him to reflect on his lifestyle "which has been one of almost unparalleled devotion to your profession, to the exclusion of that which was due to your God and even to your family, and an utter disregard of your health".

With the sabbatical in Devon over Brunel, having experienced another relapse and breakdown, fled to Europe to convalesce, and it is unlikely that he ever read the letter. Sadly, we now know Horsley was right and Brunel would soon be lost to the world at a very early age.

Fortunately for posterity, Horsley had decided to do a portrait of his friend, and although he may not have been thought of as a master painter, he undoubtedly played an important part in capturing Victorian England on canvas.

His portrait of Brunel depicted him as a man getting things done and in smart clothes at his desk, not standing before the Great Eastern's launching chains with mud on his boots.

Horsley's strong convictions were now to bring controversy. In an age of hypocrisy and prudery Horsley publicly objected to artists painting nudes and was tarred with the nickname "Clothes Horsley".

He was also to see his world change beyond belief. Having been in attendance at the birth of the royal Princess Beatrice, the dresser to the family happened to mention in royal circles that on the same day a boy had been born to an artist friend of hers (John Horsley).

The dresser was later informed that the Queen and Prince Albert had been contemplating whether there might be an equivalent male name to Beatrice and at the Queen's suggestion, they asked that a message be conveyed to the friend that perhaps the baby boy might be named Victor Alexander.

Below: Horsley's Christmas card which started a national tradition.

Above: Orestone Manor, home to Horsley for a year and now a hotel.

And so he was, and this link was not to be forgotten when, one year later, a portrait of Princess Beatrice was required and it was John Callcott Horsley who received the commission. June, 1858 saw him dodging in and out of Buckingham Palace trying to avoid Prince Albert, as the finished portrait of his one-year-old child was to be a surprise birthday present.

Meanwhile, Brunel, having returned from his European convalescence, was diagnosed as having a fatal kidney disease; and on September 15, 1859 the world lost this amazing entrepreneur at the age of 53.

With royal patronage Horsley's artistic career was now assured. Between 1875-1890 he was Rector of the Royal Academy and organiser of its first Old Master Winter Exhibition.

A keen musician and a friend of the great Mendelssohn, Horsley now contributed to *Punch* via another famous friend, John Leech. But Horsley's solemnity and prudery publicly resurfaced in a letter which appeared in The Times on May 25, 1885. Headlined "A Women's Plea" and signed "A British Matron" the letter was in fact written by Horsley.

Sympathetic replies were received, one from "The Church of England Purity Society". Horsley, wishing to remain anonymous, concocted a reply and signed it "H".

He was even more offended on another occasion when female art students were asked to view nude paintings of women. For this he was vilified at a Church of England Congress in October, 1885 and publicly ridiculed in a cartoon entitled "The Model British Matron", depicting him as a corseted Matron.

John Horsley died on October 19, 1903 just two years after his Queen and the end of the Victorian era. A Torbay Civic Society blue plaque to his memory was unveiled at the Orestone Manor Hotel in 1988.

46

PRINCESS MARIE LOUISE -
Princess of many parts

PRINCESS MARIE LOUISE was born on August 12, 1872, a granddaughter of Queen Victoria and the fourth child of Prince Christian of Schleswig-Holstein and his wife, the Princess Helena Augusta Victoria, who was the third daughter of the Queen.

THE PRINCESS HAD A CONVENTIONAL EDUCATION in England, relieved only by trips to Germany. At the age of eight she and her sister spent time at the same house as the D'Oyly Carte actor George Grossmith. For two impressionable youngsters, being entertained by a "real live actor" was exciting indeed.

Marie Louise came to understand the needs of the sick at an early age. Her mother was instrumental in setting up a State Register of Nurses, was a founder member of the Red Cross, and had tended the wounded of the Russo-Turkish War during 1878.

With the encouragement of her cousin, Emperor William II, the Princess was betrothed to Prince Aribert of Anhalt, at a lunch at Potsdam on December 6, 1890 and the wedding took place at St. George's Chapel, Windsor on July 6, 1891. The honeymoon was partly spent at Bayreuth in Germany where the Princess heard her first Wagner and where Cosima Wagner introduced her to musicians, ballet stars and musical evenings.

However, the House of Anhalt had concocted a marriage of convenience and Aribert, proving to be an unsatisfactory husband, eventually had to ask his father to intervene.

After nine years of disillusionment and unhappiness in a marriage drifting apart, the German sovereign exercised a medieval family prerogative granting an annulment to the loveless and childless marriage. Aribert wrote to his father-in-law that "he was a young man and had the right to live his life in his own way" and signed it "Your devoted and obedient son-in-law Aribert Prince of Anhalt". Marie Louise later stated: "Truly the Germans have no sense of humour".

The marriage had typified the stupidity of the "stiff upper lip" stance. Another incident, which concerned a Princess being banned from riding a bicycle because it was "not seemly", also highlighted this, the offending bicycle was even given the Royal Imperial Seal, so that it was never used again.

As a devout Christian, Marie Louise's marriage vows were sacrosanct and binding throughout life, and not something that could be put aside lightly by what the Princess termed an "arbitrary local family law". The German annulment was finalised in December, 1900 and from then her maiden name was adopted and she never remarried. She was also the last royal in Britain to hold the title of "Her Highness".

The Princess was appointed Lady of the Imperial Order of the Crown of India by Queen Victoria in 1893. Having inherited a passion for Bach from her mother and with an appreciation for Wagner she regularly attended Covent Garden, becoming a friend of the tenor Lauritz Melchior. Patron of the arts, a skilled enameller and a tireless traveller, with few corners of the world escaping her curiosity, the Princess had a huge circle of personal friends that was unusual for a member of the Royal Family at that time.

Her happiest times were between the world wars, sharing Schomberg House in Pall Mall with her sister Princess Helena Victoria, where they frequently held parties for friends in musical circles.

During half a century her devotion to charitable and social causes would include nursing lepers, assisting youths, being involved with organisations wanting greater international understanding, and helping relieve poverty. Her causes included a London boxing club, the St Christopher's Fellowship, the Navy League, Guide Dogs for the Blind, and many others.

Above: Normount, now the Bishops Court Hotel in Lower Warberry Road, often played host to the Princess.

She was most involved with University College Hospital, the South Eastern Hospital for Children and Friends of the Poor.

As a supporter of bazaars, fetes, receptions and exhibitions the Princess became proficient at committee work. Being tall and with imposing features, she brought an air of dignity to formal occasions and her speeches, "neat and pointed" in a refreshing style, would often surprise her audiences.

The 1914-18 War saw her establishing a 100-bed hospital in Bermondsey under direction of the War Office and, unique for the times, she chose not to wear any uniform. One amusing story tells of a patient refusing raw egg and iced champagne (to her Highness a delicacy) and asking for porter and eel pie. Her wondering aloud how anyone could prefer this peculiar dish brought the reply: "Princess, you ought to taste my wife's jellied eels". She was clearly on a learning curve.

A Dame Grand Cross of the Order of St John of Jerusalem, Lady President of the Order of Mercy and a keen churchwoman, the Princess lost her only surviving brother, Albert, in April, 1931, and her beloved sister, Princess Helen Victoria, in March, 1948.

Having decided to plan, build and stock an elaborate dolls' house as a gift to Queen Mary, she secured the support of the great architect Edwin Lutyens to design it. By writing no fewer than 2,000 personal letters she was able to secure the finance needed to purchase miniatures of everything for the house, which is still on permanent exhibition at Windsor Castle.

The Princess always had a lady-in-waiting, one being Evelyn Adams, whose maiden name was Wills, of the Imperial Tobacco family. Through Evelyn frequent visits were arranged to Torquay, staying at the Rainbow, with her relative Ella Rowcroft (another Miss Wills). On other occasions they stayed in the royal suite at Torquay's Imperial Hotel.

The Princess worshipped at St Michael's Church, Pimlico, when in Torquay, particularly on her birthday. In 1951 and 1952 the Princess celebrated her 78th and 79th birthdays with Mrs Rowcroft at Rainbow, when cocktail parties were arranged for local dignitaries.

Throughout her life the Princess was a voracious reader of history, biographies and detective stories. She was president of the British Empire Shakespeare Society and chaired its meetings at the Haymarket and Her Majesty's theatres. Having previously been honoured with a GBE in 1919 from King George V, she received a DGCVO from Queen Elizabeth II as late as 1953.

One visit to Torquay included an invitation to Normount, now Bishops Court Hotel in the Warberries, from owner Mrs Nelson Clover. A Torbay Civic Society plaque was unveiled there in 2002 as it is recognised as one of Torquay's best surviving Italianate villas. Built in 1844, its white stonework reflecting the marine light in its heyday must have seemed perfection to Victorians and Edwardians alike.

The Princess finally published a book of her reminiscences, *My Memories of Six Reigns*, in the year of her death. Available from November, 1956 it sold 40,000 copies within six months and was an immediate success. It portrays a penetrating style of a vanished age, and "confided intimacy and a playful disrespect for the etiquette of German Courts". It includes a loving reverence for her grandmother Queen Victoria but sadly the Princess, although able to attend the books launch event, was unable to deliver the message of greeting she had composed, due to her failing health. Days later she died.

The Princess's extraordinary family names, which had always embarrassed her, were Fransiska Josepha Louise Augusta Marie Helena Christina. She was the last surviving member of the Royal Order of Victoria and Albert and she died at her grace and favour residence at Fitzmaurice Place, London on December 8, 1956.

The congregation at her funeral included three of London's "pearly kings" who came in their gay costumes as a tribute to their friend and patron. By coincidence the funeral date fell on what was seen as the most melancholy date of the Victorian calendar, December 14, the anniversary of the death of the Prince Consort some 95 years earlier.

JOHN SALTER - Fine drawings of Torquay

DESPITE HAVING BEEN named after his father, young John Salter did not follow the family tradition of farming but chose to draw and paint - and eventually become one of Torquay's finest artists.

HE WAS BORN AT NORTH TAWTON, IN MID-DEVON, in 1825 to John and Mary Salter, and although he helped on the family farm it was not long before drawing was more important than minding the stock. He also became seriously interested in drawing on wood, or to give it its commercial name, lithography, which involved engraving wooden blocks.

This interest led to him going to London, where in 1848 he studied at Messrs Mizetelly's, a firm of lithographers. Living at 18 Charles Street, Hoxton, Salter soon exhibited a first picture, *A Mill on the Teign*, at the Royal Academy, ensuring that at just 23 he determined his career was to be within the art world.

His earliest work draws on scenes of Devon but once trained in lithography he was soon employed at the commercial premises of the *Illustrated London News*. Having always been impressed by the work of Constable, Salters own style of drawing and painting would be much influenced by the master painter.

In 1850, having produced his first successful lithograph, he returned to his native Devon to live at Torquay, where as a "professor of drawing" he set up a studio to teach art to those who found him at No 2 Park Place.

Already a prolific colourist, Salter was to be especially noted for his coastal views and the intricacy of his drawing. Most of his pictures, still of his native Devon, centre on his chosen home of Torbay. He was now painting both in watercolours and oil, and though his paintings extended to portraits they were accomplished with a photographic fidelity.

His individual style and expertise came from being able to work in a wide variety of materials which saw many panoramic views engraved on wood as well as produced as wash drawings or chalk work. There was no "artistic licence" at all, he merely interpreted very accurately exactly what he saw.

Between 1850 and 1891 he arguably became one of the best artists of his time, employing such diverse materials as pencil, pen and ink, oil, chalk and watercolour, along with engraving.

A devout Christian and a member of the Plymouth Brethren, he was throughout life a deeply religious man. The Plymouth sect ensured he was barred from belonging to any local or national association of his chosen profession, and perhaps this explains why he was largely unknown to contemporaries in the art world. Certainly, membership of the Brethren would have debarred him from the camaraderie that generally flows when fellow professionals gather. The strict code also saw him debarred from or being associated with unionism, any trade or political organisations or any non-Christian based society. It is often said that his best work was in drawing and painting "the trees and trout streams" of Devon but to some extent it was the Devon sect's code that ensured he was a less commercially acceptable artist than might have otherwise been the case.

It is believed that John Salter of Torquay should be identified as the same John (William) Salter who worked on the Geological Survey of the United Kingdom and Canada during the early 1840s through to the 1860s although this is difficult to prove.

After losing his father, John married Elizabeth Stabb of Tormohun in 1857, who during the next 18 years bore him 10 children.

The prolific number of local scenes drawn, etched or painted by Salter included those of Anstey's Cove, Babbacombe Bay, Livermead and the Waldon and Vane hills. Local buildings include The Gibbons Hotel, St Michael's Chapel, Torre Abbey Chapter House and, of course, his beloved rural scenes from around the county.

More often than not his landscapes were captured in wash drawings, watercolour or oil on canvas. A number of local prints were confirmed as being by Salter in 1977 by J. V. Somers Cocks, and these included two sets of local scenes, *Six Views of Torquay and Neighbourhood,* dated 1850, and an untitled series of six vignette views of Torquay in 1862.

Salter and his family lived first at Duncan House, Old Torwood Street, the home of Elizabeth's parents, but by 1866

Above: One of the best known Salter drawings, of Torquay harbour.

they had moved to 3 The Terrace, now Carlton House.

His ever developing skills saw him responding to an increasing demand for his services and by 1870 an expanding workload saw an art studio created at the property. Working on coastal views or shores, trees and trout streams and the inevitable landscapes, he frequently depicted his Torbay habitat.

He exhibited at the Royal Academy in 1870 for a second time, using on this occasion a painting of the "Natural Arch" on the Torquay coastline, and during the next seven years his local and Scottish scenes were exhibited on no fewer than 21 occasions at the International Exhibition, the Royal Manchester Institution and other lesser venues.

His earliest illustrations included *Behind Gibbons Hotel*, which perhaps typifies the intricacy and almost photographic detail he always captured. This picture shows the rear of No 1 Torwood Street (originally the Commercial Hotel) the Hole in the Wall public house and in the background the Holy Trinity Church spire.

During 1870 to 1889 Salter painted in many countries including Canada, Italy, Norway and Switzerland, and when at home his teaching work at Lower Terrace continued until 1878.

By the late 1880s the family had moved to Romsdal, Walnut Road (now demolished), where Salter remained for the rest of his life.

He died aged 66 on July 18, 1891 and was interred at Torquay Cemetery. Elizabeth survived him nearly 20 years until she died aged 79 in 1911.

The Torquay Directory obituary column confirms Salter as "a pious man, strong in his religious views, who did his utmost to promote spiritual advancement of those among whom he lived".

In 1926, Mary Salter, his daughter, gave many of her father's local drawings to the Torquay Natural History Society, which included a most valuable, framed watercolour of Livermead, which was painted in 1850.

This was one of his earliest works and a great prize for the society's then Pictorial Records Section, with its objectives of forming a collection and a record of illustrations and portraits, (old and modern), relating to Devonshire.

Such collections relied on benefactors of the time giving works of art, and today the society's collection at Torquay Museum includes priceless examples of those early Victorian scenes, captured long before the world of photography competed with the skills of individual artists and illustrators.

In January, 1974 an album of Salter's sketches was sold at Sotheby's, and it included many scenes from visits he had made to places that had previously not been recorded. Among them were Portsmouth and the Isle of Wight, Brighton and Hove, Hastings, Northumberland, Yarmouth and Yorkshire, as well as places in Wales and Ireland, proving that the largely unknown artist had been a much travelled Victorian.

In 1994 at Rainbow House, Torquay, an exhibition of Salter's work was arranged as part of a fund raising campaign for "Torbay and its Artists" by the Friends of Torre Abbey and Torquay Museum. Then in 1997, in conjunction with Friends' president Dr Toby Thorne, the museum arranged the most recent exhibition to display Salter's work, which remained on view for two months. That exhibition, entitled "Devon Views and Water Colours by John Salter" included many privately owned paintings never before seen in public.

In a final tribute to the artist in 1997, Torbay Civic Society unveiled a commemorative plaque at his old studios at, 30 The Terrace, now the commercial offices of solicitors Hooper and Wollen.

Below: Salter's sketch of the area behind the Gibbons Hotel, with the Hole in the Wall public house on the right.

TORBAY CIVIC SOCIETY

THE ARTIST
JOHN SALTER
1825 – 1891

LIVED AND WORKED
HERE
1878 – 1890

SIR RICHARD BURTON -
Exploring and erotica

THE BURTON FAMILY, of Franco-Irish stock, seemed forever in need of money. Brought up undisciplined by their parents, Joseph and Martha allowed their children Richard and Francis to similarly develop into what today we would call "brats".

IN THEIR TEENS JOSEPH AND HIS BROTHER FRANCIS had become interested in the Baker sisters, Martha and Sarah, having realised that they could inherit £30,000 each. But having fled to Britain after naval retirement enforced by no less a person than the Duke of Wellington himself, Joseph did marry Martha in 1820 only to discover his assumed share of the Baker fortunes was only going to be released "in dribs and drabs".

Into this maelstrom of intrigue came his son Richard, born at Torquay on March 19, 1821 one year into the marriage and baptised at Torre Church. The family left Devon one year later to live at Elstree in Hertfordshire.

As Richard grew his father envisaged he would be a churchman. The young man matriculated at Trinity College, Oxford in November 1840, where he had colloquially mastered six languages and was an expert swordsman and sportsman. His academic career spanned only five terms - less than two years.

Burton now determined it was the army for him. With the Afghan war raging he obtained a cadetship in the Indian Army and left England complete with bull terrier, to land at Bombay in June, 1842. An impatient man yet a prolific writer, he would throughout life commit to paper everything he learned.

He was intoxicated by India, with its vast landscape encompassing the equinoctial Madras and the snows of the Himalayas. He adored the multi-cultural mix of India, finding ten different races and three main languages — Semitic, Hamitic, and Japheptic or Turanian.

He witnessed the squalor of Bombay and saw limbs and heads sliding off funeral pyres as he stood silently by, disguised as an undertaker. He smelt the "roasting flesh" and watched "lizards and bandicoot rats slithering through open sewers". He loathed the cruelty of India and its harsh treatment of women and yet admired the people's knowledge of sex. This aspect coloured his life and ensured his intellectualism also had a darker side.

He discovered males trained early in the art of love-making and the so-called "retaining arts" (non-ejaculation) and that Indian women were contemptuous of European men having little understanding of the phenomenal possibilities of this art; he said of his mistress that "she had made her muscles prehensile to such a point that she was able to catch a mosquito between her toes during intercourse".

In hacking his way through the jungles of Karachi to learn about male brothels, this period led him to romanticise about women who seemingly fell into two groups - "there are the fair unattainables, and those who can be objects of fantasy, or day dreams".

He ingratiated himself fully into oriental life, passing an examination in Hindu and Gujarathi and within one year was qualified as an interpreter. His translation of Italian hydrodynamics for the Indus irrigation system gives another insight into his wide-ranging skills.

He rode, boxed, wrestled and practised swordsmanship with Indian sepoys and having been given a three-year commission to visit the Muhammadan provinces of India, his fellow officers said he lived the life of what they called a "White Nigger".

But nothing held him for long. In 1843 he was in Cairo disguised as a Persian Mirza, a Dervish and then a Pathan. He was determined to be the first European to penetrate Mecca, for which he was in disguise as a Mohammedan. Becoming Al-Haj (the pilgrim) the "infidel" made his pilgrimage to Mecca - and had the Devon born explorer been unmasked death would have been inevitable - and and visited Aden, Zanzibar and the Nile.

The years 1846 to 1848 saw him recuperating in the Nilgiri hills and convalescing in Goa. This brought his first major book *Goa and the Blue Mountains*, concerning the Todas and their language, Cameons.

The sandy deserts of Sind eventually saw him diagnosed with recurring Indian fevers, ophthalmia, chest infections and a bladder problem; so with his Sindian servant he left for England in May, 1849.

The Government, having learned of his exploits in Karachi from his various papers and five published books, were in no hurry to officially reappoint him.

Put on indefinite sick leave he travelled Europe's spas and fresh water springs, eventually returning to visit spas in Dover, Leamington and Malvern in 1850. September that year saw him meeting 19-year-old Isabel Arundell, who was besotted, but with her mother intervening, a four-year parting saw Richard torn between heterosexuality and homosexuality. He was always attractive to women but it was generally the intervention of mother's that damned any permanent liaison.

After a brief flirtation with his cousin Elizabeth a disillusioned Burton went to Boulogne where, uninvited, his sister Maria and his mother joined this ex-patriot.

His leisure pursuits included being a swordsman, poet, master of disguise, boxer, raconteur, practical joker, diplomat, pornographer and writer. His overriding zest for the unusual and erotic saw personal safety as of little consequence. Sexual liaisons gave him syphilis, he was racked with oriental ills and yet his intellectual skills made him one of the most outstanding linguists and translators of all time. He mastered no fewer than 35 oriental languages and even his signature included Arabic characters.

Visits to India, Africa and Egypt saw the British Foreign Office entrusting him to seek the source of the Nile. Like Alexander the Great, Julius Caesar and Napolean before him he failed but later, with explorer John Hanning Speke, he reached Lake Tanganyika in 1856.

No ordinary explorer, Burton often wore a fez and carried a dagger, but as a botanist, zoologist, ethnologist, archaeologist, anthropologist, physician and linguist he was often regarded as "the most interesting figure of the 19th century".

Burton was convinced that India, once conquered, must be ruled with an iron fist. He predicted that if British rule were ever driven out, the regime would return to thuggee rule on its streets, burning of widows on funeral pyres, and the Dark Ages generally. Whether or not he was a visionary, others must judge, but Britain's withdrawal from India did not bring wealth for many.

Burton was a popular author. He produced around 100 books, many being literal translations of academic topics and, as ever, voyeurism. In Syria he tells of finding the "Moabite Stone" and of the Mesha-King of the Moabites defeating the Israelites. In 1860 in America he studied the Mormons,

which resulted in his book *The City of Saints* the following year.

Within a month of return he married Isabel Arundell at the Bavarian Catholic Church, Warwick Street, London, sadly without the consent of her family. Twelve months later and appointed Consul to the Spanish Island of Fernando Po, he used the opportunity to visit the Cameroon mountains and ascend the Congo river to reach Yellala Falls.

Appointed Vice-Consul at Santos in South America he visited Brazil, Paraguay and crossed the Andes into Peru and Chile. Appointed to his most sought-after role of Consulate at Damascus, he then saw Jerusalem and Syria. His final consular appointment wass at Trieste in 1872.

Arriving in Gibraltar from Morocco in 1886 a cable announced he was to get a knighthood. In fact, although he wore his KCMG Star, he was never officially knighted by his Queen.

His most remembered translations - the saucy tales of the *Arabian Nights*, the erotica of *The Perfumed Garden* and the *Kama Sutra*, with its explanation of "asanas" (coital positions) were completed in 1886.

Sir Richard died aged 69 in Trieste, on October 19, 1890. His body was returned to Mortlake and a special mausoleum sculptured in the shape of a tent. Lady Isabel returned the following January and published a biography of him in 1893. She confirmed the 30-year marriage had been passionate, although many believed that in a fit of pique and to protect his reputation, she had destroyed Burton's last notes concerning yet another sex-manual.

This was not true, as 100 years later they emerged from a solicitor's office intact and were exhibited at the Orleans House Gallery, Twickenham, in 1998. The exhibition was entitled "Lady Burton's Gift".

Above: Lady Isabel Burton
Below: Torre Church, where Sir Richard Burton was baptised in 1821.

49

CHARLES BABBAGE - Paving the way to computers

CHARLES BABBAGE WAS a genius of almost unbelievable ingenuity.

BORN SOME 500 YARDS FROM THE Elephant and Castle, London on December 26, 1791 he was the son of a rich banker. The Babbage ancestry is traceable to the Westcountry and Benjamin, Charles's grandfather, a well known resident of Totnes. His son, also Benjamin, was a retired banker from London who came to Teignmouth where Charles spent most of his formative years.

With the family having returned to Devon, Charles was sent to school at Alphington, near Exeter, to learn English, Latin and Greek but not science. His youthful years saw him developing into a strong swimmer, a hunter, a fisherman and a competent sailor using a small boat owned by the family. One of his earliest inspirations involved apparatus he had designed to allow him to walk on water. This involved strapping sea paddles onto his feet but having attempted to walk across the Dart he was to prove the concept did not work.

On returning to London and school at Enfield, at 19 he was ensconced at Trinity College, Cambridge where he studied mathematics, chemistry and non-scientific subjects including politics, social reform and liberalism.

It was here in 1812 Charles met his future wife Georgiana Whitmore, and in the same year helped establish the Analytical Society. On leaving Cambridge in 1814, he and Georgiana returned to Teignmouth where on July 2 they married.

As an adult Charles would challenge the "conservatism" of scientists, lamenting their ignorance of social need, and despairing of industrialists who refused innovative scientific ideas to such an extent that he eventually became a scientific recluse. Undoubtedly, he was a genius and social reformer ahead of his time and many of his early ideas were adopted in the 19th and 20th centuries.

The Babbages returned to London, where their first child was born in 1816, the same year as Charles became a member of the Royal Society, the oldest and most important of Britain's scientific societies.

During the next four years Charles would be noted as a rising star by fellow scientists. Together with his great friend John Herschel, he travelled to Paris in 1819 to learn and investigate what was happening in scientific terms on the Continent.

Herschel was to become an outstanding astronomer, chemist, and photographer and like Babbage helped establish the Astronomical Society, becoming its first president.

Babbage was getting an income of £300 per annum from his father (a handsome sum at that time) which allowed him great freedom. To supplement this the Chancellor of the Exchequer, no less, awarded him an Admiralty grant of £1,500 in order that he might continue his work on his "difference machine", a device designed to undertake mathematical calculations by the utilisation of punched cards, similar to the system used on early Jacquard looms in the textile industry.

Once inputted, punched cards programmed and controlled the machine by acting as its brain (computer), which ensured it made or did anything required. Babbage, of course, wanted to generate totals of complicated calculations for astronomers, surveyors, navigators and scientists. This also led him to want to assist actuaries who required extreme accuracy when undertaking mathematical calculations for the life insurance industry.

Sadly, many of his programmes, although proven on paper, could not be reproduced by metal parts in his machines, nevertheless he left us the principles that paved the way for the electronic machines which we know today as digital computers.

Contemporaries of his time thought the work misguided, futile, time consuming, absurd and at best, utterly preposterous, whereas in fact he was one of the most far-sighted men of his generation. Fortunately, he never let their derision and scorn deter him from his early scientific work.

In 1823 he and his wife toured factories and mills in England and Scotland noting that the storage of energy was always a problem. He found that the French metric system was mathematically a far more logical way of measuring and weighing products, and on return to London tried hard to convince Britain to change from imperial to metric measure. It would take another 100 years before that particular change occurred, which even today remains controversial.

Babbage desperately wanted to construct a machine that would replace printed calculation tables. Invariably these had errors, and bankers and the scientific community wanted a machine that would work tirelessly and be relied on to give faultless results.

The year 1827 was dreadful for Babbage. His father died in February, his son Charles died in July and he lost his wife and their newly born son in August. Georgiana had given him eight children between 1815 and 1827 but only three survived into adulthood. With the death of his wife, one son was despatched to a progressive school in London while Charles, living with John Herschel, arranged for his remaining son Herschel and daughter Georgiana to be left with his mother in order that he could undertake a scientific pilgrimage abroad.

In 1828 he returned and that year became Lucasian Professor of Mathematics at Cambridge, holding the honour for two years although flatly refusing to give the lectures expected of him. By 1830 he had published *Reflections on the Decline of Science* and in 1832 his book *On the Economy of Machinery & Manufactures* was on the shelves. A partly-constructed calculating machine was completed with the intention of creating a 20-point decimal machine, but work on the difference machine ceased in 1833 due to lack of finance.

During these years Babbage stood twice for Parliament, losing on both occasions. Cartoons of the time ridiculed him, one even portraying him as a man who would make a mechanical King but, undeterred, his thoughts were already turning towards an analytical machine. This was operated by a cranked handle that turned the columns of wheels, each adding to the other to produce a grand total.

Now enter Ada Lovelace, daughter of Lord Byron and a gifted mathematician in her own right. Becoming a close friend Ada improved Babbage's punched card system and perhaps earned the right to be regarded as among the world's first programmers.

He, meanwhile, was involved in a variety of innovations including a human diving bell, safety devices for lighthouses, a speedometer, an ophthalmoscope and even a gadget to fit on

Above: The Difference Machine built to celebrate Babbage's bi-centenary.

the front of trains to clear obstacles from the track, the American "cowcatcher". His interest in theatre stage lighting resulted in the heliograph, which had the ability to send messages by light via mirrors, an essential tool where speed and accuracy of message was required. Ciphers were also examined and Babbage developed an ability to crack cypher codes.

Unable to complete his full-size working model into a calculating machine, and with the Government despairing of him, he stated: "I have sacrificed time, health, and fortune in the desire to complete these Calculating engines". It was all over by 1852. Government funding was withdrawn and the work and the "salon", his premises at East Street, London, were finally closed down.

But social issues still intrigued him. The noise levels of London due to increasing street cabbies, organ grinders, brass bands, fiddlers and street entertainers usually associated with public houses, saw him introduce a Parliamentary Bill known as "Babbage's Bill". This became law in July, 1864 and gave UK residents the right to legally "move on" unwanted rowdy individuals.

Charles Babbage died on October 18, 1871 aged 79, and was buried at Kensal Green Cemetery in London.

He is best remembered for his calculating machines, and although his ideas were mathematically sound and a major part of the Mark 2 difference machine had been produced, it took another 120 years before Babbages mechanical theories were mathematically be proved effective.

In 1991, engineers successfully built a second difference machine to celebrate the bicentenary of Babbage's birth. By then, of course, the electronic age had clearly overtaken the era of mechanical devices.

Finally a national postage stamp was issued in December, 2001 to honour the "Father of the Computer" on his 200th anniversary.

Above: The postage stamp issued in 2001.

50

ERNEST SHACKLETON - Sailor and polar explorer

ERNEST SHACKLETON, born on February 15, 1874 would often remark that he shared his birthday with the great scientist and astronomer Galileo.

H IS BIRTH YEAR, HOWEVER, WAS LESS auspicious - its disastrous Irish potato crop failure caused his father to leave the land and take his family to Dublin, where he read medicine at Trinity College. Thus Ernest was an honorary Dubliner.

With an Anglican background, Henry Shackleton and his wife Henrietta Letitia Sophia Graven had married in 1872, making their home at Kilkea, County Kildare. A typical bearded Victorian patriarch, Henry sired 10 children of which Ernest was the second, and the elder of two brothers.

Dr Henry Shackleton qualified in 1884, and the family then moved firstly to South Croydon and then Sydenham, both suburbs of London. Henrietta had become an invalid so it was left to Henry to bring up the family.

Ernest's education came via a governess at home and a Dulwich preparatory school where he was a misfit, disliking sport and becoming quickly bored. Nevertheless he somehow managed to avoid the punishment usually associated with rebels, coping well with school discipline.

Transformation came when a naval career was in view. In 1890 he was near the top of his form at Dulwich and in more ways than one was learning the ropes. It was a vital necessity to get rigging right - and his first ship, the Hoghton Tower, with 200 named ropes, Ernest had a lot to learn.

Punished by a rope with a knot each time a "clewline, halyard, lee brace or weather backstay" was misnamed, thrashings were sensibly meaningful, for an error at sea could prove fatal. With these experiences under his belt the 22-year-old Shackleton passed out as First Mate in 1896, and by April, 1898 was a certified Master qualified to command any British ship on the seven seas.

"Shacky", as he was affectionately known, now reflected on a career in which as Master he could go no higher.

Nevertheless "I would like to make a name for myself — and her" he wrote.

The "her" was Emily Dorman, a friend of his sisters, whom he had met on his return from a voyage to Japan on the ship Flintshire, which having unfortunately run aground near Middlesbrough had enabled him to return home for a surprise visit in the summer of 1897. Emily, six years older than Ernest, soon recognised he was smitten and in pursuit, the first time in fact he had been seriously in love.

A friend confirms that Shackleton "gave the impression of inexhaustible animal spirit, of exuberant vitality, of explosive energy" but with Victorian morality followed to the letter, Ernest as Don Juan thought the pursuit, not the conquest, provided at least some satisfaction.

Soon separated and on his way to China, Shackleton now wrote regularly of the pain that human separation brought. On his return he resigned the Welsh Shire Line and its Far Eastern routes to join the Union Castle Line carrying mails from England to Africa.

The summer of 1900 saw him regularly in London, and seeing Emily. But he now volunteered for the National Antarctic Expedition and on September 13, 1900 for the first time met the formidable Commander Robert F. Scott. Neither of earths Poles had yet been reached by man, and both men were seeking advancement and had both high ambition. But whereas Scott could hide his ambition Shackleton wore it on his sleeve — a distinct disadvantage.

The ship Discovery was launched at Dundee on March 21, 1901 two months after the Queen's death and the end of the Victorian era. Shackleton had meanwhile convinced himself that with Emily still in London they would sooon marry, though she was not so sure.

Sent to the Tay to supervise the additional material and requirements of a steam ship in sail, and a hull strength required to ensure it was not crushed by ice floes, Shackleton realised that the coming exploration was a unique opportunity for him or Scott to become men of history — the stuff of legend — a dream fulfilled.

With the Navy having determined that their man at the helm was to be Scott, and not Shackleton and with Emily having written to say she was in love with someone else, Shackleton was depressed and under immense strain. But as the Discovery steamed up the Thames on July 31, 1901 he witnessed his three youngest sisters signalling in handkerchief semaphore from the bank that he had replaced the interloper, Emily would after all marry him. A family soubriquet of Great Shacky (vis-a-vis Great Scott) seemed appropriate and all he now required, in true Victorian manner, was Mr Dorman's approval. With the expectant public's insatiable desire to see British flags placed on every distant land, a decision was taken that the expedition would go South rather than the expected North, the target, the exploration of the South Magnetic Pole.

Scott and Shackleton had by now become Freemasons, perhaps to ensure a union between them, or perhaps in recollection of the 18th century edict that declared: "Masonry provides… no small advantage to a man who would rise in the world". King Edward, himself a prominent Freemason, visited the ship before she sailed on an exploration that would last three years. Emily waved as Shackleton steamed out, but he still did not know if he had her father's permission to marry her.

The rest is history. He became one of the two to accompany Scott across the Ross Barrier, further south than any other person had been. Weakened and with scurvy he was invalided home in the relief ship Morning in 1903.

Shackleton married Emily at Christchurch, Westminster, on April 9, 1904. Holding the post of secretary to the Royal Scottish Geographical Society until 1905 he now planned a return to the Antarctic. He raised the necessary finance by 1907 by giving redeemable guarantees for promised lectures and written work on his return.

He left London for the South Pole in the small whaler Nimrod in August and reached the Ross Barrier in January, 1908. Heavy pack ice forced him to abandon a landing at King Edward Island but he succeeded in reaching latitude 88'23"S on the Antarctic plateau, although it was to be a competing expedition that reached the actual magnetic pole on January 16, 1909. A second group from his ship made the summit of Mount Erebus on March 10.

On his return to England Shackleton was feted as the hero of the hour, received a CVO, a knighthood and a score of medals. Parliament underwrote the £20,000 financial liability but Sir Ernest still undertook a lecture tour of Europe and America in order to defray other costs.

During his career he came to Torquay three times, staying on one occasion with his family. Together with his sister they even boarded the Nimrod and later watched as she sailed from Torquay harbour. He also gave a lecture, with Lord Clifford presiding, in the Bath Saloons (later to become the Marine Spa) only yards from the same quay.

By 1914 Sir Ernest was planning an even more ambitious mission involving two ships. The first, the Endurance, was to land a sledging party at the Weddell Sea, with the ship Aurora following to create a land depot at McMurdo Sound in the Ross Sea, to eventually welcome the trans-polar party.

But 1914 was a bad year for pack ice and the Endurance was lost on October 27, 1915, some 1,200 miles from help. Undaunted, Shacky and five companions set off for Elephant Island, which they reached on April 16, 1916. They then had to sail 800 miles in a 22-foot boat to reach South Georgia, which then had to be crossed to get to the Norwegian whaling station and help.

It was an almost impossible task but the men made it and thus wrote their own chapter in the history of polar exploration. Shackleton now made three rescue attempts to get back to his marooned men. On August 30, 1916 he succeeded, to find they had never given up on him. "If Shacky lived he would return" had been the men's belief.

Two years later he was serving as a Major assisting the North Russian expeditionary force, having vainly tried a number of commercial ventures in an effort to support his family. He even tried to get elected to Parliament. But in September, 1921 the sea called again and Sir Ernest returned to South Georgia in the vessel Quest to explore the region around Enderby Land. There, just off South Georgia in a much delayed ship with seriously faulty engines, Sir Ernest Shackleton died of angina pectoris. It was January 4, 1922. He left behind two sons and a daughter.

Below: The Endurance in the pack ice; the ship was finally crushed, leaving the crew to haul their lifeboats to open water 1,200 miles from human help.
PA Photo/Credit. Scott Polar Research Institute, University of Cambridge.

51

WILLIAM HENRY SMITH -
Newsagent & Lord of the Admiralty

THE MAN DESTINED to become newsagent to the nation was, not surprisingly, the son and grandson of newsagents.

WILLIAM HENRY SMITH, whose initials became as well known as the names he shared with his father, was the only son of a devout Methodist and was born in Duke Street, Grosvenor Square, London on June 24, 1825.

Young William was educated entirely at home, except for a few months in 1859 when he came to Devon as a boarder at Tavistock Grammar School, where his brother-in-law, the Rev W. Beal, was headmaster.

When sixteen William expressed a wish to go to Oxford and take Holy Orders but in deference to his father's wish he instead joined the family news agency business at a house in the Strand.

On attaining his majority in 1846 he became a partner and with the business recognised as a leader in its field, the young W. H. Smith decided to branch out and use the growing network of railways to further widen the scope of sales of literature.

With his father's health failing, Smith decided to establish bookstalls at all railway stations and by 1851 he had secured a monopoly on the London and North Western line to trade what some called his "pernicious literature".

Cartoonists nicknamed him "The North Western Missionary", yet his reputation and success was such that he had agreements to sell newspapers and books on all the important railway stations of the country. With the repeal of newspaper stamp duty in 1854 making newspapers more affordable W. H. Smith & Son now began to sell just about every type of journal then published.

During this period Smith also became involved with philanthropic and public work, by first joining the management committee of King's College Hospital and in 1855 getting elected to the metropolitan Board of Works.

However, most of his chosen philanthropic causes were usually connected to the Church of England.

The commercial network of WHS spawned advertising on bookstalls and having witnessed promotional techniques being used in the Great Industrial Exhibition of 1851, Smith was among the first to make use of outdoor advertising space.

Initially opposed by his father, he went on to lease all the walls of railway stations throughout Britain, creating enormous profits for the company. This led to the establishment of a circulating library within the bookstall business, which involved no fewer than 300,000 books.

Smith senior lived long enough to witness one more milestone, which involved the publishers Chapman and Hall releasing the copyright on many of their books. This enabled Smith junior to sell a much cheaper "yellow books" version of mainstream titles to the ever growing reading public.

Smith married Emily Leach, widow of his old friend Benjamin Auber Leach, in 1858 and by 1861 in his philanthropic role he was on a working committee of the Bishop of London's Fund, and was treasurer of both the Society for Promoting Christian Knowledge (SPCK) and the London Diocesan Council for the Welfare of Young Men. Smith was unquestionably the rising star of the business in his own right by the time his father died in 1865.

Wesleyan Methodists were normally presumed to be Liberal politically but in 1865 Smith was invited to stand as a "Liberal Conservative" against the Whig Captain Grosvenor and the radical John Stuart Mill for the Borough of Westminster.

He came bottom in 1868, by which time householders had been given the vote, the constituency returned him to Parliament with a large majority. His election was controversial as an enormous amount of expense had been incurred to get him elected.

An opposition petition was mounted and through the stupidity and indiscretions of his agent he came close to having to resign. A leader in The Times even

Above: Gilbert's comic depiction of W. H. Smith in HMS Pinafore.

came to his defence, observing that "a good character has, to Mr Smith at any rate, proved better than riches". A wit of the time then noted that "it may be a question whether the latter has won the seat for him, but there can be no question that the former saved it".

His maiden speech to the House of Commons centred on pauperism and vagrancy, and as he was now recognised as a substantial benefactor members of the House listened with great respect.

Together with W. E. Forster and Lord Sandon, Smith was chiefly responsible for ensuring the Government abandoned the creation of 23 school boards for the Metropolis and, more sensibly, substituted just one.

When Disraeli formed his new administration in 1874 Smith was appointed Secretary to the Treasury and three years later First Lord of the Admiralty. He and his many public offices were famously lampooned by the great satirist W. S. Gilbert in his opera HMS Pinafore in the lines: "Stay close to your desk and never go to sea, and you may all be Rulers of the Queen's Navee". The opera was a great success… just like Smith's career.

In 1880 he purchased land comprising farm dwellings and 5,000 acres at Week just outside Moretonhampstead in Devon, from a railway company. The investment value of this was perhaps dubious for the land was not connected to Brunel's Great Western Railway but the increasing price of land and a growing population moving to the Westcountry were factors that would not have escaped the notice of an astute businessman like Smith.

Gladstone was Prime Minister from 1880 until 1885 when Lord Salisbury took over. Back in Parliament by courtesy

of voters of the Strand constituency, Smith was now appointed Secretary of State for War. Salisbury turned to Smith again when Sir William Hart Dyke resigned as Chief Secretary to the Viceroyalty of Ireland. It was a difficult role to fill and one that Smith held for only a month, due to the resignation of the Salisbury Government.

When Salisbury's second term dawned and Lord Randolph Churchill resigned in 1886 as Leader of the Party, Salisbury again turned to Smith and made him First Lord of the Treasury, Leader of the House of Commons and Lord Warden of the Cinque Ports. As Gilbert might have observed, Lord of Everything!

A lifelong benefactor of good causes, Smith was greatly respected in the Commons and in High Office. He was not a brilliant orator or good debater but few men secured the honest respect and patience he was awarded. He numbered Lord Salisbury a close friend, which perhaps explains why he became a trusted parliamentarian. He was always there to be called when positions of importance demanded a shrewd but steady hand.

With his health failing, Smith made his final appearance in the House on July 10, 1891 before leaving for Walmer Castle his official home at the Cinque Ports. He died there on October 6th 1891.

It was known that the Queen had intended to create Smith the first Viscount Hambleden, and after his death Victoria bestowed the honour posthumously by allowing his wife to become Viscountess and enabling their son, Frederick Danvers Smith, to succeed to the title. It was Viscount Hambledon that finally commissioned the building of the tudor style Manor House at Moretonhampstead, with its magnificent banqueting hall and minstrels' gallery.

The Hambleden association lasted 50 years and the new Viscount, like his father, became a major benefactor to the cottage hospital and St Andrew's Church at Moreton in Devon, as well as providing housing for his estate workers. The Hambleden coat of arms still emblazons the Jacobean carved stone chimney of the manor banquet hall, with its motto Deo Non Fortuna Fretus - Relying on God not Fortune. Interestingly, both Smith and his Viscount son chose to be interred at St Andrew's Church, Moretonhampstead.

The mansion has changed hands many times since the early death of Lord Hambledon in June, 1928. Initially auctioned in November, 1928 it was purchased by the Great Western Railway Company in 1929 and converted into an hotel and 18-hole golf course. The renamed and extended North Bovey Manor became a convalescent home in 1939 since when it has changed hands many times. Then a hotel and golf club and at one time in the ownership of Mr Peter DeSavary who developed it into an up-market country club named Bovey Castle, today it has once again changed hands.

The Tudor style manor house built by W. H. Smith's son at Moretonhampstead, was constructed on land bought by his father.

ISAMBARD KINGDOM BRUNEL -
Engineer extraordinaire

ISAMBARD KINGDOM BRUNEL was born in April 1806, the only son of Sir Marc Brunel, who planned a tunnel under the Thames, which was built between 1825 and 1843.

BY THE AGE OF SIX ISAMBARD HAD MASTERED geometry, and went on to study drawing and horology. By 16 he was working in his father's office, and in his twenties became chief engineer to the Thames tunnel scheme. This first tunnel dug under the river, from Wapping to Rotherhithe, now forms part of the London Underground.

In one incident which occurred during work on the Thames project, Isambard had to be dragged from the tunnel during a terrible flooding.

Later, while convalescing from illness in Bristol, he entered a competition for a proposed new suspension bridge at Clifton, and won. This was his first major project, although he never saw it finally constructed.

He also became involved in the Bristol to London Great Western Railway (GWR), and by the time he was 30 his first acquaintance with Torquay had probably come when surveying land to extend the GWR line from Exeter to Newton Abbot. The London to Exeter line was already in place.

With two major schemes for the line extension abandoned in 1836 due to cost, it was the founding of the South Devon Railway Company in 1844 that saw his proposals for a rail link from Newton Abbot to Dartmouth conceived. Three months later, as chief engineer, Brunel was undertaking his first survey of the Torquay line.

The Exeter to Newton station (Abbot name came later) broad gauge line was officially opened in December 1846, and it initially operated for about a year, using Brunels revolutionary new "atmospheric" powering system. Requiring no engine, the carriages were driven at speed by a steam powered piston in the middle of the track. But with only a single track, and

the driving arm being unable to cross tracks, the system was bound to be inadequate and was eventually abandoned.

A reminder of the pumping house for the atmospheric line can still be seen at the old Longpark Pottery building on the Newton Road in Torquay, now the premises of fruit, flower and vegetable wholesaler Frank H. Mann. The only other surviving building is at Starcross on the Exeter line.

The branch line from Newton Abbot to Torre station opened on December 18 1848, but plans to extend it to Torquay Harbour were sadly abandoned. What a bonus that would have been for today's railway travellers.

The railway system saw little change until 1857 when the Dartmouth and Torbay Railway Company obtained Royal Assent for a Torquay to Paignton line. Only three miles long, it involved the construction of 20 bridges, a viaduct and a tunnel.

Steam-driven trains eventually reached Churston in 1861 and Kingswear Station in 1864. For many years these trains used Brunel's 7ft broad gauge track but in a colossal feat of engineering on the night of May 21, 1892 some 5,000 navvies descended upon Devon to lift the rails and completely replace them with a four foot eight and half inch standard gauge track.

It took just 31 hours, after which the broad gauge legacy that had for years created inconvenience to passengers and freight always requiring a change at Exeter, was finally and permanently removed.

Brunel and his wife Mary had regularly visited Devon and it was perhaps no surprise that they decided to retire to Torquay. Purchasing land at Watcombe from Squire Brown they rented a house and became frequent "locals", enjoying regattas, fairs and functions and, it seems, poultry exhibitions. Isambard was even appointed Patron of the Poultry Exhibition in 1853.

It says much about his character that Brunel chose to build workers' houses long before he started his own. This period of history, known as the "Hungry Forties" had seen home crops failing and imported corn heavily

Above: Brunel Manor, the house Brunel started but never lived in.

taxed, leaving bread, the staple diet of working people, in very short supply. Many of the poor were on the verge of starvation, and "bread riots" were common throughout the UK.

Torquay had its fair share, with 130 individuals being imprisoned or sent to Australia in 1847 for rioting. Navvies working on the railway were generally housed in lodgings of the worst kind - attic rooms, beer houses and the slums of central Torquay – and were often subject to the heaviest sentences. This partly explains why Brunel built his workers' houses as a priority.

Isambard and Mary purchased Watcombe Villa in September 1849 then sold it in 1857 to buy Portland Villa, nearer the site of his proposed manor. He sketched a gothic castle for the crest of Maidencombe hill but later designed an Italianate villa with a belvedere and colonnaded terrace with water fountains. Wells were dug in Moor Lane, and a water pumping station was built in his lifetime.

Completion of the London to Exeter line had seen Brunel building a railway village at Swindon, and now he purchased a two-acre field at Barton to develop 10 detached cottages, a church and school at Barn Close for his workers in Devon. Sadly, he would not complete the church and school and this project was left for his wife Mary to fulfil in 1875 in his honour.

In 1851 Brunel took his Barn Close residents to visit the Great Exhibition in London. The local newspaper recalls that "they occupied the bodies of two carriages and started in high spirits. They were met by a guide at Paddington and conducted to the Crystal Palace, the British Museum, the Thames Tunnel and other Lions of London." All expenses and wages for working hours lost were reimbursed.

Taking a lead from Brunel, HRH Prince Albert made

provision to exhibit "model housing" at the Great Exhibition, and later awarded Brunel £250 for this social innovation.

Two years later, Mary and Isambard, always concerned for their workers, laid on a lavish garden party in 1853, which saw 70 of their workers children enjoying races and other amusements before tucking into tea, buns and tarts. Later in the day the parents received Dublin stout, followed by some serious eating.

Proposals to resite the Torwood Gardens gasometer at Babbacombe Beach were strongly opposed by Brunel and in committee he stated the original site had been inadequate, emphasising the mistake should not be made again. His argument, repeated in the House of Lords, was persuasive and the proposals were rejected. The local authority gasometer was eventually built near a beach, at Hollicombe.

As an artist, architect and engineer, Brunel had been responsible for the building of dozens of tunnels and bridges in the South West, while also undertaking marine design and engineering projects including the building of the dredger Bertha, and becoming involved in gunnery and hospital equipment. His SS Great Britain was launched in 1843 and the SS Great Eastern in 1857. With this schedule and pace of life his output was phenomenal. In 1857 the first section of Brunel's Saltash bridge was floated into place on the Tamar, but now with his health failing he was becoming seriously ill. Diagnosed with nephritis, in a desperate bid to recover he went to Europe to convalesce.

He returned in 1858 seemingly recovered but it was not to be. In August 1859 the Exeter to Paignton line was officially opened but two months later, on September 15, 1859, aged 53, Isambard Kingdom Brunel died. Fate also decreed a most damaging storm in Torquay that autumn. On October 25 and 26 the new Meadfoot road and Livermead walls were swept away, allowing seawater to lap at Livermead House when Brunel's railway embankment was lost. At Abbey Sands seven-ton stones used to construct the seawall were similarly tossed across the road, and six-foot deep water flooded in and reached the Spanish Barn.

After his death the Brunel local connection continued, as Mary visited Torquay for another 20 years and completed her husband's wish for a church and school at Watcombe. Their son Henry, aged 18 in 1860, completed the small bridge started by his father which spanned the Teignmouth road at Watcombe.

Torbay Civic Society has unveiled blue plaques to Brunel at Barn Close, Barton, Bishops Close at Paignton and at the Hookhills viaduct at Goodrington. Finally in Brunel woods at Watcombe visitors can see a sculpture of the great man plus a totem pole depicting his work, carved from the storm damaged trees.

TORBAY CIVIC SOCIETY

BARN CLOSE

AN ESTATE OF
HOMES, SCHOOL & CHAPEL

PLANNED FOR HIS
WORKERS BY

I. K. BRUNEL

1806 ~ 1859

Commemorative Blue Plaques

Many of the individuals featured in this book have been honoured by the installation of a commemorative Blue Plaque to their memory. The plaques usually honour the individual or sometimes an associated building. Below is complete list of plaques associated with the individuals featured in this book together with an address where they may be discovered.

Elizabeth Barrett – Vaughan Parade Torquay
Isambard Kingdom Brunel – Barn Close, Watcombe, Torquay
      – Bishops Place, Paignton
      – Hookhills Viaduct, Broadsands Rd, Churston.
Robert Sheddon Cary – Torre Abbey, Torquay
Agatha Christie – Barton Road, Torquay
Angela Burdett Coutts – English Riviera Centre, Chestnut Avenue, Torquay
Charles Darwin – Meadfoot House, Hesketh Crescent, Torquay
William Froude – Manor House, Chelston Cross, Torquay
Robert Ranke Graves – Vale House, Greenway Road, Galmpton
Oliver Heaviside – Barclays Bank, Palace Avenue, Paignton
John Callcott Horsley – Orestone Manor, Rock House Lane, Maidencombe
Rudyard Kipling – Rock House, Rock House Lane, Maidencombe
William Kitson – Vaughan Parade, Torquay
Sir Edwin Lutyens – Drum Inn, Cockington, Torquay
Frank Matcham – A plaque has recently been unvieled in Newton Abbot
Thomas Newcomen – A personal plaque to Mr Newcomen can be found at
      Royal Avenue Gardens, Dartmouth
William Pengelly – Kents Cavern, Ilsham Road, Wellswood, Torquay
Eden Phillpotts – Oakhill Road, off Teignmouth Road, Torquay
Bishop Henry Phillpotts – Palace Hotel, Babbacombe Road, Torquay
Ella Rowcroft – The Rainbow, Avenue Road, Torquay
John Salter – Hooper & Wollen, The Terrace, Torquay
Isaac Merritt Singer – Oldway Mansion, Paignton
Colonel Robert Smith – Redcliffe Hotel, Marine Drive, Paignton
Edward Vivian – The Piazza, Fleet Street, Torquay
      – Woodfield, Lower Woodfield Road, Torquay
Herbert Whitley – Primley House, Totnes Road, Paignton
Oscar Wilde – Babbacombe Cliff, Beach Road, Babbacombe, Torquay
Richard Wolston – Saxon Heights, New Road, Brixham

Index

What is a Civic Society ?

The National Civic Society movement emerged throughout the United Kingdom following the formation of The Civic Trust in 1957. Parliament had decreed there should be an independent charitable body set up that would involve individuals giving of their time on a voluntary basis to ensure their local area had vitality and sustainability of good design in buildings, whilst also encouraging and hopefully improving the local environment.

Today that charitable body is still called the Civic Trust. It is supported by no less than 700 officially affiliated local Civic Societies made up of residents who are either full or life members of their individual Society. They are also able to directly support the National Civic Trust should they wish which ensures they then receive all Civic Trust publications. Most people however prefer to be associated with their local Society, which generally monitors planning issues, keeps an interest in local parks and the built heritage and of course the countryside. Being a member of a locally based institution like a – Resident Association, Preservation and Conservation group, History, Heritage or an Environment group is also a way of supporting the civic movement, although often these groups are not affiliated to the Civic Trust itself.

Many groups of this type were formed long before the emergence of the Civic Trust movement and today a large number of civic groups still use the term Society, the Skegness Society and the Sid Vale Society (established in Devon in the 19th century) are typical of societies that in reality are true locally based Civic Societies. .

The voluntary civic movement today is huge, it numbers hundreds of thousands of groups all of which have individual subscribers. All of these groups help to protect and preserve the local heritage and the living environment. As an affiliated member of the Civic Trust members of the Torbay Civic Society committee attend meetings of the regional committee which then reports back to the National Committee of the Civic Trust. However, like other Societies it retains its individuality and independence whilst continuing to adhere to its mission statement which promises; "to promote public interest in Civic Design and to stimulate public conscientiousness and appreciation of the beauty, history and character of the (Torbay) area". The object of our Society is – "to encourage the preservation, development, and improvement of features which enhance the attractiveness of the three towns of Torbay".

Torbay Civic Society was formed after the merging of the Friends of the Pavilion group and other local resident associations in 1976 to create a local Civic Society which today is a registered charity. With a small but active committee it arranges local meetings, study groups, literature and lectures whilst also installing blue plaques, supplying merit certificates and undertaking a variety of community based functions to help improve the local environment. In its lobbying role the Society monitors all planning applications and works with a number of local agencies to further the cause of its mission statement. During the past thirty plus years the Society has installed over forty commemorative blue plaques, planted literally thousands of trees whilst leaving to posterity a number of public gardens, seats and commemorative memorials. Membership is open to all citizens irrespective of age, creed, race or colour, gender, sexual orientation, marital status or disability.